**Marketing
Decision
Models**

Marketing
Decision
Models

Edited by

Randall L. Schultz
School of Management and Administration
The University of Texas at Dallas

Andris A. Zoltners
Kellogg Graduate School of Management
Northwestern University

North Holland
New York · Amsterdam · Oxford

Elsevier Science Publishing Co., Inc.
52 Vanderbilt Avenue, New York, New York 10017

Distributors outside the United States and Canada:

Elsevier Science Publishers B.V.
P.O. Box 211, 1000 AE Amsterdam, The Netherlands

Library of Congress Cataloging in Publication Data

Main entry under title:

Marketing decision models.

    Includes bibliographical references and index. 1. Marketing management—
Decision making—Mathematical models. 2. Marketing—Mathematical
models. I. Schultz, Randall L. II. Zoltners, Andris A.
HF5415.135.M37   658.8   80-20618
ISBN 0-444-00426-2

Manufactured in the United States of America

To Lee and Joyce Clemen— R.L.S.
To Aurelia, Greg, and Jennifer— A.A.Z.

Contents

Chapter 4. Models of Market Mechanisms   77
Leonard J. Parsons

Chapter 5. Subjective Versus Empirical Decision Models   99
Philippe A. Naert and Marcel Weverbergh

Chapter 6. New Product Models   125
Gert Assmus

Chapter 7. A Model for Product Management   147
Edgar A. Pessemier

Preface

It has now been over 20 years since the appearance of the first significant work dealing with what we have come to call marketing decision models. Prompted by foundation interest and support and by a general impatience in the business community for scientific help in management, academic and professional marketing researchers set out to bring some rationality to the process of making decisions. The results of this effort are mixed; there have been successes and, inevitably, failures. In this book we report on the state of the art of marketing decision models so that, in the future, we will have a benchmark for judging the next generation of modeling activity.

Decision models are aids to making decisions, and hence their worth is intimately related to their actual use or implementation in organizations. This implies that decision model building is an applied research task. But decision models, if they are to improve organizational decisions, must be representative of real markets and observed marketing behavior. There must be some tangible evidence that what a model purports to be true is, with some likelihood, really true. A decision model that fails to pass such a test of validity cannot be regarded as aiding the manager in a direct and unambiguous way. This key point accounts for our special concern with measures of organizational improvement that go beyond accounting for implementation. So, to the extent that we are concerned with such phenomena as sales response and organizational behavior, research on marketing decision models is decidedly scientific.

Although the issue of whether or not decision models are actually used seems transparent, it was only recently that the process of model implementation came under research scrutiny. Anecdotal evidence aside, there was not (indeed still is not) much knowledge about how organizations react to and adopt the technology of decision making. What we have is a situation where more and better information, particularly of the "what is the big picture" nature, should enable model builders and model users to work together more closely and more effectively toward mutual goals. The purpose of this book is to provide this kind of information.

The chapters in this volume have been written by leading marketing scholars, each of whom has made original contributions to the literature on marketing decision models. The authors also bring to their subject considerable experience in working with marketing organizations on the utilization of their research. In short, they are marketing research professionals.

Although tempered by individual style and expression, each chapter fits into an integrated framework. The book first discusses organizational design and how models are natural complements to human resources in the general decision-making process. Then, the way organizations do make decisions (descriptive models or decision rules) is contrasted with the way they should make decisions (normative models). The key mechanism of sales response is discussed, and subjective and empirical approaches to response measurement are critically compared. New product models are reviewed, first in general and then with a particular focus.

The next chapters of the book deal with decision calculus models, stochastic brand choice models, and strategic planning models. Finally, the volume concludes by examining the application of such models to the public sector and other nonprofit organizations and by looking into the issue of how any model is implemented and what is meant by implementation success.

We acknowledge the help of three groups of people in putting this volume together: first, the authors, who believed in the project and thus gave it its vitality; second, our colleagues at Purdue and Northwestern, who show no signs of relaxing their high standards of research and scholarship and hence stimulate others to do the same; and third, our editor at Elsevier North Holland, Ken Bowman, who has a knack for focusing creative energy on projects without losing sight of creative freedom.

Randall L. Schultz
Richardson, Texas

Andris A. Zoltners
Evanston, Illinois

Contributors

Gert Assmus, Dartmouth College
Robert C. Blattberg, University of Chicago
Michael D. Henry, Purdue University
James M. Hulbert, Columbia University
Leonard M. Lodish, University of Pennsylvania
Philippe A. Naert, European Institute
  for Advanced Studies in Management
Leonard J. Parsons, Georgia Institute of Technology
Edgar A. Pessemier, Purdue University
Randall L. Schultz, University of Texas at Dallas
Dennis P. Slevin, University of Pittsburgh
Charles B. Weinberg, University of British Columbia
Marcel Weverbergh, University of Antwerp
Yoram Wind, University of Pennsylvania
Andris A. Zoltners, Northwestern University

**Marketing
Decision
Models**

1

Marketing Models
and Organizational Design

Dennis P. Slevin

Marketing decision models have been developed over the past two decades with one explicit purpose in mind: to enhance the decision making of marketing managers. The objectives of the marketing manager include the final goal of changed buyer behavior. As shown in Figure 1, the decision making of the marketing manager, if successful and implemented, will by definition lead to changed buyer behavior. Historically, most of the emphasis concerning ways to obtain changed buyer behavior has been on the development of improved decision models for marketing decision makers. The emphasis has been on the "decisional" aspects of the marketing manager's job more than on the "implementation" aspects.

However, behavioral research concerning the nature of managerial work over the past two decades has led us to conclude that the manager's job may be much less decisional and much more implementation oriented than believed by the classical management theorists. An example is the study of five chief executives (five days of observation each) of smaller firms by Henry Mintzberg [17, 18]:

Seventy-eight percent of their time was spent in verbal (oral) communication.

Half of their activities lasted less than 9 minutes each.

Forty percent of their contact time was spent on activities devoted exclusively to the transmission of information.

Ninety-three percent of the verbal contacts were arranged on an ad hoc basis.

The five chief executive officers—the leaders of their firms—initiated on their own, that is, not in response to something else, a grand total of one piece of mail per day each.

Figure 1. The marketing manager's job.

The chief executives met a steady stream of callers and mail from the moment they arrived in the morning until they left in the evening.

An excellent review of research on managerial work by McCall, Morrison, and Hannan [16; see p. 6] has concluded that managers are high-energy people whose days are full of activity. "A number of studies of the activity rate of first level supervisors have shown at least 100 separate activities (incidents or episodes) during a typical 8-hour day. These studies reported averages of up to 583 incidents per day and individual rates as high as 1,073 per day [6, 20, 23, 24]." I have often wondered about the current status of that poor chap who had 1000 incidents per day. In a similar vein, the manager's work is fragmented, characterized by brevity, and fraught with interruptions. Luijk's study [14] of senior executives found that it was not unusual for them to have 40 telephone conversations and 30 visitors each day, for a total of 70 interruptions!

In summary, behavioral science studies investigating the micro aspects (day-to-day, hour-to-hour, and minute-to-minute activities) of practicing managers' jobs have concluded that managers live in a world of role overload, frenetic activity, fragmentation, interruptions, and superficiality. A maximum amount of time seems to be spent in short-term interpersonal interactions, and a minimum amount of time seems to be spent in reflective decision-making activities. As a consequence, managers spend much of their time in implementation activities rather than in classical decision making, and much of this implementation may have substantial impact on the basic structure of the organization in which the manager works.

Thus it may be possible to augment Figure 1 to include the inputs of marketing models and the implementation effects on organizational behavior and organizational structure.

As can be seen from Figure 2, and can also be concluded from a basic knowledge of organizational behavior, there are many steps between development of a marketing decision model and the final goal of changed buyer behavior. These implementation steps can have a tremendous impact on the behavior of the organization and the actual structural design of the organization itself. The purpose of this chapter is

(1) to provide an explanation of how marketing models result in changed organization design,

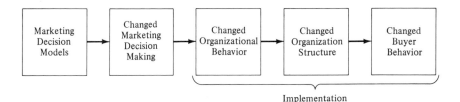

Figure 2. The impact of marketing models on organizational structure.

(2) to provide a basic framework for organizational design, and
(3) to suggest a procedure for evaluating marketing models and the needed changes that they imply in organizational design for successful implementation.

Marketing Models and Behavior Change: A Hypothetical Case

In order to show more specifically the potential impact of a marketing model on organization design, a hypothetical case is presented. Figure 3 shows a traditionally organized firm, consisting of a functional vice president in each of the departments of finance and accounting, production, marketing, and personnel. Let us look at how the implementation of a marketing model might have an impact throughout this hypothetical organization.

1. The first person to be affected is the vice president of marketing. He looks at a model, say ADBUDG, and decides to double his advertising expenditures for the next quarter. He has been "assured" by his analyst that this will increase sales by 30%.
2. The V.P. Marketing gets approval from his president.
3. He then tells his manager of advertising to double expenditures—with the same general campaign as current.
4. The manager of advertising tells her staff to get cracking on this project and they do.
5. The manager of advertising requests execution of the purchase order for increased advertising from a buyer in the purchasing department.
6. The buyer solicits approval from the vice president of purchasing, who grants it.
7. The V.P. Purchasing routinely notifies the V.P. Finance of an additional purchasing commitment.
8. The V.P. Finance tells his manager of cash flow to cash some certificates of deposit to cover the increased cash flow needs starting in about 30 days.
9. The V.P. Marketing notifies the V.P. Production that they hope to get a 30% increase of sales by the end of the quarter.

4

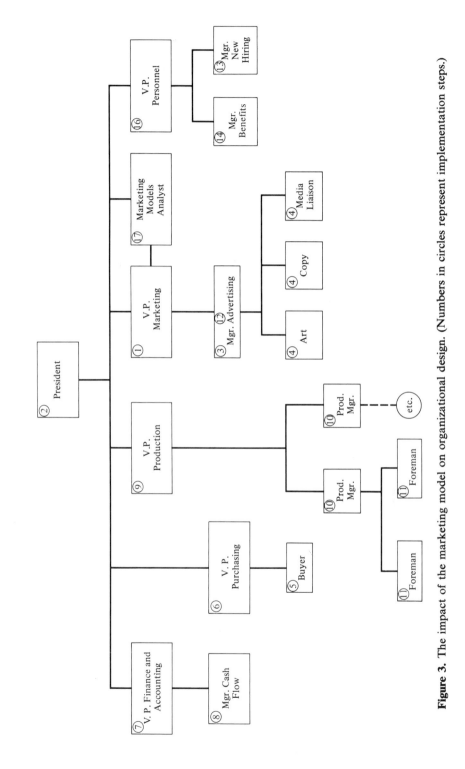

Figure 3. The impact of the marketing model on organizational design. (Numbers in circles represent implementation steps.)

10. The V.P. Production notifies his production managers.
11. The production managers notify their foremen to plan on hiring 15% more workers in order to minimize overtime.
12. The media liaison tells the manager of advertising that she needs two additional staff members for the quarter.
13. The manager of new hires receives the requests from both the production department and the manager of advertising for new workers. The manager of new hires places notices in newspapers, beginning the recruitment process.
14. The manager of benefits finds her staff with an increased work load from explaining their benefit packages to the new hires.
15. Sales increase by 40%!
16. The V.P. Personnel meets the V.P. Marketing at an after-work function and says," Business sure is booming. We've been hiring like crazy." The V.P. Marketing says with a smile, "It's all due to ADBUDG."
17. The next day the V.P. Marketing asks his marketing modeler, "Can we do it again—I mean double advertising again to four times the level of 4 months ago? What does the model say?" The marketing analyst takes a deep breath and says, "Let me experiment with it for a day or two and get back to you."
18. We have not even considered the impact of this seemingly straightforward implementation of the ADBUDG model in our hypothetical organization in other areas:
    A. Inventories increase.
    B. Plant capacity is needed.
    C. Warehouse space is needed.
    D. The purchasing of raw materials is increased.
    E. Stock price goes up.
    F. Preferred stock is issued to finance additional expansion.
    G. And so on.

The trail of communication flows is shown in Figure 4. Virtually the entire organization is affected by the operational implementation of a decision recommended by the marketing modeler.

A Clear Message

The message is clear. Marketing decision models, if they are to be successful in changing buyer behavior, must have an impact on organizational decision making and structure. This idea is not new or revolutionary, but merely has not been attended to that much by organizational theorists and marketing modelers. Alfred D. Chandler, Jr., in his book *Strategy and Structure* [3], an intensive study of General Motors, Du Pont, Standard Oil of New Jersey, and Sears Roebuck, made a strong point that *structure follows strategy*. The hypothetical example presented here focuses primarily

6

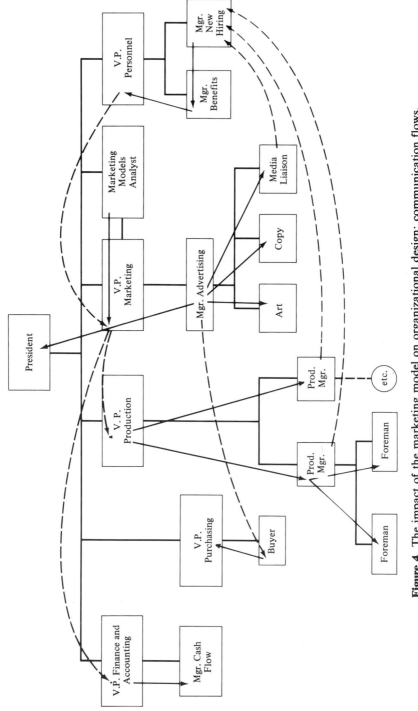

Figure 4. The impact of the marketing model on organizational design: communication flows.

on an operating decision rather than strategic decision making. Even at the operating level, if such ADBUDG-stimulated decisions were made frequently, a number of changes in organization structure would undoubtedly occur, as in these examples:

The personnel department (or some portion of it) might be subsumed within manufacturing to increase the speed of response to staffing needs.

A buyer specializing in media purchasing might be assigned to the marketing department.

Increased budget authorization and independence might be given to marketing.

Personnel might be added to the marketing staff to collect and refine data going into the model.

The manager of advertising might see her department, along with her authority to hire interim help as needed, expanded.

The president of the company might even eventually call in a major consulting firm to determine whether the company should move its current functional design more toward a product organization structure.

As shown in Figure 5, the causal arrow clearly goes in the direction of marketing models affecting organization design. In our hypothetical example, we used a relatively straightforward change in an operating decision (increase advertising expenditures). Imagine the greater impact on organization design that would be caused by changes in strategic decisions. If marketing models are used in this area, to which many of them are clearly well suited, then their impact on organization structures will be even greater.

Consequently, the marketing model builder and the decision maker should also have an appreciation for theories of organization design. What follows is an organization design framework that is intended to help both the modeler and the manager to do a better job of implementing marketing models through changes in organization structure.

Figure 5. Marketing models affect organizational design.

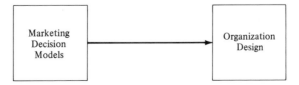

Organization Design: Some Basics

Two major concepts that must be understood and managed for effective organization design are differentiation and integration. They are fundamental general systems concepts, but have very real implications for organization structure.

Differentiation

Lawrence and Lorsch [12, pp. 3–4] have defined differentiation as "the state of segmentation of the organizational system into subsystems, each of which tends to develop particular attributes in relation to the requirements posed by its relevant external environment."

To this author, differentiation means different people doing different things. It is captured primarily by the concept of *specialization* and this author prefers to think of it largely as equivalent to specialization when applied to real-world design problems. However, other scholars, such as Pfeffer [19] and Kast and Rosenzweig [9], in looking at previous literature prefer to describe two types of differentiation: horizontal and vertical.

Horizontal differentiation is viewed primarily as specialization, while vertical differentiation is viewed as the hierarchy and number of levels in an organization. We will comment more on these two types of differentiation later.

Integration

Integration is defined [12, p. 4] as "the process of achieving unity of effort among the various subsystems in the accomplishment of the organization's task."

To this author the concept of integration is synonymous with *coordination*. Although different people must do different things in any organization (differentiation), at the same time their efforts must be coordinated so that a unity of effort is achieved. Bonoma and Slevin [1] have suggested that there are three levels of integration. These will be examined in greater detail in a later section.

Selected Research Results

The classic work concerning differentiation and integration was done by Lawrence and Lorsch in the mid-sixties and reported in their book *Organization and Environment* [13]. While it is not possible to critique their methodology and results comprehensively here, a few comments will be made and some summary results presented.

Lawrence and Lorsch completed a field study in which they measured differentiation and integration in both high- and low-performing firms in three industries. Their contention was that the degree of change found in the industry environment would have an impact on structural variables in the firms. Lawrence and Lorsch define differentiation as "the difference in cognitive and emotional orientation among managers in different functional departments" [13, p. 11] and they put this concept into operation with four variables: goal orientation, time orientation, formality of structure, and interpersonal orientation. The interpersonal orientation is measured by Fiedler's [4] least-preferred co-worker instrument, which is really a measure of leadership style. This author feels that this particular variable is more a measure of the personalities of the role occupants than a structural variable in the organization. If we are making true measures of organizational structure, they should be independent of the idiosyncracies of the role occupants of particular positions.

Lawrence and Lorsch put integration into operation by asking people the degree of collaboration and unity of effort between their departments. A copy of the format appears in Figure 6.

One criticism that can be made of their approach to integration is that it was not more precisely subdivided into the three stages, as suggested by Bonoma and Slevin [1] and developed further in the next section.

Nonetheless, in spite of methodological problems and small sample sizes, the Lawrence and Lorsch research had a tremendous impact on the field. Their summary results are presented in Table 1. Although the data are limited, this author has drawn some hypotheses that seem to bear up under the test of a conceptual analysis.

First, notice the impact of the degree of environmental change on the level of differentiation experienced in the industry. A high-performance and a low-performance firm were selected for study from each industry, and it can be seen that the more dynamic the environment, the higher the average level of differentiation. Even the low-performance plastics firm has

Figure 6. The format for measuring organizational integration. *Source*: Lawrence and Lorsch [13, pp. 259–260].

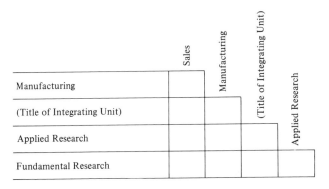

Table 1. Relationship of Environment to Differentiation and Integration

Industry	Organization	Differentiation	Integration
Plastics (very dynamic)	High performance	10.7	5.6
	Low performance	9.0	5.1
Foods (moderately dynamic)	High performance	8.0	5.3
	Low performance	6.5	5.0
Containers (stable)	High performance	5.7	5.7
	Low performance	5.7	4.8

Source: Lawrence and Lorsch [13, pp. 259–260].

a higher average differentiation level than the high-performance foods firm. Consequently, we might conclude that *a dynamic environment requires more differentiation.*

Second, as you look at the integration column in Table 1, you will notice that the high-performance firm in each industry has a higher level of integration than the low-performance firm. Thus we might formulate the second conclusion: *Higher levels of integration result in higher levels of performance.*

No attempt has been made here to test for statistical significance, and in fact, the empirical support is tenuous at best, but the conclusions make conceptual sense. A dynamic environment filled with change and variety requires a large number of specialized departments, and a well-coordinated firm is more likely to succeed than one that is less integrated.

A related conceptual conclusion might be suggested here. That is, integration and differentiation are antagonistic to each other. As Hall [7, p. 146] has said, "Both horizontal and vertical differentiations present organizations with control, communication, and coordination problems.... The greater the differentiation, the greater the potential difficulties in control, coordination and communications." Thus it appears that the secret to success is to match the differentiation to the environment, and then to provide the integration needed to bring back together the differentiated subsystems. Further specifics on organization design steps are given in the last section.

A Closer Look at the Concepts

Types of Differentiation

Horizontal differentiation can best be measured by the degree of task specialization [19]. Task specialization logically leads to departmentalization, and one surrogate for horizontal differentiation may be the number of departments and subdepartments in the organization. The three primary bases of departmentalization are (1) function, (2) product, and (3) location [9].

Vertical differentiation is based on the vertical division of labor and may be measured by the number of levels in the organization. Another variable that may provide insight into the vertical differentiation in an organization is the distribution of salary from the top to the bottom [19]. Salary level may also provide an interesting surrogate measure for another aspect of vertical differentiation—the time span of the job. Elliott Jaques [8] defines the manager's time span as the time required to complete the longest job in his in-basket. Jaques maintains that in order for there to be proper morale in an organization, there must be a correlation between time span and felt fair pay (what people in the organization feel the job is worth). The equitable pay levels (felt fair pay levels) for the Eastern United States in 1978 as computed by Jaques are shown in Table 2.

Thus we can conclude that one method of vertical differentiation is the time span of the job itself, and this usually is correlated with pay level. Taller organizations would obviously have greater vertical differentiation than wider ones. In the formal organization, the "chain of command" up through various levels further specifies the vertical differentiation. Any marketing model, to be successfully implemented, must have an impact throughout a variety of differential levels. These levels must then be coordinated with appropriate integrative mechanisms.

Types of Integration

In the hypothetical case concerning the implementation of an ADBUDG recommendation, the need for coordination to accomplish a doubling in advertising expenditures and a 40% increase in sales was evident. As you can see from Figure 4, a tremendous amount of integration had to occur throughout the organization in order to accomplish this marketing model

Table 2. Correlation of Felt Fair Pay with Time Span

Time span	Felt fair pay U.S. 1978
10 years	$250,000
5	125,000
3	65,000
2	34,000
1	20,000
3 months	

Reprinted by permission of the *Harvard Business Review*. Exhibit from "Taking Time Seriously in Evaluating Jobs" by Elliott Jaques (September/October 1979). Copyright 1979 by the President and Fellows of Harvard College; all rights reserved.

implementation. However, there are different types of integration and we should specifically define these concepts.

Bonoma and Slevin [1] have defined three stages of integration; in order for organizational integration to occur, three different coordinative variables must be addressed:

information exchange—by definition no integration may occur unless information is exchanged. Thus information is a necessary condition for all three levels of integration.

agreement on the decision—required in stage 1 and stage 3.

agreement on decision authority—required in stage 2 and stage 3.

Stage 1: Instantaneous Integration. This is the type of integration that occurs in an ad hoc meeting where people quickly coordinate where they stand on some issue. Its fundamental requirements are

information exchange, and

agreement on the decision.

An example of this in our hypothetical case might be the quick meeting between the vice president of marketing and the president to approve the increase in advertising expenditure.

Stage 2: Process Integration. The fundamental elements in process integration are

information exchange, and

agreement on decision authority.

An example of this might be the vice president of marketing requesting the manager of advertising to double the expenditure. The manager of advertising might have felt that this was an incredibly stupid thing to do, but she agreed that the vice president of marketing had the authority to make such a decision and consequently would, in an integrative fashion, cooperate with the decision.

Stage 3: Composite Integration. Composite integration requires

agreement on decision, and

agreement on decision authority.

An example of this level of integration might occur if the vice president of marketing saw fit to have an extensive meeting with his marketing modeler and his manager of advertising to persuade the manager of advertising of the wisdom of the decision. This composite integration would eventually occur if the manager of advertising could be brought on board with the decision, and this would eventually be needed for long-term morale in the organization.

A comprehensive questionnaire [2] for diagnosing the amount of each type of integration in an organization is given in the Appendix.

Organization Design Steps

A variety of organization design approaches have been described in the organization design literature. Kilmann [10, 11] provides an empirically based computer-analyzed macro design approach in his MAPS technology.

Figure 7. The organizational design process.

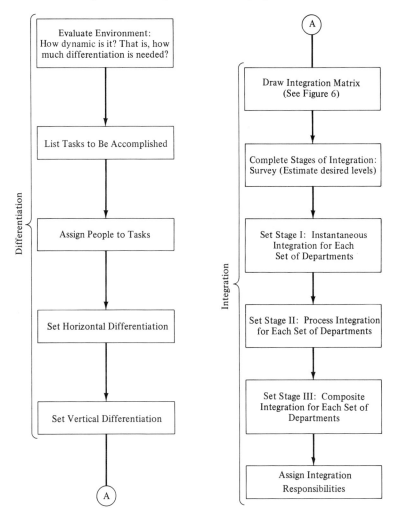

His approach requires a substantial intervention in the firm and significant participation by all of the affected role occupants. Since it is comprehensive, it requires commitment on the part of the target organization, and its empirical base provides important inputs into the design process. Galbraith [5] in his book *Organization Design* describes in detail a theoretical and pragmatic approach to design problems. His use of case studies provides additional assistance to the design.

In this section, we attempt to provide marketing modelers with a reasonably comprehensive and yet pragmatic approach to the design problem. Although not as complete as those developed by Killman and Galbraith, the orderly set of organization design steps presented here should be of use to the practitioner. The flowchart in Figure 7 shows how this process works. First, the environment is sensed to determine the degree of differentiation needed. The differentiation is then set for the organization. Finally, based on the differentiation that has been established, the integration needs are met.

In the case of an internal marketing decision model, the model implementers must make a careful analysis of the differentiation needs and the

Table 3. Organization Design Needs of Marketing Models

	Differentiation needs		Integration needs		
Model	Horizontal (number of departments)	Vertical (number of levels)	I. Instantaneous (agree on decision)	II. Process (agree on decision authority)	III. Composite (agree on decision and decision authority)

integration needs of their implementation. As we showed in our hypothetical case, a good model may require dramatic changes in the differentiation and integration needs of organizations. To help in this process, Table 3 is included; it provides an orderly approach to assessing different types of differentiation and integration needs of marketing models. The reader might wish to use it to make a general assessment of the organization design needs for a model about to be implemented.

Overview

The marketing modeler's job is a difficult one. He must be able to develop data from what often is a highly noisy and unpredictable environment. He must be able to match appropriate models to the types of buyer behaviors that he is attempting to predict. He must also have a keen sense for model validation. In other words, the modeler must be good at developing models with high technical validity [21, 22].

But a technically valid model is only the beginning for successful implementation. At this point, the marketing modeler must become an effective organizational modeler. He must use whatever techniques he has available to develop the organization design needed for successful implementation. If modelers begin to worry more about these downstream implications of their models, undoubtedly implementation success will be enhanced. This chapter attempted to present a framework for demonstrating the impact of marketing models on organization design and an orderly design process for the model implementer.

Appendix
Stages of Integration Survey

In order to assist the marketing modeler in the determination of the types of integration needed in any implementation, the stages of integration survey [2] is reproduced here by permission.

The purpose of this instrument is to measure the degree of integration that exists between your department and a group of target departments that you select.

Definitions

Integration—the quality or state of collaboration that exists between your department and the target department that is required to achieve unity of effort by the demands of the environment.

Information Exchange—the degree to which the desired level of information exchange exists between your department and the target department. It can range from 0% (extremely poor) to 100% (optimal).

Agreement on Specific Decisions—the extent to which there exists a consensus between your department and the target department on specific decisions affecting the two of you. This consensus can range from 0% to 100%.

Agreement on Decision Authority—the extent to which there exists a consensus concerning *who* makes decisions that affect your department and the target department. In other words, is there agreement concerning the individual that possesses the *authority* to make decisions? It can range from 0% to 100% (complete consensus).

Departments

We are going to ask you to complete this questionnaire concerning the relationship between your department and key departments with which you must coordinate. Please specify your department and these key departments on the list below.

Then answer the questions about your department's relationship with department A, department B, department C, and so forth.

Your Dept. _____

Target Dept. A _____   Target Dept. D _____

Target Dept. B _____   Target Dept. E _____

Target Dept. C _____   Target Dept. F _____

THREE QUESTIONS (Answer each of these questions for Department A by placing the letter "A" on each scale; then "B," and so forth.)

Information Exchange—How much information exchange is there between your department and the target department? (% of optimum)?

0%   10%   20%   30%   40%   50%   60%   70%   80%   90%   100%

Agreement on Decision—To what extent does there exist basic agreement on decisions that are made affecting your department and the target department?

0%   10%   20%   30%   40%   50%   60%   70%   80%   90%   100%

Agreement on Decision Authority—To what extent does there exist agreement on decision authority between your department and the target department?

0%   10%   20%   30%   40%   50%   60%   70%   80%   90%   100%

PLOTTING YOUR THREE STAGES OF INTEGRATION

Stage 1: Instantaneous Integration (Plot A, B, C,...)
   Plot the answers to the questions on information exchange and agreement on decisions on the Stage 1 matrix of Figure 8.

Stage 2: Process Integration (Plot A, B, C,...)
   Plot your answers to the questions on information exchange and agreement on decision authority on the Stage 2 matrix of Figure 8.

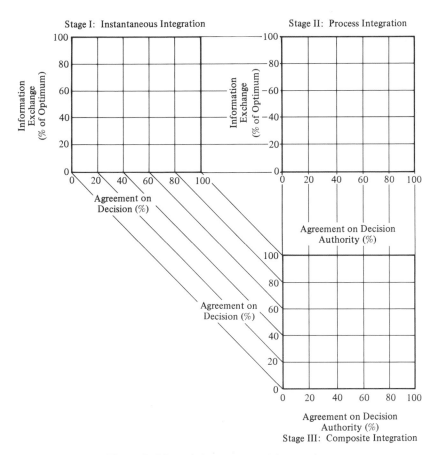

Figure 8. Map of three stages of integration.

Stage 3: Composite Integration (Plot A, B, C,...)

Plot your answers to the questions on agreement on decision and agreement on decision authority on the Stage 3 matrix of Figure 8.

References

1. Bonoma, Thomas V., and Slevin, Dennis P. *Executive Survival Manual*. Belmont, California: Wadsworth, 1978.
2. _____ and Narayanan, Vidake K. "Organizational Integration: Three Roads to More Effective Management," Working Paper No. 210, University of Pittsburgh, February, 1977.
3. Chandler, Alfred D., Jr. *Strategy and Structure*. Garden City, New York: Doubleday, 1966.
4. Fiedler, F. E. "A Contingency Model of Leadership Effectiveness" in L. Berkowitz (ed.), *Advances in Experimental Social Psychology*, Vol. I. New York: Academic Press, 1964, pp. 149-190.

5. Galbraith, Jay R. *Organization Design*. Menlo Park, California: Addison-Wesley, 1977.
6. Guest, R. H. "Of Time and the Foreman," *Personnel* 32, 478–486 (1956).
7. Hall, Richard H. *Organizations, Structure and Process*. Englewood Cliffs, New Jersey: Prentice-Hall, 1972, p. 46.
8. Jaques, Elliott. "Taking Time Seriously in Evaluating Jobs," *Harvard Business Review* 124–132 (September–October, 1979).
9. Kast, Fremont E., and Rosenzweig, James E. *Organization and Management, A Systems Approach*. New York: McGraw-Hill, 1979.
10. Kilmann, Ralph H. "MAPS as a Design Technology to Effectively Mobilize Resources for Social and Organization Problem Solving," in Ralph H. Kilmann, Louis R. Pondy, and Dennis P. Slevin (eds.), *The Management of Organization: Design, Strategies and Implementation*, Vol. I. New York: Elsevier North-Holland, 1976.
11. _____.*Social Systems Design, Normative Theory and the MAPS Design Technology*. New York: North-Holland, 1978.
12. Lawrence, Paul R., and Lorsch, Jay W. "Differentiation and Integration in Complex Organizations," *Administrative Science Quarterly* 1–20 (June, 1967).
13. _____.*Organization and Environment*. Boston Division of Research, Harvard University Graduate School of Business Administration, 1967.
14. Luijk, H. "How Dutch Executives Spend Their Day," in G. Copeman, H. Luijk, and F. de P. Hanika (eds.), *How the Executive Spends His Time*. London: Business Publications, 1963.
15. Mackenzie, Kenneth D. *Organizational Structures*. Arlington Heights, Illinois: AHM Publishing Corp., 1978.
16. McCall, Morgan W., Jr., Morrison, Ann M., and Hannan, Robert L. *Studies of Managerial Work: Results and Methods*. Greensboro, North Carolina: Center for Creative Leadership, May 1978.
17. Mintzberg, Henry. *The Nature of Managerial Work*. New York: Harper & Row, 1973.
18. _____. "The Manager's Job, Folklore or Fact," *Harvard Business Review* 53, No. 4. 49–61 (July-August, 1975).
19. Pfeffer, Jeffrey. *Organizational Design*. Arlington Heights, Illinois: AHM Publishing Corp., 1978.
20. Ponder, Q. D. "The Effective Manufacturing Foreman," in E. Young (ed.), *Proceedings of the Tenth Annual Meeting of the Industrial Relations Research Association*, New York, 1957, pp. 41–54.
21. Schultz, Randall L., and Slevin, Dennis P. *Implementing Operations Research/Management Science*. New York: American Elsevier, 1975.
22. _____. "Introduction: The Implementation Problem," in R. Doktor, R. L. Schultz, and D. P. Slevin (eds.), *The Implementation of Management Science* (TIMS Studies in the Management Sciences, Vol. 3). Amsterdam: North-Holland, 1979.
23. Thomason, G. F. "Managerial Work Roles and Relationships," Part I, *Journal of Management Studies* 3, 270–284 (1966).
24. _____."Managerial Work Roles and Relationships," Part II, *Journal of Management Studies* 4, 17–30 (1967).

2

Descriptive Models of Marketing Decisions

James M. Hulbert

Attempts to improve the quality of marketing decisions have included devoting considerable effort to the development of normative decision models, to which the other chapters of this book bear witness. In some respects, however, it might be argued that we have been trying to run before we have properly learned to walk. Few observers would disagree that there is a considerable amount of judgment and creativity, if not art, involved in being a successful marketing manager, or that the behavioral problems involved in changing accustomed patterns of decision making are considerable. Despite these mores, however, there is a lack of formal descriptive research on marketing decision making.

In many ways, this is a curious state of affairs, especially when compared with the body of work on consumer decision making. The onslaught of customer-oriented notions of marketing has led to an explosion of descriptive research on customer decision making. To companies, the potential payoff of such research is evident—and may often be expressed in dollars and cents. To academic researchers, the subject has proved inherently interesting as well as quite challenging. Such work, then, is the stuff of much market research, as suggested by Table 1, cell I. Marketers have shown less interest in normative models of customer behavior (Table 1, cell II), but others have been less reticent. The economic theory of consumption, as well as bidding models and the like, are evidence of this effort. Likewise, consumer advocates and regulators, among others, have often promoted normative views of consumer decision [53].

There is a rich variety of work on normative decision models for managers (cell III). The theory of the firm provides a sound theoretical foundation, and much of the applied modeling in marketing has focused

Table 1. Decision Research in Marketing

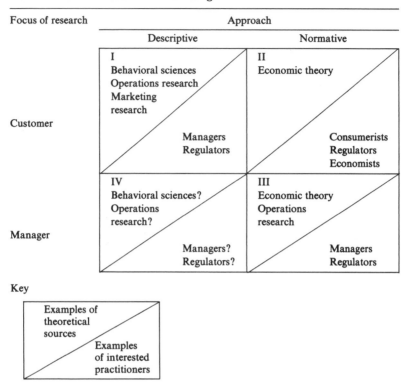

Focus of research	Approach	
	Descriptive	Normative
Customer	I Behavioral sciences Operations research Marketing research Managers Regulators	II Economic theory Consumerists Regulators Economists
Manager	IV Behavioral sciences? Operations research? Managers? Regulators?	III Economic theory Operations research Managers Regulators

Key

Examples of theoretical sources / Examples of interested practitioners

on estimating or "guesstimating" elasticities or response curves to facilitate the application of microeconomic decision rules [48, 49].

However, it is with cell IV, descriptive research on marketing manager's decisions, that this chapter is concerned, and it is not by chance that the entries in this cell are tentative. There is a gulf in our knowledge and understanding of how marketing managers make decisions. Although some knowledge has been gleaned, marketing has no developed tradition in research of this type despite early recognition of its importance [29], and many of the existing studies are flawed.

Why does this state of affairs exist? Has it stemmed from lack of pragmatic payoff, or from other less significant causes? It would seem that several very pragmatic benefits might result from expanded research efforts. First, the general literature on attempts to implement management science is supportive of the importance of organizational context to successful implementation [20, 69, 70]. Thus, a priori there is reason to suppose that good understanding of current decision-making methods can facilitate attempts to improve the quality of decisions by implementation of normative models. Furthermore, some work suggests that model building should be directly related to the individual manager's decision-making style, further reinforcing the argument [37, 43].

Second, good descriptive research on executive decision making may provide very useful inputs to the formulation of competitive strategy by aiding the understanding and prediction of competitors' decisions. Oligopolistic market structures mean that great importance is (or should be) attached to the actions and reactions of competitors. In such markets competitive behavior should always be a key consideration in strategy planning, and it has been argued that today the competitive element is more important than ever [61].

Third, some research suggests that simple (linear) decision models developed from the decision maker's own rules and behavior may outperform the decision maker himself. This phenomenon, dubbed bootstrapping, works by eliminating the error component introduced by the decision maker [8, 34]. This interesting finding is examined in more detail later in the chapter.

There are also several peripheral benefits to the organization that has developed good descriptive understanding of its marketing decision-making systems. Identifiable problems, biases, and oversights in the system may, of course, be corrected [12]. System description can also serve a variety of teaching and training objectives [15]. In addition, the information-processing and decision-making network of the company does, of course, have important implications for organization structure [77]. Finally, there are evident public policy issues inherent in patterns of executive decision making, particularly in concentrated industries [15].

All in all, there are more than enough arguments to justify expanded research efforts in this area. A number of methodological problems have undoubtedly presented difficult barriers to research. Nonetheless, marketing could well take a lead from research in other areas of executive decision making, some of which is beginning to yield useful insights for researcher and practitioner alike.

Research on Executive Decision Making

Although usually more informal than formal, there has been a long history of "research" on executive decision making. This overview, however, will focus on work that has evinced some concern for methodology, or has contributed to conceptual or methodological development. More or less formal research on decision making, however, still admits a great variety of approaches. In the marketing area, for example, Lanzillotti's [42] "post-prandial" survey of pricing objectives is a classic of sorts. Fogg [26] reports on a single strategic decision, while Abell [1] has used content analysis of marketing cases quite innovatively to develop a typology of strategies. Even more common an approach is the survey of managerial practice, often restricted to the purely descriptive [78, 79], but sometimes treated more analytically [9, 10].

In this chapter we shall limit our purview to research that has approached executive decision making as a complex process rather than as a "black box." In other words, we shall focus predominantly on studies concerned with the kinds of information that are sought by executives and with how that information is processed in the course of making a decision. In consumer research, Bettman [6, p. 71] distinguishes this approach as one in which "the process by which choices are made has been scrutinized, rather than merely the choices themselves." We shall use the label "decision process research" to indicate work that exhibits concern with process rather than just output of decisions.

Development of Decision Process Research

While many approaches to studying decision making express concern with process [38], Newell and Simon's work was seminal in stimulating the concept of the human as an information processor [58, 59]. In the classic tradition, subjects are asked to talk aloud as they solve a problem. The resulting "protocol" is the raw material from which the decision process model is built, in most cases depicting the problem-solving activity as a sequential binary choice process. In practice, other materials and methods have been used to augment or sometimes replace the protocol [36, 51, 54], but the last is still the preferred choice of decision process researchers, where feasible. Further, although some recent work in psychology has questioned the ability of respondents to report on mental processes [60, 73], both the internal and the predictive validity of models thus derived have been quite good.

Some of the early decision process models dealt with a trust officer's choice of a stock portfolio [16] and department store pricing [17]. Subsequently, there have been a variety of applications to consumer buying behavior [3, 5, 27, 62, 68], and the related development of a fairly comprehensive theory of consumer choice [7].

There have been other "micro" approaches to the study of executive design. Huber [34, p. 229] argues that a simple linear model "is able to make extremely good approximations of most decision processes." Bowman [8] used this approach to investigate production management decisions, and work has continued in this tradition [18, 66]. One of the more interesting implications of this research tradition has been the possibility of gain by substituting a model of the manager's decisions for the manager's own decisions. This phenomenon has been termed "bootstrapping" and works because the random error of the decision maker is replaced by the nonrandom error of the model [34, p. 229]. We should note, however, that the criterion here is prediction, and such approaches do not (directly) generate descriptions of decision makers' information processing; that is, they are basically black box approaches.

Type of Decision

Simon [71] distinguishes between programmed and nonprogrammed decisions on the basis of repetitiveness versus novelty. Others have introduced further distinctions. Howard [29, 30] prefers a three-way breakdown, characteristics of the three types of decision being shown in Table 2, while Robinson, Faris, and Wind [67] use a similar system to classify industrial buying decisions.

The bulk of the earlier work on executive decision processes focused on programmed decision, or Howard's "routinized response behavior." Easily predictable, however, was the emergence of interest in higher-order decision processes. Strategic decisions are scarcely "programmed," yet these must be a key concern for research on executive decision making.

Soelberg's [74] study of job choice was one of the earliest attempts to deal with unprogrammed decision, although not in an organizational context. In marketing, the work on price and volume forecasting decision processes by Farley, Howard, and Hulbert [22] represented an intermediate step. Here the decisions studied were somewhat above the routinized level, but were generally viewed as operating rather than strategic decisions, with the possible exception of list-price setting. The methodological problems involved in research on strategic decision processes

Table 2. Classification of Decision Processes

Type	Element			
	Information inputs	Content	Information outputs	Array of alternatives
Routinized response behavior (RRB)	Prespecified and predictable in detail	Prespecified and predictable in detail	Prespecified and predictable in detail	Completely specified
Limited problem solving (LPS)	Partially structured	Prespecified in general form and partially predictable	Prespecified in form	Partially specified
Extensive problem solving (EPS)	Developed as content is developed	To be developed	Developed as content is developed	Not specified

Source: Howard, Hulbert, and Farley [33]. Reprinted by permission of the publisher. Copyright 1975 by Elsevier North Holland, Inc.

are clearly substantial, and a protocol approach would generally be infeasible. Despite these handicaps, however, several pieces of work have recently appeared, although none are marketing oriented. Mintzberg, Raisinghani, and Théorêt's [54] paper, based on an analysis of 25 strategic decisions, is probably the best known, and develops some useful methodology as well as providing a conceptual structure. As with most pioneering work, there are some unresolved methodological and substantive issues, but as the authors themselves point out, we have "barely scratched the surface of organizational decision making" [54, p. 274]. They conclude that there is still great need for empirical research on organizational decision—a conclusion that seems equally valid in the marketing domain.

Models of Marketing Decisions

The previous section noted that decision process studies have most frequently been performed in structured and repetitive problem situations. Most of the applications in marketing have been of this type, and have typically focused on one element of the marketing mix. This part of the chapter is therefore organized in a similar manner. Although the compilation of studies to be discussed is believed to be comprehensive, there may well be other research not included here.

Pricing Decisions

Pricing decisions have been the most frequently studied mix decisions. No doubt the central role of price in economic theory, its tangibility and apparent unidimensionality, as well as its practical importance, have been causal factors. However, the fact that one of the earliest decision process studies chose to focus on price was also probably influential [17]. The discussion is best divided into two parts, the first dealing with price adjustment decisions, the second focusing on setting of list price.

Price Adjustments. As would be expected, all price adjustment decisions that have been studied are reaction programs. The commonest initiating cue, as in the Howard–Morgenroth [32] model shown in Figure 1, is a competitive price change or customer requests for discounts (often prompted by competitive price cuts), although unsatisfactory sales levels can also initiate price adjustments [17, p. 140]. The elaborateness of subsequent processing, however, appears to be dependent on a number of characteristics of the marketing environment or, as Newell and Simon [59] would describe it, the task environment. Companies facing the same set of competitors in each end-use market retain quite centralized price adjustment decision processes. In such environments, pricing changes are easily communicated to competitors, and price changes in one end-use market

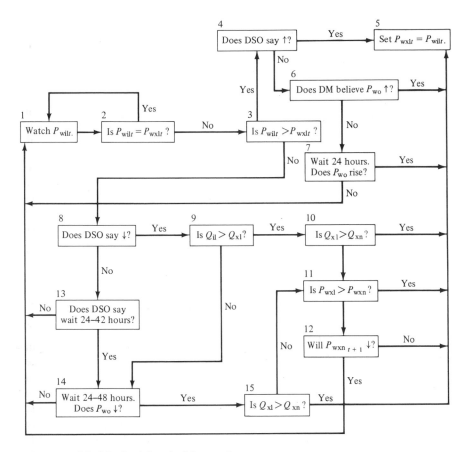

Figure 1. Model of pricing decision node.

Source: Howard and Morgenroth [32]. Reprinted by permission from "Information Processing Model of Executive Decisions," *Management Science* 14 (March), 416–428 (1968), copyright 1968 The Institute of Management Science.

Symbols

P—Price
w—Wholesale
x—Our company
o—Other major competitors in local market
i—Initiator
t—Time, at present
Q—Quantity, i.e., sales volume in physical terms
1—Local market wherein price change in being considered

n—Nearby market with funnel influences
DSO—District Sales Office (District Sales Manager)
= —Is equal to
≠ —Is not equal to
> —Is greater than
↑—Raise price
↓—Drop price
DM—Decision maker

usually have very rapid repercussions in other unrelated markets. Thus, although price adjustment decision processes in these situations may restrict participation to a limited number of executives and involve very streamlined processing activity [24], nonetheless, fairly high organization levels—executive V.P.s [22] or division managers [57]—personally make or approve decisions. An example of such a pricing decision structure is shown in Figure 2.

For companies with greater product, market, or competitive heterogeneity, where seller or buyer concentration ratios are low and/or purchase amounts tend to be quite small, it is not at all uncommon to find much greater decentralization of the pricing decision. Discretionary limits may be hierarchically ordered [11] or the pricing decision may be made entirely at the department level [17].

A further useful distinction can be made between "uniform" prices and "differential" prices. In industrial markets differential pricing is quite widely practiced (subject, of course, to Robinson–Patman constraints in the United States), whereas the existing models suggest uniform (across customer) pricing for companies marketing to the final consumer [17; 39, p. 541].

Information requirements, of key importance to would-be information system builders, show some uniformity, although likely method variance suggests caution in generalizing. In most cases, quite detailed information on competition and customer [21, 22]; and even on the department store buyer monitored competing price levels [17, p. 144], is required. In most industrial companies studied, customer information was more readily available than competitive information, and effective management of differential pricing suggests a need for better/more formal pricing information systems.

List Price Determination. Particularly for industrial marketers, but also for many consumer products, the proportion of sales made at list prices is less than half of the total, sometimes practically zero. Nonetheless, list prices serve at least three useful purposes. First, list prices can be advertised and promoted, whereas this is virtually impossible for actual prevailing prices. Second, list prices provide a base level from which to develop discounts and deals. Finally, list prices also perform a "signaling" function, particularly important in oligopoly.

List price determination processes have been studied in fewer companies than price adjustment decisions, but some observations are in order. First, some decision processes are explicitly [12] or implicitly [24] cartelized, that is, price setting was collusive. Second, the oligopolistic character of most of the companies studied means that government takes a direct [23] or indirect [22] role in the decision process. List price decisions were normally taken at the executive vice president or director's level in the companies studied [21–23] but involved wider participation and more extensive information processing than normally took place for individual price adjustment decisions. In all companies except the completely cartelized, there was extensive monitoring of environmental variables, with high concordance of variables tracked among the different companies studied. Data included competitor and substitute price levels, costs, market shares, capacity and capacity utilization, profits, and profitability.

Method variance and the developing nature of appropriate statistics [6, 24] make formal comparison difficult, if not impossible, at this stage. However, given similar market environments, there seems to be considerable similarity in the pricing decision processes that have evolved. Morgenroth reached a similar conclusion, noting similarity across decision makers within company [57, p. 22]. The most striking aspect of the observed similarities is that they occur within company, despite absence of organizational specification of any standard operating procedure, as well as across organizations. It does not, therefore, seem unduly optimistic to expect that useful generalizations about company pricing activities will emerge.

Advertising Decisions

Although less extensively explored than the pricing decision, a number of models of advertising decisions have been developed more or less independently. Advertising decisions for which models have been developed include selection of items for retail advertising [64, 65], media decisions [25], budget decisions [12, 51], agency–client relationships [13], and new/special campaign decisions [12, 13]. As for pricing, this section will concentrate on findings that suggest possible generalizations and hypotheses for further research.

Budget Decisions. Advertising budget decisions have been a class of decisions where academics have assailed what appeared to be fairly widespread industry practice. Kotler [39], for example, points out that

> the widely used percentage-of-sales method has little to justify it on theoretical grounds. It uses circular reasoning,...discourages experimentation,...militates against the planning of long-range advertising programs,...does not provide a logical basis for the choice of a specific percentage,...[and] suggests that all allocations be made at the same percentage of sales.[1]

Clearly, blind and unreasoning adherence to percentage-of-sales rules can produce problems. For example, advertising and marketing budgets must

---

[1] Reprinted from Philip Kotler, *Marketing Management: Analysis, Planning, and Control*, 2nd ed., copyright 1972, p. 670, by permission of Prentice-Hall, Inc., Englewood Cliffs, New Jersey.

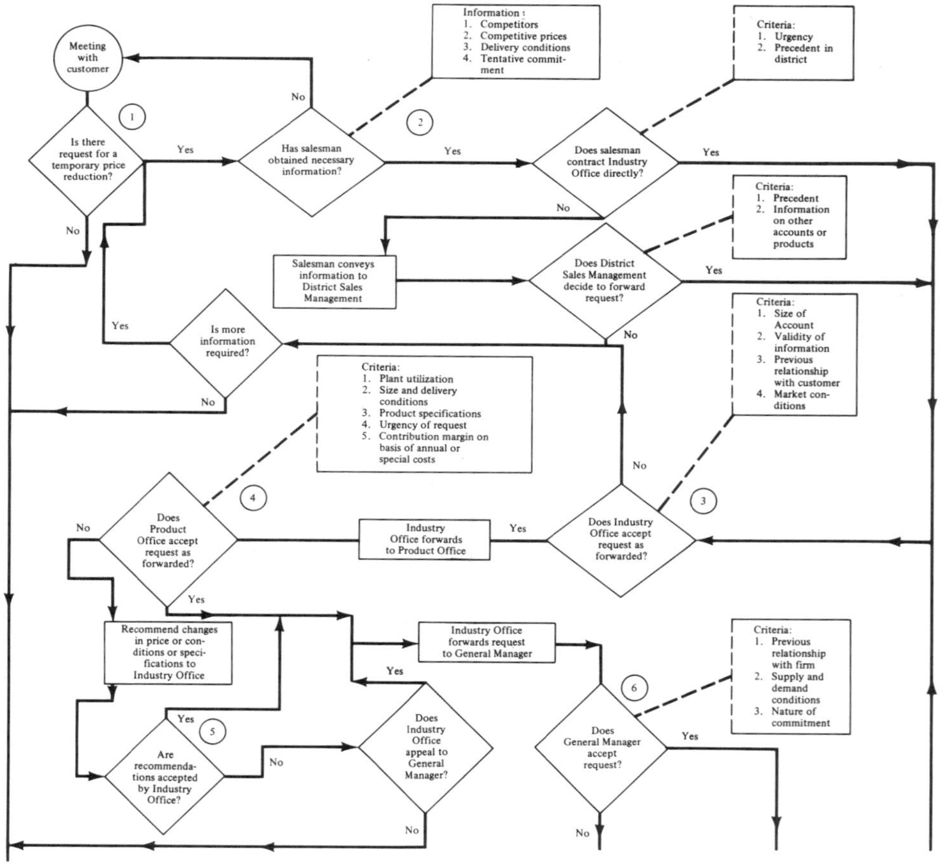

Figure 2. A feedback decision structure. *Source:* Howard, Hulbert, and Farley [33]. Reprinted by permission of the publisher. Copyright 1975 by Elsevier North Holland, Inc.

KEY

B_I — Advertising budget, approved by management for the coming time period

C — Estimated media production costs to put B_I into effect

B_{II} — Space and time budget, to be apportioned

S — Total sales of branded "Guardian" gasoline, including both regular and premium grades, in U. S. direct-supplied territory during the previous year

P — Total sales of "Guardian Premium" gasoline, same

$M_1, M_2, \ldots, M_{126}$ — Listing of markets where Guardian gasoline is sold on a direct basis

Flowchart elements:

Meeting with customer

(1) Is there a request for a temporary price reduction?

(2) Has salesman obtained necessary information?

Does salesman contact Industry Office directly?

Criteria:
1. Urgency
2. Precedent in district

Information:
1. Competitors
2. Competitive prices
3. Delivery conditions
4. Tentative commitment

Salesman conveys information to District Sales Management

Does District Sales Management decide to forward request?

Criteria:
1. Precedent on other accounts or products

Is more information required?

(3) Does Industry Office accept request as forwarded?

Criteria:
1. Size of Account
2. Validity of information
3. Previous relationship with customer
4. Market conditions

Industry Office forwards to Product Office

(4) Does Product Office accept request as forwarded?

Criteria:
1. Plant utilization
2. Size and delivery conditions
3. Product specifications
4. Urgency of request
5. Contribution margin on basis of annual or special costs

Recommend changes in price or conditions or specifications to Industry Office

(5) Are recommendations accepted by Industry Office?

Industry Office forwards request to General Manager

Does Industry Office appeal to General Manager?

(6) Does General Manager accept request?

Criteria:
1. Previous relationship with firm
2. Supply and demand conditions
3. Nature of commitment

Advise Vice President Marketing

Criteria:
1. Impact on overall strategy
2. Implications for industry pricing patterns

Vice President Sales evaluates request with General Manager

(7) Do we need review by Vice President Sales? Yes / No

General Manager conveys all information to Vice President Sales

Was an adjustment granted? Yes / No

Industry Office advises sales personnel

General Manager advises Industry Office of Decision

Is decision appealed by District Sales Management? Yes / No

Is there new market information? Yes / No

Incorporate new information in request

(8) Negotiate with customer on basis of adjusted terms

(9) Negotiate with customer on basis of original terms

Does customer accept? Yes / No

Obtain commitment

Lose order

Is there new information on market or plant utilization? Yes / No

---

$s_1, s_2, \ldots, s_{126}$ — Branded Guardian gasoline sales, regular and premium grades, in $M_1, M_2, \ldots, M_{126}$, through direct-supplied service stations, during the previous year

$p_1, p_2, \ldots, p_{126}$ — Guardian Premium gasoline sales, same

$M_{t1}, M_{t2}, \ldots, M_{t6}$ — Selected 50% test markets, in which advertising expenditures are to be kept at a constant level for an indefinite period in order to test the impact of advertising

$M_{t7}, M_{t8}, \ldots, M_{t12}$ — Selected 150% test markets, same

A — Prime multiplier

G — Total "profit" gallons, giving double weight to premium gallons

g_i — "Profit" gallons sold during the previous year in M_i (any market)

$y_1, y_2, \ldots, y_{126}$ — Prime market budgets

x_i — Budget for M_i

of necessity be high as a percentage of sales dollars or units early in the life cycle of a brand or product, but typically decrease as sales mature [63]. Nonetheless, as some recent work has shown, under certain conditions percent-of-sales budgeting rules may be optimal [cf. 41].

The percent-of-sales controversy illustrates why, once again, better knowledge of decision processes—in this case for advertising budgeting— would be useful. Yet, there are only two studies that deal with this

Figure 3. Advertising budget allocation model.
Source: Marschner [51]. Reprinted from the *Journal of Business* by permission of the University of Chicago Press. copyright 1967.

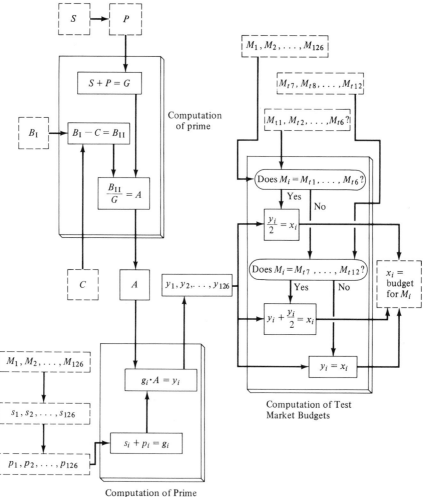

Computation of prime

Computation of Test
Market Budgets

Computation of Prime
Market Budgets

decision. Capon and Hulbert [12] briefly describe the process of setting the total advertising budget for an industrial company. Although their process description is rather vague, it is evident that the overall budget-setting process is quite crude, for "the main determinant of the budget is the previous year's expenditure" [12, p. 156].

More detailed and more interesting is Marschner's study of the allocation decision process used to determine how, given a total budget, spending levels in particular submarkets were established for a gasoline and a coffee manufacturer [51]. One of his objectives was to compare practice in these two companies with normative approaches to the allocation decision. The gasoline company model, shown in Figure 3, is clearly a percent-of-sales method; the coffee company process, although more complex, likewise reduces to a similar basis [51, p. 301].

Marschner's evaluation of these decision processes pointed out that neither explicitly took into account concepts of sales decay, response rates, or saturation levels, nor did they deal with competitive spending levels [51, pp. 298–299]. Both models can be summarized by their tendency to spend most heavily where sales have been heaviest, and there is a strong tendency for routinization and compromise to dominate the resulting decisions.

Media Decisions. Fleck [25] presents a two-part media selection model, the first part of which is shown in Figure 4. Tests were limited to choice of media for five products, but in each case the model performed well in predicting the media chosen by the agency. Budget allocations among media were not modeled for a variety of practical reasons.

Noticeable in Figure 4 is the first binary choice (node 2), supporting the notion of the importance of last year's advertising decisions, as noted by Capon and Hulbert [12]. The model is a simple sequential binary choice network that uses heavily the kinds of media information that might be used in an optimizing model. Fleck comments that the expenditure patterns were affected by special media deals that might be available to buyers, but that allocation to media was related to the model-assigned media weights [25, p. 18]. The resulting budget, we might speculate, could therefore be quite similar to what would result from a weighted cost-per-thousand approach, a widely used heuristic [72].

Other Advertising Models. Rados's study [64, 65] dealt with weekly advertising decisions in a large supermarket chain. The model developed to simulate the decision to advertise the product (BF) is reproduced in Figure 5. Notable is the complete absence of any sales feedback, perhaps explained by the relative unimportance of the decision. The information-processing activity for this repetitive and routinized decision was abbreviated and precedent derived. Although a different type of advertising decision, there was some similarity to the budget and media decisions

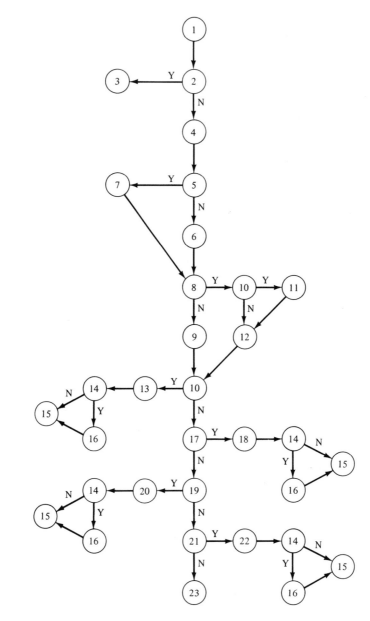

Figure 4

Symbol	Definition
1	Start.
2	Was the last media plan completely acceptable?
3	Use last fiscal year's media plan.
4	Generate target audience.
5	Is the campaign to be completely national in nature with no regional "heavy-ups"?
6	Add 1 to spot television.
7	Add 2 to all national media weights.
8	Is the primary target audience upper income or college educated?
9	Eliminate upper income–college media.
10	Is the primary target audience male?
11	Eliminate all nonupper income and all noncollege educated media.
12	Add 1 to all print media.
13	Select male media.
14	Secondary audience?
15	Go to media refiner.
16	Select media for secondary audience. Use secondary audience as if it were the primary. Reduce all media weights for secondary audience by 1.
17	Primary audience female?
18	Select female media.
19	Primary audience children?
20	Select children's media.
21	Primary audience male and female or mass?
22	Select mass media.
23	Error terminal.
Y	Yes.
N	No.

Figure 4. Primary media selector model.
Source: Fleck [25].

in that past actions were again explicitly used to determine future actions.

Flow charts of decision processes for campaign initiation [12, 13] and monitoring of agency–client relationships [13] afford little scope for generalization. None were formally replicated by decision, decision maker, or organization.

Product Decisions

Retailer buyer decisions can also be viewed as their product policy decisions, since they determine the line of products they will offer for sale. Two models of this type of decision process have been developed. The first [52] deals with a department store's procedure for deciding which manufacturer's lines to carry in the major appliance department. The second model, on the other hand, deals with a supermarket's decision whether to accept manufacturers' new product offerings [55]. Finally Capon and Hulbert [12] present a flowchart of the new product development decision process for a British industrial manufacturer.

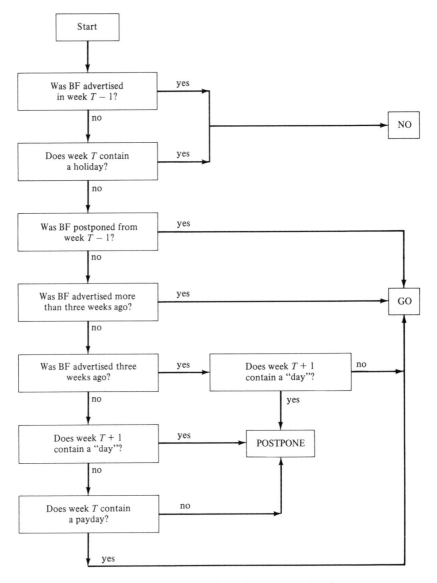

Figure 5. Model of retailer's decision to advertise.
Source: Rados [64].

Massy and Savvas's model (Figure 6) suggested, as did some of the advertising models, that precedent—the results of past decisions—was a key influence on current decisions. For example, they comment that

> gross margin (last year's sales multiplied by markup) is used as the buyer's primary criterion for ranking lines. For lines not carried now, he looks at his weakest major competitor's sales. Thus, his method for forecasting gross margin is biased in favor of products he now carries [52, p. 34].

Similarly, fairly minimal satisficing criteria determined whether or not products were retained in the "carry" list, and whether or not new products were even considered for addition to the line. For this particular decision, either buyer or seller could benefit from the development of such a process model. For example, poor service and distribution strength in discount stores both operated so as to remove the alternative from active consideration.

Montgomery's "gatekeeping" model is not a decision process model as we have discussed them. However, its methodological innovations are important and merit discussion. Like most decision process studies, in which models are painstakingly developed from protocols, interviews, and other records, Montgomery used a preliminary interview stage, but "to identify a list of potentially important variables" [55, p. 4] rather than to build a process model. Based on this list, a structured personal interview was developed and used to obtain ratings from 3 buyers for 124 product addition proposals. However, the processing model shown in Figure 7 was developed not from the actual information-processing activity of buyers, but by a hierarchical thresholding analysis:

1. Search for a variable and for a value of that variable which will enable us to reach a classification decision for all or a part of our sample (see step 2) while making very few errors. In effect, we seek a variable and a value of that variable above or below which there is little or no overlap in the sample distributions from the two populations. This search may be made on the basis of prior logic and/or heuristic methods.

2. Remove from the data base those observations which we are ready to classify.

3. Return to step 1 with the remainder of the data. Repeat until sample sizes become extremely small, or no variables can be found which will achieve the objective, or you are satisfied with the classification success [56, p. 261].

Montgomery's approach has implicit benefits and costs. Among its advantages is that it appears to be a less labor-intensive way of developing a process model than more traditional methods. On the other hand, there is no assurance that the resulting model has any descriptive validity. Rather, the approach provides a heuristic for developing an "optimal" node sequence, "optimal" in the sense that it appears to minimize the amount of

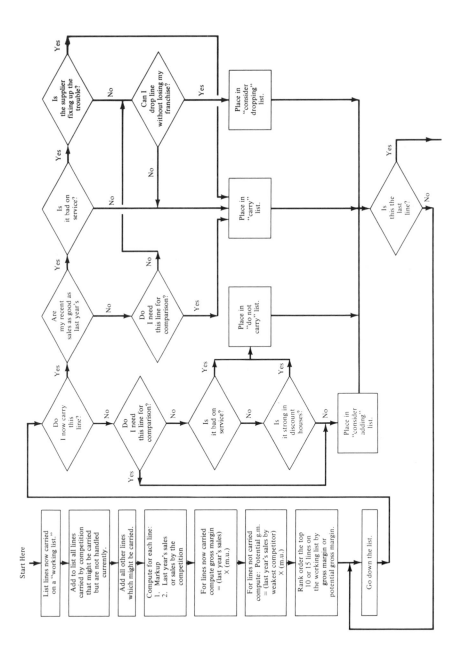

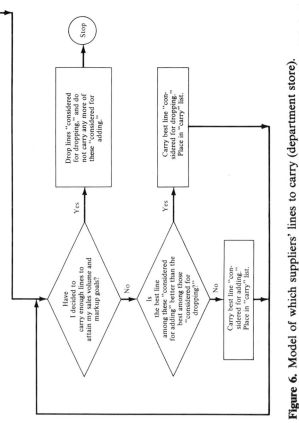

Figure 6. Model of which suppliers' lines to carry (department store). *Source:* Massy and Savvas [52]. Published by the American Marketing Association.

38

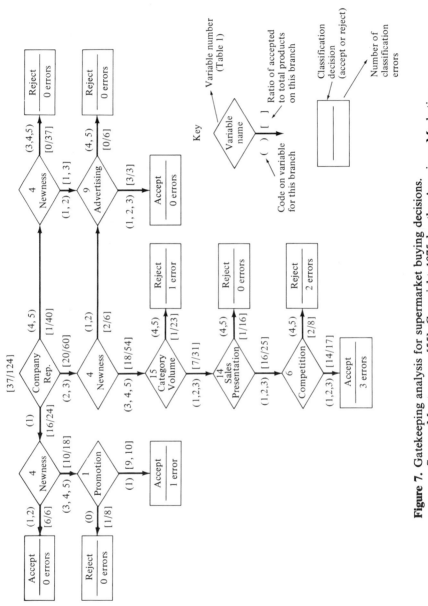

Figure 7. Gatekeeping analysis for supermarket buying decisions. *Source:* Montgomery [55]. Copyright 1975 by the American Marketing Association.

information processing necessary to arrive at a decision. Such an approach offers a means to attain parsimony [27], and a criterion by which to evaluate and perhaps to attempt to modify descriptively valid information-processing models [6].

In terms of the *content* of Montgomery's gatekeeping model, the role of company reputation is striking. Although the importance of this "source" effect has previously been suggested [44]—and disputed [14]—for these supermarket buyers it is key. Sales presentation quality (found more important than reputation for a sample of industrial buyers [45]) was here less important, but newness, promotional support, category volume, and moderate to heavy advertising were of some importance. It is also interesting to note the attenuated processing structure for the extremes (high- and low-reputation companies) and more extended processing for intermediate-reputation companies. Montgomery's model predicted extremely well (94%, 93.3%, and 89.3% hit rates for the three buyers, respectively), but its node structure was not validated as representative of any of the buyers' decision processes. From a normative perspective, it might be argued that the model shows, overall, little regard for directly estimating future profitability of these products, even when compared to Massy and Savvas (Figure 6). However, many of the cues are presumed surrogates for future sales success, so that profit potential is indirectly considered.

The new product development decision process depicted by Capon and Hulbert [12] (Figure 8) corresponds more closely to a normative view of product addition decisions. Notice, however, that this description was developed for a manufacturer, not a retailer, and the economic implications of a nonsimilar (node A) product are considerable. Despite the evident concern with market potential, profitability, and so on, some aspects of the process remained surprisingly informal. There were no organized sources of information on past or present development projects, no clear objectives or policies during the idea phase, and new product activities were essentially part-time responsibilities for all, competing with current operations for managers' interest and attention [12, pp. 156–159].

Forecasting

Forecasting processes have been most widely studied in the industrial marketing studies referred to earlier [11, 12, 15, 21, 22, 24]. In-depth studies of seven companies in equivalent though often geographically disparate market situations have found heavy reliance on sales force composite forecasting systems, sometimes augmented by other approaches. In general, these forecasting systems have corresponded to the overall process depicted in Figure 9.

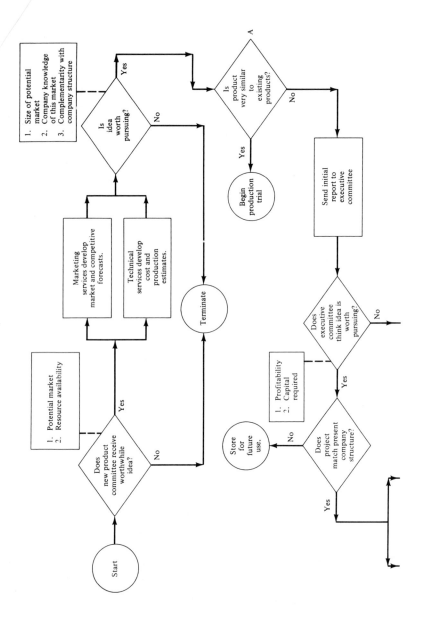

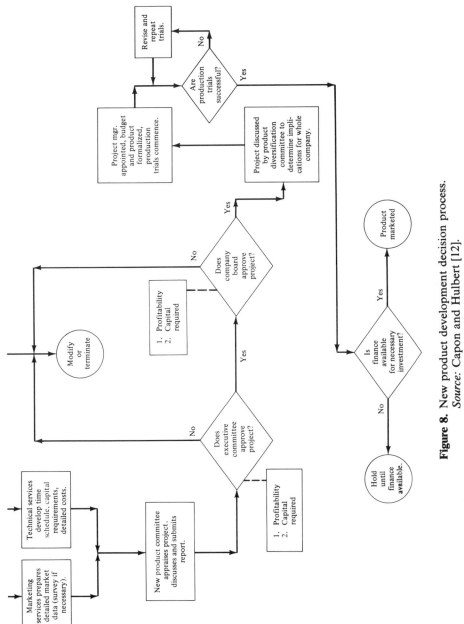

Figure 8. New product development decision process. *Source:* Capon and Hulbert [12].

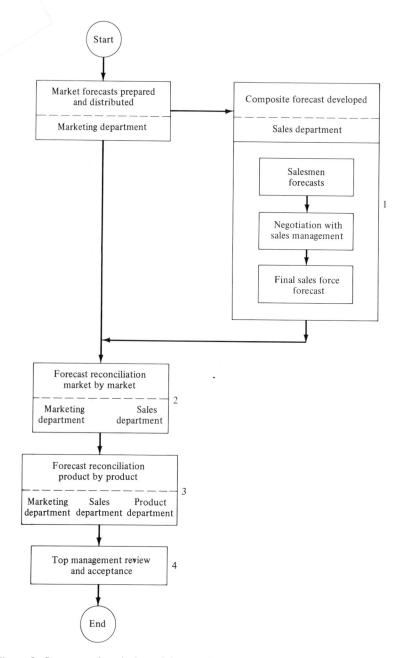

Figure 9. Summary description of forecasting system.
Source: Capon and Hulbert [11], Proceedings of the American Institute for Decision Sciences, copyright 1972.

These decision processes are examples of coordination by plan [50]. Triggered on a regularly scheduled basis, the forecasting process in these firms involves considerable breadth and depth of organizational involvement [24]. In consequence, the processes are extremely labor intensive, and their net benefits must be sought in a broader view of a participative planning process, rather than forecasting per se.

Despite the fairly widespread literature on composite systems and some of their problems, they remain in common use, particularly by industrial manufacturers. Unfortunately, there is little evidence that companies themselves have diagnosed the weaknesses of these operationally oriented forecasting and planning activities. Indeed, their modification and/or obsolescence seems more likely to result from the current wave of interest in strategic planning than any careful internal audit [35].

The forecasting model developed by Cyert and March was a by-product of their overall study [17, pp. 134–135]. Perhaps as a result, they are not particularly forthcoming about its development and descriptive validity:

> We do not mean to imply that the department consciously uses such a rule. Although the rule was inferred from a study of actual behavior, the head of department did not describe his estimation rule in these terms [17, p. 134].

The rule to which they refer is one that bases the forecast on dollar sales for the corresponding period in the preceding year. This basic rule, with a few refinements, predicted 95% of monthly forecasts within 5%, and while the authors felt that further accuracy could have been obtained, they also adjudged unwise the allocation of further effort to this activity. Notable once again in this study was the overriding importance of precedent, with a built-in conservative (downward) bias [17, pp. 134–135].

Despite the immense effort devoted to developing forecasting models, and the substantial number of surveys and laboratory studies of forecasting behavior [75, 78, 79], there is still a relative paucity of data on forecasting processes within the firm. In most companies forecasting is or should be an integral part of planning activities, and the implications of the various conflict resolution processes embodied in boxes 1–4 of Figure 9 are of key importance to the firm and to a descriptive understanding of its functioning. Recognized as central to a behavioral theory of the firm [17], these processes have witnessed considerable theoretical and laboratory development. Field studies, however, have not kept pace, with consequent gaps in knowledge.

Research Decisions

There exists sound normative theory dealing with the value of research information [4]. However, despite widespread recognition and discussion of the fact that research activity is often politicized and research findings noninfluential on decisions [40], once more there appears to be little detailed descriptive study of research decisions.

Capon and Scammon present a description of a fairly lengthy decision process in an advertising agency. They point out the key gatekeeping role of the account executive, who is normally untrained in research. Also noteworthy is the marked ambivalence of the agency research group, which wishes both to initiate research ideas and to avoid putting effort into projects that will not be accepted by the client. Finally, in the agency studied there was great reluctance to present recommendations along with research findings. Capon and Scammon [13, p. 10] conclude that this is "a risk-avoidance strategy on the part of the agency."

Conclusions

This chapter has reviewed descriptive models dealing with a fairly broad range of marketing decisions. The areas of pricing, advertising, and volume forecasting, in particular, have received the most attention. A number of substantive and methodological issues arise from this research, and these will now be explored.

Assessment of Research

Given the fragmented nature of most of the research discussed in this chapter, it is difficult to develop generalizations. However, a number of tentative conclusions may be drawn. First, the importance of precedents—of past decisions—was evident in a number of the models that were reviewed. Lindblom [46, 47] has noted similar incremental behavior among decision makers in government and elsewhere. For some of the repetitive advertising and stocking decisions reviewed in this chapter, incrementalism was quite evident.

Not unrelated to this first point was the relative simplicity of the rules used by many of the individual decision makers. Although this simplicity was not always evident to the decision maker [57, p. 21], its emergence is consistent with the propositions of organizational theorists [50]. Simple structure would appear to facilitate the task of developing information system support for the decision makers, insofar as the information to be supplied is linked to existing decision processes.

Another important observation concerns the relationship of normative to descriptive models of decision making. While most (but not all) of the descriptive models demanded informational inputs similar to those that a normative model would have required, there was little formal evidence that this information was being processed according to normative rules. Marschner's [51] attempt to compare normative and descriptive approaches was a useful concept in this regard, and could well be emulated by other would-be builders of descriptive models.

Finally, it also seems evident that more important marketing decisions are best viewed as part of an organizational decision system. Only some of the most simple and repetitive of decisions could be treated as essentially individual. This is not a surprising observation, but it has important methodological implications, which will be discussed in the last part of the chapter.

Table 3 presents a summary assessment of the research reviewed in this chapter. One key aspect of the state of this research is revealed by the first column. Of the decisions typically made by such individuals as brand,

Table 3. Assessment of Descriptive Research on Marketing Executive Decision Making

Decision area	Study	Models developed?	Formal validation on decision Sample?	Replication? Across decision makers	Across company?
Pricing	Cyert, March, and Moore	√	√	Joint	×
	Howard and Morgenroth/ Morgenroth	√	√	√	×
	Capon/Farley/ Howard/Hulbert	√	×	Joint	√
Advertising	Marschner	√	√	Joint	√
	Rados	√	√	×	×
	Capon and Scammon	√	×	×	×
	Fleck	√	√	Joint	×
	Capon and Hulbert	√	×	×	×
Product	Massy and Savvas	√	?	×	×
	Montgomery	√	√	Joint	×
	Capon and Hulbert	√	×	×	×
Forecasting	Cyert, March, and Moore	√	Limited	×	×
	Capon/Farley/ Howard/Hulbert	√	×	Joint	√
Research	Capon and Scammon	√	×	×	×

Key: √, yes; ×, no; ?, unclear; joint, model development apparently involved more than one decision maker.

market, or sales managers, quite a few are omitted. Thus, we have no descriptive studies of decision processes in areas as distribution, sales force allocation, or sales promotion, let alone studies of the trade-off decisions that must often be made among such mix elements as advertising and sales promotion or advertising and selling [76]. Further, even within mix decision areas that have been studied, there are relatively few pieces of research and often considerable divergence in the specific decisions that were studied.

Also of concern should be the fact that most of the research reviewed in this chapter has dealt with repetitive decisions, sometimes of rather mundane type. Table 4 reproduces a typology of strategic decisions, developed by Abell [2]. Few would argue with the important role of marketing in all row 1 and row 2 decisions, while Abell [2] and others [19] see important marketing aspects to decisions of the row 3 type. At best, the decision process models reviewed in this chapter deal with one element in the marketing mix, and might conceivably qualify for a position in the row 1, column 2, cell of Table 4. However, to tackle decisions affecting all mix elements—marketing strategy decisions for a product line, for example—will demand an upward shift of research focus, analogous to that which has occurred elsewhere [54]. So far, there is little sign that this shift is taking place—indeed, the fairest characterization of the state of descriptive research on marketing managers' decision making might well be "moribund." However, emerging interest in higher-level decisions among theoreticians [2, 31] might augur well for the future; there is certainly plenty of opportunity for empirical contributions.

Methodological Issues

A number of the major obstacles to the development of descriptive models of decision making are methodological, and some of these, at least, are reflected in Table 3. For example, the lack of follow-through in most of the studies is evident, for there is not one full row of check marks. There are at least two good reasons for this. First, developing the flowchart models is itself very labor intensive and the process of full validation is in some ways even more so. Thus, it is curious indeed to inspect an area of research and find an overwhelming dominance of single studies by an author(s), many of which were Ph.D. theses. Only one group of researchers has been involved in more than one of these studies. Second, the goal of most scientific research is to develop useful generalizations or lawlike propositions. Yet, decision process research is essentially idiographic; it does not foster the emergence of generalizations, and the attempt to do so is further impeded by the lack of suitable descriptive statistics. This problem is being approached on several fronts [6, 24], but further development is still needed.

Table 4. Matrix of Strategic Decisions

Level of decision	Decision categories		
	Product market strategy	Functional strategy	Portfolio/resource allocation strategy
Product/market segment level	"Positioning"	Marketing mix	Not applicable? Management may view segments of demand as parts of a portfolio?
"Business" unit level	Business definition/ configuration	Manufacturing policy, service policy, R&D policy, procurement policy, etc.; control policies, financial policies	Portfolio of products within a "business": resource allocation decisions
Corporate level	Corporate diversification strategy	Not applicable? Corporations may have a distinct marketing mix and set of other functional policies that transcend individual products and segments?	Portfolio of "businesses" within a corporation: resource allocation decisions

Related to the statistical issue is the problem that we call level, which arises in several studies and serves as a further impediment to the development of decision process research in organizational settings. Briefly, the origins and much of the early application and development of information-processing models were at the level of the individual decision maker. Yet, as researchers turn their attention to more strategic decisions, more persons inevitably become involved in a given decision process. Consequently, researchers are faced with a painful choice. To attempt to develop flowchart models for the forecasting process, for example, at the same level of specificity as has been attained for some of the repetitive individual level decisions we have discussed would entail enormous networks, and inordinate development and testing effort. Evidently, some more summary method is necessary for dealing with what we call organizational decision processes. Hulbert, Farley, and Howard [36] combine and compact node sequences by the use of criteria "boxes" that list briefly the various criteria that might usually be processed sequentially by the respective decision maker. However, no formal convention or rule to cover the collapsing process is presented. At any level above that of the individual decision maker, then, the utility of network statistics to compare decision processes is potentially compromised by this lack of control. Note also that similar problems can easily exist at the individual level; cf. Cyert and March's comments [17, p. 134] about their forecasting model.

The labor intensiveness problem is unlikely to be greatly ameliorated, particularly in the absence of more programmatic, replicative research efforts. Although Montgomery's approach [55] and that of others [28] have shown that the development of a model that predicts well need not be a laborious process, the development and testing of a model that purports to describe the actual process by which decisions are made is likely to remain time consuming.

A final problem is indicated quite clearly in Table 3. Development of appropriate conventions and statistics that enable generalization and improved model building methods are laudable tasks, but are only means to the end of developing better understanding of marketing executives' information processing and decision making. To develop this understanding will require much more effort and many more studies than are currently under way. Quite apart from the omission of important decision areas from the research effort (which was discussed in the first part of this section), decision process work in marketing has been remiss in its efforts to expand the data cube. For example, most of the studies summarized in Table 3 have looked at either samples of repetitive decisions [17, 55, 64] for a decision maker within a company or at the process for the same decision in different companies [e.g., 24]. Marschner's study is the only one that looked at samples of decisions in two different companies [51].

In some ways more problematic is the way in which some of the studies approach the issue of "the decision maker." In describing decision process research for consumer buying decisions, Bettman comments that

> ...the importance of this class of studies is that they focus on decision processes, use a deterministic, detailed, and individualistic approach in detail; [2] emphasize using situational variables; and support the use of nets as a first approximation of how human decision-makers combine attributes [6, p. 72].

While Bettman's work has been consistent with these precepts [5], some of the studies we have reviewed have not been. Some of the models described in this chapter were built by synthesizing protocols and/or other information from several decision makers [55; 57, p. 21; 64] and these we characterize as "joint" in Table 3. However, it is perhaps unfortunate that the synthesis was not made explicitly, so that comparison of different decision makers [e.g., 36] would be possible. Since the processes we have discussed are rarely organizationally prescribed [57], much of the potential research interest focuses on similarities and dissimilarities in process struc-

---

[2] Bettman [7, p. 9] has since modified this view somewhat, to admit a stochastic component.

ture among individual decision makers, types of decisions, and firms. That so few studies have been performed and that replications are so rare are, therefore, discouraging aspects of the field.

Nonetheless, there are strong arguments to buttress the importance of this kind of research. Better understanding of the marketing decision maker is not only a desirable research goal, it can also benefit normative model building, information system development, marketing teaching, and last but not least, the quality of marketing decisions.

References

1. Abell, Derek F. "Competitive Market Strategy: Some Generalizations and Hypotheses," Report #75-107. Cambridge, Massachusetts: Marketing Science Institute, 1975.
2. _____. "Alternative Strategies for Strategy Research in Marketing," Report #78-100, Cambridge, Massachusetts: Marketing Science Institute, 1978.
3. Alexis, Marcus, Haines, George, and Simon, Leonard. "Consumer Information Processing: The Case of Women's Clothing," in Proceedings of the American Marketing Association Fall Conference, *Marketing and the New Science of Planning*, 1968, pp. 197–205.
4. Bass, Frank M. "Marketing Research Expenditures: A Decision Model," *Journal of Business* 36 (January), 77–90 (1963).
5. Bettman, James R. "Information Processing Models of Consumer Behavior," *Journal of Marketing Research* 7 (August), 370–376 (1970).
6. _____. "Toward a Statistics for Consumer Decision Net Models," *Journal of Consumer Research* 1 (June), 71–80 (1974).
7. _____. *An Information Processing Theory of Consumer Choice*. Reading, Massachusetts: Addison-Wesley, 1979.
8. Bowman, E. H. "Consistency and Optimality in Management Decision Making," *Management Science* 9, 310–321 (1963).
9. Brandt, William K., and Hulbert, James M. "Organizational Structure and Marketing Strategy in the Multinational Subsidiary" in Proceedings of the American Marketing Association, *Marketing: The Challenges and the Opportunities*, 1975, pp. 320–325.
10. _____ and Hulbert, James M. "Patterns of Communication in the Multinational Corporation: An Empirical Study," *Journal of International Business Studies* 7 (Spring), 57–64 (1976).
11. Capon, Noel, and Hulbert, James. "Decision Systems in Industrial Marketing: An Empirical Approach," in *Proceedings* of the American Institute for Decision Sciences, November 1972, pp. 112–117.
12. _____ and Hulbert, James. "Decision Systems Analysis in Industrial Marketing," *Industrial Marketing Management* 4, 143–160 (1975).
13. _____ and Scammon, Debra. "Advertising Agency Decisions: An Analytic Treatment," in J. M. Leigh and C. R. Martin, Jr. (eds.), *Current Issues and Research in Advertising*. Ann Arbor: University of Michigan Press, 1979.
14. _____, Holbrook, Morris B., and Hulbert, James. "Industrial Purchasing

Behavior: A Reappraisal," *Journal of Business Administration* 4 (Fall), 69–77 (1972).

15. _____, Farley, John U., and Hulbert, James. "Pricing and Forecasting in an Oligopoly Firm," *Journal of Management Studies* 12 (May), 133–156 (1975).
16. Clarkson, Geoffrey. *Portfolio Selection: A Simulation of Trust Investment.* Englewood Cliffs, New Jersey: Prentice-Hall, 1962.
17. Cyert, Richard M., and March, James G., *A Behavioral Theory of the Firm.* Englewood Cliffs, New Jersey: Prentice-Hall, 1963.
18. Dawes, Robyn M., and Corrigan, Bernard. "Linear Models in Decision Making," *Psychological Bulletin* 81 (February), 95–106 (1974).
19. Day, George S. "Diagnosing the Product Portfolio," *Journal of Marketing* 41 (April), 29–38 (1974).
20. Ein-Dor, Phillip, and Segev, Eli. "Organizational Context and the Success of Management Information Systems," *Management Science* 24 (June), 1064–1077 (1978).
21. Farley, John U., and Hulbert, James. "Sistemas de Planejamento Mercadológico de Uma Firma Multinacional Sediada no Brasil," *Revista de Administração de Empresas* 15 (January–February), 7–14 (1975).
22. _____, Howard, John A., and Hulbert, James. "An Organizational Approach to an Industrial Marketing Information System," *Sloan Management Review* 13 (Fall), 35–54 (1971).
23. _____, Hulbert, James M., and Weinstein, David. "Marketing Planning Systems in European Multi-Market Industrial Companies," paper presented to the Academy of International Business, Fontainebleau, 1975.
24. _____, Hulbert, James M., and Weinstein, David. "Industrial Market Planning By Two European Multinational Companies: A Study of Decision Processes," Working Paper, Graduate School of Business, Columbia University, 1978.
25. Fleck, Robert A., Jr. "How Media Planners Process Information," *Journal of Advertising Research* 13 (April), 14–18 (1973).
26. Fogg, C. Davis. "Planning Gains in Market Share," *Journal of Marketing* 38 (July), 30–38 (1974).
27. Haines, George H. "Process Models of Consumer Decision Making," in G. David Hughes and Michael L. Ray (eds.), *Buyer/Consumer Information Processing.* Chapel Hill: University of North Carolina Press, 1974.
28. Heeler, Roger M., Kearney, Michael J., and Mehaffey, Bruce J. "Modeling Supermarket Product Selection," *Journal of Marketing Research* 10 (February), 34–37 (1973).
29. Howard, John A. *Marketing: Executive and Buyer Behavior.* New York: Columbia University Press, 1963.
30. _____. *Marketing Management*, 2nd ed. Homewood, Illinois: Richard D. Irwin, 1963.
31. _____. "Progress in Modeling Extensive Problem Solving: Consumer Acceptance of Innovation," Research Working Paper #147A, Graduate School of Business, Columbia University, August 1978.
32. _____ and Morgenroth, William M. "Information Processing Model of Executive Decisions," *Management Science* 14 (March), 416–428 (1968).
33. _____, Hulbert, James, M., and Farley, John U., "Organizational Analysis

and Information System Design: A Decision Process Perspective," *Journal of Business Research* 3 (April), 133–148 (1975).

34. Huber, Joel. "Bootstrapping of Data and Decisions," *Journal of Consumer Research* 2 (December), 229–234 (1975).

35. Hulbert, James M. "Composite Forecasting Systems: Avoiding the Pitfalls and Problems," Working Paper, Columbia University, December 1978.

36. _____, Farley, John U., and Howard, John A. "Information Processing and Decision Making in Marketing Organizations," *Journal of Marketing Research* 9 (February), 75–77 (1972).

37. Huysmans, Jan H. B. M. "The Effectiveness of the Cognitive-Style Constraint in Implementing Operations Research Proposals," *Management Science* 17, (September), 92–104 (1970).

38. Janis, Irving L., and Mann, Leon. *Decision Making*. New York: Free Press, 1977.

39. Kotler, Philip. *Marketing Management: Analysis, Planning and Control*, 2nd ed. Englewood Cliffs, New Jersey: Prentice-Hall, 1972.

40. Kover, Arthur J. "Marketing Research and Two Kinds of Legitimacy," *The American Sociologist* 6 (Supplementary Issue), 69–72 (1971).

41. Lambin, Jean-Jacques, Naert, Philippe A., and Bultez, Alain. "Optimal Marketing Behavior in Oligopoly," *European Economic Review* 6, 105–128 (1975).

42. Lanzillotti, Robert F. "Pricing Objectives in Large Companies," *American Economic Review* 48 (December), 921–940 (1958).

43. Larréché, Jean-Claude. "Managers and Models: A Search for a Better Match," unpublished doctoral dissertation, Stanford University, August 1974.

44. Levitt, Theodore. *Industrial Purchasing Behavior: A Study of Communications Effects*. Boston: Division of Research, Graduate School of Business Administration, Harvard University, 1965.

45. _____. "Industrial Purchasing Behavior: A Bayesian Reanalysis," *Journal of Business Administration* 4 (Fall), 79–81 (1972).

46. Lindblom, Charles E. "The Science of Muddling Through," *Public Administration Review* 19, 79–99 (1959).

47. _____. *The Intelligence of Democracy*. New York: Free Press, 1965.

48. Little, John D. C., and Lodish, Leonard M. "A Media Planning Calculus," *Operations Research* 17 (January–February), 1–35 (1969).

49. Lodish, Leonard M. "CALLPLAN: An Interactive Salesman's Call Planning System," *Management Science* 18 (December), 25–40 (1971).

50. March, James G., and Simon, Herbert A. *Organizations*. New York: Wiley, 1958.

51. Marschner, Donald C. "Theory vs. Practice in Allocating Advertising Money," *Journal of Business* 40, 286–302 (1967).

52. Massy, William F., and Savvas, Jim D. "Logical Flow Models for Marketing Analysis," *Journal of Marketing* 28 (January), 30–37 (1964).

53. Maynes, E. Scott. *Decision-Making for Consumers: An Introduction to Consumer Economics*. New York: Macmillan, 1976.

54. Mintzberg, Henry, Raisinghani, Duru, and Théorêt, André. "The Structure of 'Unstructured' Decision Processes," *Administrative Science Quarterly* 21 (June), 246–275 (1976).

55. Montgomery, David B. "New Product Distribution: An Analysis of Super-market Buyer Decisions," Research Paper 104, Graduate School of Business, Stanford University, August 1972.

56. _____. "New Product Distribution—An Analysis of Supermarket Buyer Decisions," *Journal of Marketing Research* 12 (August), 255–64 (1975).

57. Morgenroth, William M. "A Method for Understanding Price Determinants," *Journal of Marketing Research* 1 (August), 17–26 (1964).

58. Newell, Alan, and Simon, Herbert A. "Elements of a Theory of Human Problem Solving," *Psychological Review* 65 (May), 151–166 (1958).

59. _____ and Simon Herbert A. *Human Problem Solving*. Englewood Cliffs, New Jersey: Prentice-Hall, 1972.

60. Nisbett, Richard E., and Wilson, Timothy DeCamp. "Telling More Than We Can Know: Verbal Reports on Mental Processes," *Psychological Review* 84, 231–259 (1977).

61. Oxenfeldt, Alfred R., and Moore, William L. "Customer or Competitor: Which Guideline for Marketing?" *Management Review* 67 (August) 43–48 (1978).

62. Payne, John W., and Ragsdale, Easton K. "Verbal Protocols and Direct Observation of Supermarket Shopping Behavior: Some Findings and a Discussion of Methods," in Proceedings of the Association for Consumer Research, *Advances in Consumer Research* 5, 571–577 (1978).

63. PIMSletter No. 10. "The Senior Executive Tight-Wire Act: Balancing the Portfolio of Businesses." Cambridge, Massachusetts: The Strategic Planning Institute, 1978.

64. Rados, David L. "Simulation of the Selection of an Item for a Grocery Ad," *British Journal of Marketing* 4 (Summer), 70–79 (1970).

65. _____. "Selection and Evaluation of Alternatives in Repetitive Decision Making," *Administrative Science Quarterly* 17 (June), 196–206 (1972).

66. Remus, William Edward. "Testing Bowman's Managerial Coefficient Theory Using a Competitive Gaming Environment," *Management Science* 24, 827–835 (1978).

67. Robinson, Patrick V., Faris, Charles W., and Wind, Yoram. *Industrial Buying and Creative Marketing*. Boston: Allyn and Bacon, 1967.

68. Russ, Frederick A. "Consumer Evaluation of Alternative Product Models," unpublished doctoral dissertation, Carnegie-Mellon University, 1971.

69. Schultz, Randall L., and Slevin, Dennis P. (eds.). *Implementing Operations Research/Management Science*. New York: American Elsevier Publishing Company, Inc., 1975.

70. _____ and Henry, Michael D. "Implementing Decision Models," Institute Paper No. 684, Krannert Graduate School of Management, Purdue University, February, 1979.

71. Simon, Herbert A. *The New Science of Management Decision*. Englewood Cliffs, New Jersey: Prentice-Hall, 1960.

72. Sissors, Jack Z., and Petray, E. R. *Advertising Media Planning*. Chicago, Illinois: Crain Books, 1976.

73. Smith, Eliot R., and Miller, Frederick D. "Limits on Perception of Cognitive Processes: A Reply to Nisbett and Wilson," *Psychological Review* 85, 355–362 (1978).

74. Soelberg, Peer O. "Unprogrammed Decision Making," *Industrial Management Review* 8 (Spring), 19–29 (1967).
75. Staelin, Richard, and Turner, Ronald E. "Error in Judgmental Sales Forecasts: Theory and Results," *Journal of Marketing Research* 10 (February), 10–16 (1973).
76. Swinyard, William R., and Ray, Michael L. "Advertising-Selling Interactions: An Attribution Theory Experiment," *Journal of Marketing Research* 14 (November), 509–516 (1977).
77. Tushman, Michael L., and Nadler, David A. "Information Processing as an Integrating Concept in Organizational Design," *Academy of Management Review* 3 (July), 613–624 (1978).
78. The Conference Board. *Forecasting Sales*, Study in Business Policy No. 106, New York: National Industrial Conference Board, 1964.
79. The Conference Board. *Sales Forecasting Practices*, Experiences in Marketing Management No. 25, New York: National Industrial Conference Board, 1970.

3

Normative Marketing Models*

Andris A. Zoltners

Compared with descriptive and predictive models, normative models have recently assumed a secondary role in marketing model development. This trend can be contrasted with early marketing model building activity, which produced many normative models. Early marketing modeling textbooks, such as those by Montgomery and Urban [13] and Kotler [9], have a decidedly normative orientation compared to more recent textbooks, such as that of Naert and Leeflang [15], which are significantly more descriptive. The inclination toward descriptive modeling also distinguishes marketing models from models in other business disciplines, such as operations management and finance, in which normative models have a significant presence. Several reasons for this trend are cited in this chapter.

It can be argued, however, that normative models should be an integral part of many model-assisted marketing decision systems. With this position in mind, this chapter also describes how normative models fit into the marketing decision process, characterizes various types of normative models, and suggests future directions for normative marketing model building.

Marketing Models and Marketing Decisions

Frequently, marketing models evolve from a decision process similar to the one described in Figure 1. A manager is faced with one or more marketing decisions. For example, (a) a brand manager may be faced with determining an advertising and promotional plan for a brand; (b) a group product manager may have to decide whether or not to introduce a new product, determine a positioning strategy, and establish an introductory marketing

*I would like to thank Randy Schultz and Prabhakant Sinha for their helpful comments.

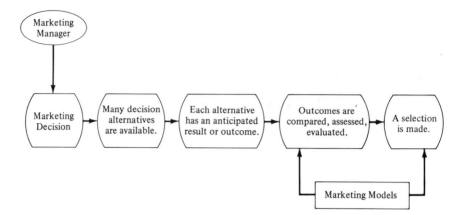

Figure 1. A marketing decision process.

program; (c) in view of recent product, market, and competitive changes, a vice president of sales may be faced with deciding upon a new sales force size, an improved product, market and account sales effort allocation, and a modified sales force organization; (d) the media staff at an advertising agency may have to assist a client in selecting the most effective media mix.

Usually there are numerous decision alternatives available to the decision maker. The brand manager in (a) can choose from among a variety of marketing plans for each of several brand budget levels. Similarly, the vice president of sales in (c) can choose among many sales force sizes (e.g., 0–1500), can allocate sales effort in numerous ways among the firm's products and markets, and can organize the sales force geographically, by market, or by product. Frequently, decision makers do not acknowledge the huge number of alternatives available to them. They implicitly tend to reduce the set of choices to a manageable number. Good marketing strategies may be overlooked when the set of decision alternatives is reduced by the decision maker.

The selection of the best marketing decision from the set of decision alternatives is usually based on an assessment or evaluation of the decisions in terms of one or more forecasted business outcomes. Sales, market share, long-term profits, short-term profits, and growth are among the business outcomes generally used.

Decision makers can look to marketing models to help them assess the business outcomes associated with various marketing decisions and to help them select among the available alternatives.

Descriptive and Predictive Models

Many marketing models have been developed to enable decision makers to understand and assess the marketplace and to predict the business outcomes resulting from their marketing decisions. Models that serve these functions have been called descriptive models and predictive models. Descriptive models attempt to provide detailed and accurate representations of the marketing phenomenon under investigation. Models have been developed to describe consumer and industrial buyer behavior, distributor behavior, competitor behavior, and market behavior. Predictive models, on the other hand, are concerned with forecasting outcomes of specific marketing decisions, plans, and events. They are frequently used to examine the likely impact on performance measures of changes in marketing decision variables. They have been used to estimate product class sales, brand sales, and market shares for new and established products. The following is an example of a predictive model:

$$m_t = 1.003 - 1.157 \frac{P_t}{\bar{P}_t} + 0.016 \frac{A_t}{\bar{A}_t} + 0.566 \frac{P_{t-1}}{\bar{P}_{t-1}} + 0.276 m_{t-1};$$

where

m_t is the market share of a brand in period t,

P_t is the price of a brand in dollars,

$\bar{P}_t$ is the average industry price (weighted by volume),

A_t represents the advertising expenditures for a brand, and

$\bar{A}_t$ represents the average industry advertising expenditures.

Models can be both descriptive and predictive. In fact, many good predictive models are a consequence of sound descriptive theory.

It may be a difficult task to build a good descriptive or predictive model. As Little [10] points out, "good models are hard to find" and "good parameterization is even harder." Marketing phenomena are complex, ill structured, and difficult to formulate, involving behavioral and creative aspects. Marketing is a dynamic, rapidly changing area where the time scale of change is often short relative to the time scale of observations. The following list of factors describes some of the components that can add to the complexity of marketing models:

An uncertain relationship between marketing strategies and the consequent sales response

Multiple marketing instruments and their interaction

Multiple levels of behavioral response to marketing activities; for example, awareness, trial, repurchase, switching, or sales

Delayed response and carry-over effects

Competition

Environmental influences, public policy, and technology

Multiple objectives and goals

Uncertainty and risk

Multiple and differing markets, multiple products; for example, the emergence of the multinational–multiproduct corporation

The availability of data, specifically, the quality, quantity, or variability of existing data

The modeling user's modeling and integrative abilities

The organizational structure of the firm; the interaction between marketing, financial, production, and purchasing decisions

Descriptive and predictive model building has recently become an active area. A larger number of models have been developed incorporating such methodologies as stochastic consumer behavior, econometrics, simulation, macro flow modeling, utility theory, diffusion processes, and subjective market behavior estimation. The relative importance of these models to quantitative marketing is suggested by Naert and Leeflang [15, p. 42]: "Future models will be of the predictive and descriptive, rather than the normative variety."

However, if models are to be used for decision making they must also contribute to the decision selection process. Normative models provide a basis for choosing a good, possibly even optimal, strategy from among alternative courses of action. The remainder of this chapter focuses on normative models in marketing.

Normative Marketing Models

As Figure 1 shows, a manager faced with a marketing decision must ultimately select one of several (more likely, numerous) decision alternatives. Normative models are designed to aid in the selection process. These models can be classified and discussed in various ways. Figure 2 describes a classification scheme that will be used here.

Theoretical and Decision Models

Normative models may be classified as either theoretical models or decision models. Contrasting the two approaches, we note that theoretical models are designed to develop normative theory, whereas decision models are designed to provide specific solutions to specific decision problems. Decision models are frequently reapplied, since the marketing decision may be faced repeatedly by a single firm or since various firms may encounter similar decision problems. Decision models have a "real-world"

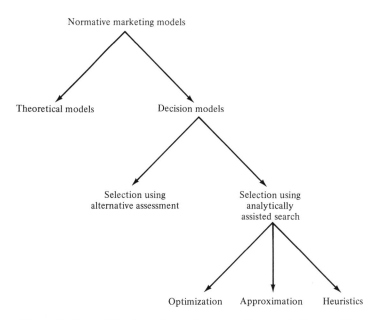

Figure 2. A classification scheme for normative marketing models.

focus and many good decision models have seen practical implementation. A final point of difference between theoretical and decision models is that theoretical models are primarily descriptive whereas decision models are usually predictive.

Media selection models, such as MINI-COMPASS [1], MEDIAC [11], HIGH ASSAY [14], ADMOD [2], and BENCHMARK,[1] are examples of decision models. They have been designed to help media planners develop good media schedules. They attempt to incorporate all of the relevant media factors and are parameterized using available data and/or subjective judgments. Several of these models are utilized daily by advertising agencies.

Normative theoretical models, on the other hand, employ theoretical mathematical representations of market behavior. They are generally solved analytically or embedded within a simulation analysis. The solution of these models usually suggests generalizable normative strategies for decision makers. As an illustration of a theoretical model, Dorfman and Steiner in a classic article [7] postulate the following theoretical relationships among profits, sales and costs, and the marketing mix:[2]

---

[1]BENCHMARK is marketed by TELMAR Corporation.

[2]Also see Kotler [9]. It should be noted that the basic analysis presented by Dorfman and Steiner has been extended subsequently by other researchers.

Company demand function

$$Q = q(P, A, D, R),$$

where

Q is the quantity produced,
P is the price of the product,
A is the promotion expenditure (that is, advertising and personal selling),
D reflects the distribution investment, and
R is an index or rating of the product's overall quality in the marketplace.

Company cost function

$$C = c(Q, R)Q + A + D + F,$$

where the unit cost c is a function of Q and R, and F represents the sum of nondiscretionary fixed costs.

Short-run profit function

$$Z = PQ - C$$
$$= Pq(P, A, D, R) - c(Q, R)Q - A - D - F$$
$$= Pq(P, A, D, R) - c[q(P, A, D, R), R]q(P, A, D, R) - A - D - F.$$

It can be shown that profits are greatest when

$$e_P = \frac{PQ}{A} e_A = \frac{PQ}{D} e_D = \frac{P}{c} e_R,$$

where

$$e_P = -\frac{\partial Q}{\partial P} \frac{P}{Q}$$

is the price elasticity of demand,

$$e_A = \frac{\partial Q}{\partial A} \frac{A}{Q}$$

is the advertising elasticity of demand,

$$e_D = \frac{\partial Q}{\partial D} \frac{D}{Q}$$

is the distribution elasticity of demand, and

$$e_R = \frac{\partial Q}{\partial R} \frac{\partial R}{\partial c} \frac{c}{Q}$$

is the product quality elasticity of demand.

Theoretical results such as these are useful for subsequent decision making. Specifically, Dorfman and Steiner suggest that a profit maximizing marketing mix occurs when the price, advertising, distribution, and product quality elasticities of demand are equal. It is anticipated that theoretical models address decision problems that occur frequently in practice. Whenever one of these decisions is encountered for which a decision model is inappropriate (incomplete data, insufficient time for a thorough analysis, etc.), the decision maker can elicit fairly general decision rules provided by the theoretical models. Thus theoretical models can be used to develop decisiveness through skill in recognizing the proper form of an optimal solution even when a problem is not completely formulated in mathematical terms. As another illustration, consider the adoption by many marketing managers of decision rules such as the following: When allocating a limited marketing resource (such as an advertising budget) to marketing entities (such as geographic regions), best results are obtained when the marginal returns from the marketing entities are equal.

As mentioned earlier, decision models address specific marketing problems. They rely on a predictive model that forecasts the outcome(s) of the decision alternatives. Through utilization of the predictive model, decision alternatives can be evaluated, assessed, and compared. A decision is usually made after comparing the decision alternatives. Two decision evaluation and selection procedures have been employed by model builders and model users.

Assessment Models

Assessment models are primarily predictive models in which the model user develops marketing strategies, evaluates them using the model, and selects a good strategy based upon a comparison of predicted outcomes. The search over the set of decision alternatives is made by the model user. The model functions as an assessor of potential marketing strategies.

Little's ADBUDG [10] is an example of an assessment model. ADBUDG is a model of sales response to advertising designed to aid a brand manager or advertising manager in determining a reasonable budget for a product. The heart of the model is the following relationship between the market share for the brand and various advertising variables:[3]

$$ms_t = m_0 + \frac{m^- - m_0}{m_i - m_0}(ms_{t-1} - m_0) + (m^+ - m^-)\frac{DA_t^\gamma}{\delta + DA_t^\gamma},$$

where

$$DA_t = e_t c_t A_t$$

---

[3] See Little [10] for a more detailed description of the model.

and

t is an index for time, usually budget periods, such as quarters,

ms_t is the brand's market share in period t,

m_i is the initial market share at the beginning of the planning period,

m^- represents the brand market share that could be expected after one time period if the brand management cut advertising to zero, given a starting market share of m_i,

m^+ represents the brand market share that could be expected after one time period if the brand management increased advertising a great deal, given a starting market share of m_i,

m_0 represents the brand market share that could be expected in the long run if the brand management ceased to advertise,

e_t is a media efficiency index in period t,

c_t is a copy effectiveness index in period t,

A_t represents the advertising expenditure for the brand in period t, and

δ, γ are subjectively determined sales response parameters.

The process required to implement ADBUDG illustrates how an assessment model could be used. The model is first parameterized using existing data or subjective judgment. Following the parameterization of the model, good candidate brand advertising budgets are developed by the brand management team. The candidates are evaluated by the model in terms of forecasted profits, sales revenue, and market share. A sensitivity analysis is usually performed. Model robustness relative to marketing parameters e_t and c_t and relative to response parameters m_i, m^-, m^+, and m_0 is ascertained. If the model results are exceedingly sensitive to these parameter estimates, additional marketing research can be performed to determine their accuracy and derive more accurate estimates if necessary. After comparing budget alternatives relative to the performance criteria, a budget selection is made.

Analytically Assisted Decision Models

Analytically assisted decision models are decision models that provide the model user with a facility to search the set of feasible decision alternatives. Such a model assists the model user in the decision selection process by providing analytically developed search routines that capitalize on the model structure. Since the number of decision alternatives can become quite large, analytically assisted decision models are frequently computerized or automated. A decision maker using an assessment model also employs heuristics (or analytics) to limit his or her search over the set of decision alternatives. These heuristics are a result of practical real-world experience and an adaptive learning that comes from assessing numerous alternatives using the model. However, the subset of alternatives suggested by the decision maker should be among those examined by an effective automated search procedure. Hence, an analytically assisted decision model will provide solutions at least as good as those provided by an assessment model. When the number of candidate decision alternatives reaches many billions, an automated search facility can have a significant advantage.

Three types of analytical search procedures have been developed. These are optimization, approximation, and heuristics. Traditionally, optimization procedures have been defined as search procedures (either closed form or algorithmic) that are guaranteed to produce the best solution to a theoretical or decision model. Approximation procedures, on the other hand, are search procedures that are guaranteed to produce a solution within a prescribed tolerance of the optimum, for example, within 5% of the optimum. Implicit in both definitions is that a single performance measure be used as a criterion for comparing decision alternatives. In view of one of the new directions for normative marketing modeling, which will be suggested in the last section of this chapter, optimization will be redefined here as a complete search (either implicit or explicit) over the set of decision alternatives to produce a set of undominated solutions. To date, approximation models have seen very little use in marketing. For completeness, however, approximation models will be redefined as a search over the set of decision alternatives to produce a set of nearly undominated solutions.

Finally, heuristic procedures are search procedures that produce good solutions to decision models. A heuristic solution may be optimal. However, there is no guarantee of this optimality nor is there any evidence of its proximity to optimality. One expects good solutions because heuristic search procedures are usually founded on clever decision rules.

Multiple modeling approaches have been developed for many marketing decision problems. For example, the sales resource allocation decision faced by most sales force managers has seen extensive model development.[4] Zoltners and Sinha [21] provide a list of over 25 sales resource allocation models that have appeared in the literature. These models address various sales resource allocation decisions: aggregate sales resource allocation, such as the allocation of salespeople and sales budget to products, markets, and channels of distribution; disaggregate allocation, such as the allocation of sales calls or sales time to the accounts and prospects constituting a sales territory; and so on. Both theoretical and decision models have been

---

[4]See Zoltners and Sinha [21] for a summary of the numerous models that have been developed for this area.

developed. Optimization and heuristic search procedures have been employed.

A specific illustration of the diversity of modeling approaches is the theoretical investigation by Wellman [19] of how a sales force budget should be allocated to geographic areas. He used linear, concave, and S-shaped sales response functions to derive allocation rules. Lodish [12] developed a decision model for determining how a salesperson's time should be allocated across accounts and prospects. His decision model is solved by using a heuristic search procedure. Zoltners, Sinha, and Chong [22] also developed a decision model for salesperson time management. However, their model employs an optimization search procedure.

Optimization and Heuristic Search Procedures

Comparing the three decision procedures mentioned above, we see that optimization appears to be preferred. Why would anyone settle for a suboptimal decision? Yet, many marketing model builders opt not to build optimizing decision models. Recall the position stated by Naert and Leeflang that future models will be of the predictive and descriptive, rather than the normative (optimizing), variety. Several reasons can be cited for this view. Decision making using optimization models tends to preclude the incorporation of managerial judgment. Managers may thus feel uneasy with model-produced solutions, particularly if they feel that the decision problem may be incorrectly defined. A model is a representation of reality. As such, it is very likely that it is an imperfect representation and human judgment can be included to enhance the decision. Optimization models tend to omit this important aspect of planning.

Perhaps the most compelling argument against optimization is that to date the model assumptions required by most optimization models are excessively restrictive when it comes to modeling complex marketing behavior. As an illustration, consider the following linear programming formulation of the media selection decision:

$$\text{maximize} \quad \sum_{j=1}^{n} e_j x_j$$

$$\text{subject to} \quad \sum_{j=1}^{n} c_j x_j \leqslant B,$$

$$l_j \leqslant x_j \leqslant u_j \quad \text{for} \quad j = 1, 2, \ldots, n$$

where

j is an index of advertising media $j = 1, 2, \ldots, n$,

x_j is the number of ads placed in medium j in the planning period (decision variable),

e_j is the exposure value of an ad in medium i,

c_j is the cost of an ad in medium j,

B is the advertising budget for the planning period,

l_j is the minimum number of ads to be placed in medium j in the planning period, and

u_j is the maximum number of ads to be placed in medium j in the planning period.

This model was introduced with considerable fanfare by a large New York advertising agency as the model that would make media selection scientific. Yet the linearity assumptions inherent in its formulation render it a weak representation of the media selection problem. For example, the model assumes that each exposure has a constant effect. It assumes constant media costs (no discounts). The decision variables can assume fractional values in the optimal solution, producing unimplementable media schedules. The model cannot accommodate the problem of audience duplication and replication. Finally, it fails to indicate when advertisements should be scheduled.

In addition to the linearity assumption implicit in linear programming, other optimization models require alternate assumptions about market behavior. Several illustrative examples are developed below.

The Lagrange multiplier technique for nonlinear constrained optimization is a popular approach for marketers. When applying this technique, market behavior is usually represented by differentiable concave functions, such as the following function employed by Buzzell [4] when deciding the optimal mix of direct and wholesale salesmen for an industrial manufacturer:

$$S = \overline{S}(1 - e^{-aN}),$$

where

S is the estimated dollar sales per period,

$\overline{S}$ is the saturation level of sales per period,

a is the rate at which sales approach the saturation level of sales, and

N is the number of direct or wholesale salesmen.

Several geometric programming models [3, 5] have recently been developed for various marketing decision areas. These models assume that demand and cost functions have multiplicative forms similar to the one derived by Balachandran and Gensch for a marketing mix application:

$$\text{Sales} = 16.212 + 3.937 A2_{t-1}^{0.91} B_t^{1.31} - 0.00021 A1_{t-1}^{-0.95} P_t^{-0.68} T_t^{-0.84} c_t^{-0.28}$$
$$- 0.00305 Ac_t^{-0.18} Q_t^{1.76} - 0.0046 I_t^{-0.9} S_{t-1}^{-1.1} - 0.0053 P_t^{-0.76} D_t^{-1.12},$$

where

$A1_t$ is relative advertising expenditure for advertising emphasizing price, that is, ratio of the firm's expenditure to that of the total industry,

$A2_t$ is relative advertising expenditure for mood or image advertising,

B_t is relative package appeal,

P_t is retail price divided by the average price charged by competing firms,

T_t represents the deals or special discounts the firm allows its wholesalers and retailers,

C_t is the relative price differential from previous period, that is, the change in retail price from one period to the next divided by the average retail price in the industry,

Ac_t is the percentage of the population between 18 and 24 years of age divided by the average long-term percentage in this group,

Q_t is the perceived relative quality of the brand,

I_t represents the relative expenditures for in-store promotions,

S_{t-1} is the sales force effort measured in terms of total salary and commissions,

D_t is the availability of the firm's brand expressed as a percentage of weighted retail outlets that carry the firm's brand.

Several marketing applications of integer programming have assumed that the sales response to marketing instruments can be represented by a discrete function. For example, the sales resource allocation models developed by Zoltners and Sinha [21] assume that sales response to sales effort can be adequately represented by functions of the type appearing in Figure 3.

As a final illustration, continuous-time optimal control models assume that market behavior can be specified by a differential equation:

$$\frac{d}{dt} x(t) = h(x(t), u(t)), \qquad t \in [0, T],$$

where

$x(t)$ represents the state of the system at time t, and

$u(t)$ represents the control input at time t.

To represent marketing behavior more adequately, marketing model builders have tended to build more complete and consequently more complex decision models. To date, optimization models have not been able

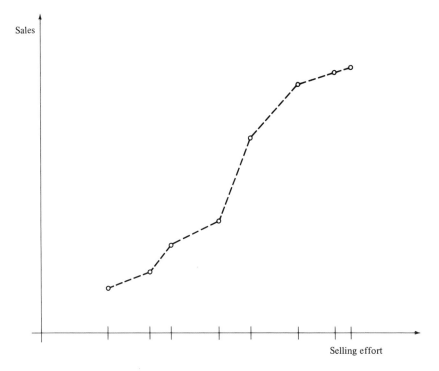

Figure 3. Discrete functions representing the sales response to selling effort.

adequately to accommodate this increased complexity. As a result, numerous heuristic search procedures have been developed to search the set of decision alternatives.

Heuristic search procedures are simple and/or sophisticated decision rules that partially search the set of decision alternatives. They are usually ad hoc, attempting to exploit the model structure. Several heuristic search strategies have been employed. The most popular is the marginal analysis strategy. This strategy is basically a gradient search in which decision variables are incremented as long as a performance criterion can be improved. Various versions of this approach exist. The "greedy" marginal heuristic is one in which decision variables are incremented in the direction of the greatest immediate improvement. The procedure stops when an improvement is no longer possible. Alternatives to the greedy heuristic incorporate "look ahead" procedures and alternative starting points.

Some heuristic algorithms solve approximations of the original model. This approach can be successful when the approximation is easy to solve and when the approximation is reasonably close in the neighborhood of the optimal solution of the original model. Finally, some heuristic algorithms are partially corrective trial-and-error procedures. Usually ad hoc,

Table 1. A Computational Comparison of an Optimal Solution with Two Heuristics for a Class of Media Selection Problems

Problem number	Solution value, m$		
	Optimal solution[a]	Control theory solution	Little–Lodish heuristic
1	0.342	0.346	0.298
2	0.753	0.761	0.761
3	1.167	1.172	0.762
4	1.579	1.573	1.600
5	1.314	1.171	0.821
6	2.790	2.705	2.005

[a] The optimal solution is not truly optimal since a piecewise linear approximation was used in its derivation. It provides a close lower bound on the true optimum.

they may systematically or randomly modify model solutions looking for improvement or they may incorporate "look ahead" and "look back" procedures to examine the effects of model solution changes.

The reaction to increased model complexity has been the reduced utilization of optimization models. Yet, several strong arguments can be made for optimization. The following reasons for optimization have been set forth by Geoffrion [8].

First, significant opportunities may be overlooked when an optimal solution is not obtained. These lost opportunities can be significant at times. Srinivasan [17] compares the Little–Lodish heuristic [11], an optimal control heuristic, and an optimal solution to a class of media scheduling problems. This comparison is reproduced in Table 1. Whereas the optimal control heuristic performs very well, it should be observed that some heuristics can lead to significantly suboptimal solutions.

It is often maintained that simpler, nonoptimizing methods are likely to perform just as well as truly optimizing methods when the model data contain substantial errors. Geoffrion argues:

> The fallacy of this is that unbiased random errors tend to cancel one another and preserve the relative ranking of alternative solutions. Computational experiments have confirmed this effect. It follows that if one solution is better than another under the estimated data, then it will probably still compare favorably under the (unknown) true data. Thus the use of truly optimizing methods is warranted even when the available data contain (unbiased) errors. Of course, no approach, computer-assisted or otherwise, can be immune from the possible deleterious effects of serious biased errors in the data.[5]

---

[5] This and the following quotation reprinted from "A Guide to Computer-Assisted Methods for Distribution" by Arthur M. Geoffrion, *Sloan Management Review* (Winter 1975), pp. 25–26, by permission of the publisher. Copyright 1975 by the Sloan Management Review Association. All rights reserved.

Second, the marketing analyst or consultant, who is frequently the model builder and model user, should keep in mind that to overlook a superior solution to a marketing model is to risk loss of credibility. It could be very embarrassing if a marketing executive were to suggest a better solution than the one proposed by the model.

Third, without optimization it is meaningless to perform sensitivity analysis and "what if" analysis. One can never be certain whether solution differences are attributable to model parameter sensitivity or to the solution wobble inherent in nonoptimization procedures.

Finally, Geoffrion argues that

> optimization methods usually lend themselves more readily to tracking down the sources of the inevitable data input errors. The reason is that input errors are revealed and diagnosed via their influence on the model's output. This influence is much easier to trace back through the precision logic of an optimizing method than through the 'mushier' innards of most nonoptimizing methods. Needless to say, thorough input validation is absolutely essential.

To summarize several of the points made above, marketing models are becoming more and more complex, whereas optimization models tend to be restrictive, yet the latter have several significant advantages. In light of this, one may question whether model complexity and optimization are compatible. It is too early to answer this question. Zoltners and Sinha have had moderate success in developing optimization models for several actual sales force decision model implementations. Together with Chong [22], they have shown that a class of salesperson time management problems can be solved optimally. Previously, this model had been solved by Lodish [12] using a heuristic algorithm.

Sinha and Zoltners [16] have also helped a firm allocate its entire sales effort across products and markets. Several decision models evolved as more information became available, model restrictions became apparent, and more decision criteria were incorporated. An algorithmic evolution paralleled the model evolution. Three optimization algorithms were developed before the implementation was completed. This research revealed that an algorithmic orientation is required if optimization models are to be developed for complex marketing problems. A direct application of a "canned" optimization model or algorithm does not seem to be adequate for many marketing problems.

Several Optimizing Search Strategies

Existing optimization techniques can provide a good starting point for anyone interested in developing a customized search algorithm for a complex marketing model. Three optimal search approaches, which are potentially useful for marketing applications, will be described briefly.

Detailed descriptions of the last two, dynamic programming and branch and bound, can be found in most operations research textbooks.[6]

Quick-and-Dirty Complete Enumeration

Occasionally the number of decision alternatives is sufficiently small that a complete enumeration can be accomplished efficiently. A complete enumeration may be feasible if a small number of decision alternatives is contemplated for each decision variable and if the aggregate decision formed by combining these decision variables is enumerable.

A simple search such as this should not be overlooked. For example, ADBUDG, the advertising budgeting model discussed in an earlier section, has been used by many student groups in conjunction with a classroom case analysis (Castle Coffee [6]). Several of my student groups have complained of the numerous trial advertising budgets that were required before good budget alternatives could be derived. Assuming a four-quarter budgeting analysis, a complete enumeration and evaluation of annual budget alternatives is feasible if the number of quarterly budget alternatives can be kept reasonably small, say 10 or fewer. Such an enumeration would provide an optimal solution relative to the smaller set of alternatives. If after analyzing the results it is felt that the set of alternatives is too small, the model user can restart a subsequent search from the optimal solution derived from the initial enumeration.

Dynamic Programming

Dynamic programming has been used to determine optimal solutions to numerous marketing models. It can be applied if the following properties exist:

1. The marketing problem can be divided into sequential stages, each stage consisting of states (see Figure 4).
2. For each state, say j_k, there is a set of decisions $D(j_k)$ available to the decision maker.
3. The system will enter exactly one state in each stage and only one decision from the set $D(j_k)$ can be chosen for each j_k.
4. There are two consequences of adopting decision $d_{j_k} \in D(j_k)$:
   (a) A system utility is obtained or a disutility is incurred.

---

[6] These optimization techniques are intended to be illustrative of some of the approaches the author thinks are potentially useful for complex marketing problems. Certainly other optimization procedures, utilizing Lagrange multipliers, optimal control, mathematical programming, etc., will be developed as well.

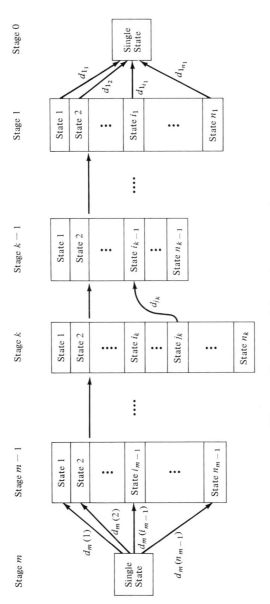

Figure 4. Overview of dynamic programming.

(b) The state entered at stage $k-1$ is a function of the state in which the system found itself at stage k and the adopted decision. For example, if decision d_{j_k} is adopted at state j_k in stage k, then the system must enter decision state i_{k-1} at the subsequent stage.

5. The stages are independent; that is, the optimal sequence of decisions subsequent to any state j_k (that is, decisions $d_{j_k}, d_{i_{k-1}}, \ldots, d_{i_1}$) does not depend on how the system arrived at state j_k. Put another way, the decision streams before and after j_k are independent.

Dynamic programming gains its efficiency from the fact that the effort involved in determining the optimal sequence of decisions subsequent to each state j_k at stage k is greatly reduced when the optimal sequence of decisions subsequent to each state in the $(k-1)$st stage is known. The search begins by solving stage 1 optimally and backtracks through all the stages until it solves the mth stage optimally.

Branch and Bound

Branch and bound is a search technique that has been applied to various artificial intelligence problems and that has been used frequently to solve complex mathematical programming problems. Branch and bound employs a divide-and-conquer strategy. The decision alternatives are partitioned. One decision partition is analyzed at a time. It is assumed that the partition analysis can be easily accomplished and that continual refinement of partitions (further partitioning of partitions) will ultimately lead to decision partitions that can be solved optimally, hence guaranteeing an optimal solution to the original model.

Strategies for partition analysis may include any of the following:

1. Direct solution of the model relative to the partition. It may be possible to solve a complex model optimally on a reduced set of decision alternatives.
2. Solution of a model relaxation relative to the partition. For example, some of the model complexity may be relaxed, thus forming an easier model to solve.
3. Solution of a model approximation relative to the partition. As an example, complex sales response functions may be approximated by concave functions, thus forming an easier model to solve.
4. Solution of a model transformation if such a transformation is easier to solve.

Information about each partition is determined from the partition analysis. This information may include (a) an optimal partition solution, (b) an estimate of how good the best solution in the partition is apt to be, and (c) an estimate of how much more the partition will have to be refined or divided before the partition optimum can be obtained.

An optimally solved partition can be dropped from consideration. best of the optimal solutions to the partitions is maintained. This solution can be called the incumbent. Partitions can also be dropped when it is discovered that the best solution in the partition under analysis cannot be better than the incumbent. Partitions that cannot be dropped are repartitioned and the new partitions analyzed. This continues until all partitions can be dropped, at which time the incumbent is declared to be the optimal solution to the original model.

A Final Observation

The state of the art in optimization has not progressed to a point where all complex models can be solved optimally. It probably never will, since the rate at which models are developed will probably always exceed the rate at which new optimization theories and approaches are developed. Occasionally, approximation approaches can be used when model complexity precludes the efficient determination of an optimal solution. The efficacy of approximation approaches is based on the empirical observation that very good solutions, and often optimal solutions, are frequently discovered early in the solution process. Verification of optimality usually requires considerably more effort than is required to find the optimal solution. In these situations approximation approaches can provide good solutions quickly. Finally, heuristic search procedures must be used whenever efficient optimization and approximation techniques are unavailable. However, normative model builders should keep in mind that some marketing models that were solved heuristically yesterday may be solved optimally today [12, 22].

Several Future Directions for Normative Marketing Models

The integration of assessment and analytically assisted decision models and the development and implementation of multiple-criteria normative models are two viable future directions for normative marketing models. Each will be discussed briefly in this section.

A decision maker facing a marketing problem uses both specified and unspecified decision criteria. Market share, profits, and sales are examples of specified criteria. Generally, decision models are built upon specified criteria. However, decision makers usually incorporate unspecified criteria (for example, organizational, political, and interpersonal factors) into their decision making. Frequently, unspecified factors may even dominate specified factors. The integration of assessment and analytically assisted decision models would facilitate decision making using both criteria. The analytically assisted decision model would be driven by the specified factors and the assessment model would be used to explore the consequences of decisions based on the unspecified factors.

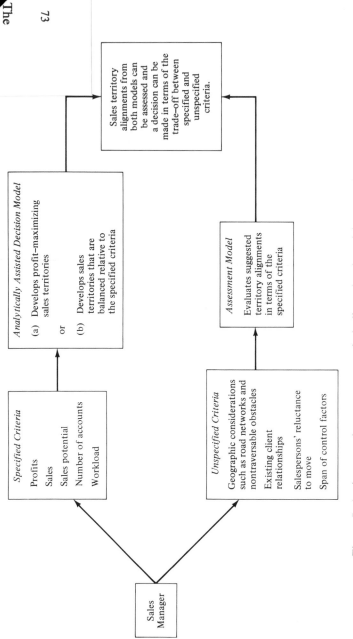

Figure 5. An integrated assessment, analytically assisted model approach for sales territory alignment decisions.

The analytically assisted decision model would produce good decision strategies in terms of the specified criteria. Modifications to these strategies, motivated by the unspecified criteria, or new strategies based entirely on unspecified criteria can be evaluated by the assessment model. Along the way, the trade-off between specified and unspecified criteria can be ascertained. As an example, an integrated decision assessment model for sales territory alignment decisions is illustrated in Figure 5.[7]

Most marketing decisions are multicriteria decisions. Usually the decision consequences on multiple criteria such as market share, profits, sales, ROI, and risk must be examined before a decision can be made. A significant literature on multiple-criteria decision making is emerging. Several recent books [18, 20] have been devoted to this topic. The infusion of this research into marketing decision making will have an impact on normative marketing models.

Finally, it is likely that models will become more and more complex in order that marketing behavior can be adequately represented. Consequently, assessment and analytically assisted decision models will also become more complex. As a result, the development and implementation of analytically assisted decision models will have to become more algorithmically oriented to keep pace with the model complexity. Dynamic programming and branch and bound, described in this chapter, are two algorithmic approaches that have been successfully implemented with complex marketing models. There seems to be a strong future for such optimization methods in marketing modeling.

References

1. *A Non-Technical Outline of MINI-COMPASS*. Chicago, Illinois: Leo Burnett Company, undated report.
2. Aaker, D. A. "ADMOD: An Advertising Decision Model," *Journal of Marketing Research* 12 (February), 37–45 (1975).
3. Balachandran, V., and Gensch, D. H. "Solving the 'Marketing Mix' Problem Using Geometric Programming," *Management Science* 21, No. 2 (October), 160–171 (1974).
4. Buzzell, R. D. *Mathematical Models and Marketing Management*. Boston: Harvard University, Division of Research, 1964, pp. 136–156.
5. Corstjens, M., and Doyle, P. "Channel Optimization in Complex Marketing Systems," *Management Science* 25, No. 10 (October), pp. 1014–1025 (1979).
6. Day, G., Eskin, G., Montgomery, D., and Weinberg, C. *Cases in Computer and Model Assisted Marketing: Planning*. Palo Alto: The Scientific Press, Hewlett-Packard Company, 1975.

---

[7]A review of decision models for sales territory alignment can be found in Zoltners and Gardner [23].

7. Dorfman, R., and Steiner, P. O. "Optimal Advertising and Optimal Quality," *American Economic Review* (December), 826–836 (1954).
8. Geoffrion, A. M. "A Guide to Computer-Assisted Methods for Distribution Systems Planning," *Sloan Management Review* (Winter), 17–41 (1975).
9. Kotler, P. *Marketing Decision Making: A Model Building Approach.* New York: Holt, Rinehart and Winston, 1971.
10. Little, J. D. C. "Models and Managers: The Concept of a Decision Calculus," *Management Science* 16, No. 8 (April), 466–485 (1970).
11. _____, and Lodish, L. "A Media Planning Calculus," *Operations Research* 17, No. 1 (January–February), 1–35 (1969).
12. Lodish, L. M. "CALLPLAN: An Interactive Salesman's Call Planning System," *Management Science*, 18, No. 4, Part II (December), 25–40 (1971).
13. Montgomery, D. S., and Urban, G. L. *Management Science in Marketing.* Englewood Cliffs, New Jersey: Prentice-Hall, 1969.
14. Morin, W. T. "Practical Media Decisions and the Computer," *Journal of Marketing* (July), 26–30 (1963).
15. Naert, P. A., and Leeflang, P. S. M. *Building Implementable Marketing Models.* Leiden: Martinus Nijhoff, 1978.
16. Sinha, P., and Zoltners, A. A. "Integer Programming Model and Algorithmic Evolution: A Case for Sales Resource Allocation," Working Paper, Northwestern University, September 1979.
17. Srinivasan, V. "Decomposition of a Multi-Period Media Scheduling Model in Terms of Single Period Equivalents," *Management Science* 23, No. 4 (December), 349–360 (1976).
18. Starr, M. K., and Zeleny, M. (eds.) *Multiple Criteria Decision Making* (TIMS Studies in the Management Sciences, Vol. 6), Amsterdam: North Holland, 1977.
19. Wellman, H. R. "The Distribution of Selling Effort Among Geographic Areas," *Journal of Marketing* 3, No. 3 (January), 225–239 (1939).
20. Zionts, S. *Multiple Criteria Problem Solving.* New York: Springer-Verlag, 1978.
21. Zoltners, A. A., and Sinha, P. "Integer Programming Models for Sales Resource Allocation," *Management Science* 26, No. 3 (March), 242–260 (1980).
22. _____, Sinha, P., and Chong, P. S. C. "An Optimal Algorithm for Sales Representative Time Management," Working Paper #78-44, Northwestern University, January 1978; *Management Science* 25, No. 12 (December), 1197–1207 (1979).
23. _____, and Gardner, K. "A Survey of Sales Force Models," Working Paper, Northwestern University, October 1979.

4

Models of Market Mechanisms

Leonard J. Parsons

Marketing managers would like to choose the mix of marketing instruments that will best achieve their objectives, taking into consideration any constraints they might face. The notion "best" implies the use of a normative model that tells the managers what they should do. Imbedded in any such normative model must be a predictive (or descriptive) model that specifies how current marketing actions will produce current and/or future marketing results. Such a predictive model is called a model of the market mechanism. The purpose of this chapter is to elaborate what such a market mechanism might encompass.

A market mechanism is likely to be a system of relationships involving a sales response function, competitive reaction functions, vertical market structures, cost functions, and other behavioral relationships. A market mechanism specifies the connections among these relationships as well as among individual variables such as demand, sales, and consumption.

After a review of the various components of a market mechanism, the sales response function will be examined in some detail. The shape of the sales response function is generally believed to be nonlinear; the shape might be concave or S-shaped. The response function could include threshold, saturation, and supersaturation effects. Moreover, there might be asymmetry in response to changes in a marketing instrument. Finally, systematic variation in the effectiveness of marketing instruments is a possibility. Insight into the nature of the sales response function might be gained by micro modeling, although the complexities of sales response functions are not well understood.

Elements of a Market Mechanism

Sales Response Functions

A simple example is the case of a monopolist that deals directly with its customers. Suppose that the monopolist wants to achieve maximum profits (PFT).[1] In addition, assume that the monopolist can control the price p, can set the advertising expenditures a, and would experience the same variable cost per unit c, irrespective of the volume sold for its product. Then the problem is

$$\max_{p,a} PFT = (p-c)q - a$$

with

$$q = f(p, a).$$

The market mechanism in this case consists simply of a sales response function. The sales response function expresses unit sales q as a function f of the marketing instruments and any other factors that might affect sales.[2]

The monopolist might find that its market is influenced by autonomous environmental conditions such as personal income per capita y and the prime rate of interest i. The sales response function can then be written

$$q = f(p, a; y, i).$$

Note that the sales response function now contains two variables, personal income and the interest rate, that are not under the control of the monopolist. In order for the monopolist to determine the marketing mix that achieves optimal profits, a model for predicting future values for the autonomous environmental variables is also necessary.

The values of an autonomous variable might simply be subjectively set by the monopolist. This may be the only way to handle some anticipated events, such as a change in government regulation. More likely is the use of time series analysis to project past behavior into the future. Thus, the monopolist might use relationships like

$$y = f(y_{-1}, y_{-2}, \ldots),$$

where the subscripts indicate past values of the variable. Of course, more complex models, which would include other variables, could be constructed. For many autonomous variables, especially ones that are macroeconomic variables, service organizations sell their predictions. In any

---

[1] For simplicity, fixed costs will be ignored. Thus, what is called profit is really contribution to profits and overhead.

[2] The actual decision will be based on statistical estimates of the parameters in the model of the market mechanism. Making decisions with estimation uncertainty must be done carefully [25].

event, a model of a market mechanism must specify how values for any autonomous variables in the sales response function are determined.

Competition and Competitive Reaction Functions

Although the case of a monopolist might be appropriate in some market segments, most firms must face competition. The sales response function can be expanded to include relevant competitive actions. Minimally, the actions of the competition can be included as arguments of the sales response function:

$$q_b = f(p_b, a_b; p_{c1}, a_{c1}, p_{c2}, a_{c2}, \ldots)$$

where the subscripts b and ci represent marketing decision variables for our brand and for competitor i, respectively. Alternatively, the sales response function can be expressed in terms of an industry sales response function Q and a market share response function (ms); that is, $q = ms \times Q$. Where primary demand is stable, the industry sales response function is often a function of autonomous environmental variables, such as

$$Q = f(y, i),$$

and market share is a function[3] of the marketing decision variables,

$$ms_b = f(p_b, a_b; p_{c1}, a_{c1}, p_{c2}, a_{c2}, \ldots).$$

Where primary demand is expansible, marketing activities of the firm and its competitors would also appear in the industry sales response function.

The firm must be able to predict the values for the competitors' marketing instruments. If the competitors make their decisions without regard to our actions, then time series analysis might be used to project future values for their marketing activities. If the competition reacts to our actions, then reaction functions[4] must be constructed:

$$a_{c1} = f(a_b, p_b, a_{c2}, p_{c2}, \ldots),$$

$$p_{c1} = f(a_b, p_b, a_{c2}, p_{c2}, \ldots),$$

$$a_{c2} = f(a_b, p_b, a_{c1}, p_{c1}, \ldots),$$

$$p_{c2} = f(a_b, p_b, a_{c1}, p_{c1}, \ldots),$$

$$\vdots$$

---

[3] Market share models should be logically consistent. That is, these models should predict that the values for each market share fall between zero and one and that the sum of all market shares equals one. For details on how to specify and estimate market share models, see Bultez [9] and Koehler and Wildt [26] and the references therein.

[4] In *estimating* a model of the market mechanism, specification of each firm's own decision rule for determining the levels of individual elements in its marketing mix might be necessary. Joint marketing decision making is possible. The level of one marketing instrument may affect or be affected by levels of other marketing instruments within the same firm [21].

Empirical evidence suggests that prompt and vigorous competitive reaction is common. See, for instance, Wildt [61]. If the competitors react to our changing one decision variable with only a change in the same decision variable, then we have a simple reaction function. If the competitors react to a change in one decision variable by changing other marketing instruments, then we have a multiple reaction function [29].

A set of theoretical conditions for the existence of primary demand, primary sales, competitive, and mixed effects of advertising have been derived by Schultz and Wittink [52]. The existence of primary demand effects has important practical implications. Metwally [36] found that in certain saturated markets the marketing efforts of competitors canceled each other out. Moreover, when coupled with competitive reaction functions, the result was a futile escalation of marketing effort.

Vertical Market Structures

The types of firms considered thus far have sold directly to their customers. A more common situation would require one or more intermediaries in the channels of distribution. Consider a simple channel involving a manufacturer, a retailer, and consumers. Factory sales equal retailer purchases and retail sales equal consumer purchases. Now there are two sales response functions, one for the manufacturer and one for the retailer:

$$q_m = f(p_m, a_m, \ldots),$$

$$q_r = f(p_r, a_r, a_m, \ldots).$$

In the long run, the two sales figures must be equal. The retailer cannot sell a product if the manufacturer does not supply it. On the other hand, the retailer will not buy more product if current inventories are high.

If the retailer uses just a traditional markup on cost in setting prices and does only cooperative advertising, then a manufacturer can behave as if retailers did not exist (assuming no out-of-stock situations occur). A manufacturer would

$$\max_{p_m, a_m, a_{coop}} \text{PFT} = (p_m - c)f\big[(1 + \text{mu}) \times p_m, k \times a_{coop}, a_m\big] - a_{coop} - a_m,$$

where p_m is the factory price, mu the retailers' markup on cost, a_{coop} the cooperative advertising allowance, k the cooperative advertising multiplier, and a_m the advertising by the manufacturer.

In general, the manufacturer cannot be treated as dealing directly with the consumer. The omission of intermediaries in the channel of distribution can be a serious error that materially alters the normative implications of a model. Equilibrium prices and advertising expenditures cannot simply be carried forward to the consumer level. Steiner [56, p. 61] concluded that the advent of manufacturers' brand advertising in a previously unpromoted product category can, and usually does, drive down consumer prices, while factory price levels may be unchanged or even increased. Consequently, if a model of the market mechanism fails to represent adequately either the manufacturer–retailer or retailer–consumer interface, it will be severely limited in its usefulness as an evaluative tool [19, p. 2].

The case of a duopoly in which each manufacturer distributed its product through an exclusive franchised retailer has been explored by Doraiswamy, McGuire, and Staelin [13]. Under the assumption that the market does not discriminate in its response between the advertising expenditures of the manufacturer and those of the retailer, they found that the entire direct cost of advertising will be carried by either the manufacturer or the retailer, with no explicit sharing of costs. The choice of who will advertise was a function of product substitutability and was relatively independent of the market's responsiveness to advertising.

A model for evaluating alternative short-run, tactical promotional programs for a manufacturer of a branded, frequently purchased food product was developed by Frank and Massy [19]. Their model provides a means for relating manufacturer allowance offers to retailer promotional activity to consumer demand. Provision is also made for estimating the likely actions of competing brands and their impact on retailers and, ultimately, on consumers.

Cost Functions and Experience Curves

The cost per unit, exclusive of marketing costs, is usually assumed to be constant. In most situations this is a satisfactory approximation. However, there are times when more attention should be given to the cost function. For instance, price promotions cause not only consumer sales but also factory shipments to be uneven. Irregular factory shipments often mean higher production and/or inventory costs.

Perhaps the most important exception occurs in the case of technological innovations, including consumer durables. The Boston Consulting Group [8] has noted that total unit costs usually decline as experience with a product is gained. An operational definition of experience is the cumulative units of production. The experience curve can be written as

$$c = f\left(q, \sum_{\alpha} q_{-\alpha}\right).$$

When a significant proportion of total costs can be reduced through experience, important cost advantages can be achieved by following a strategy that places its emphasis on accumulating experience faster than competitors. Knowledge that costs should fall favors a penetration pricing strategy because lowering price increases sales. Determination of optimal dynamic pricing policies are discussed by Robinson and Lakhani [49], Bass [4], and Bass and Bultez [6].

Costs may vary across brands for a number of reasons, one of which is product quality. Schmalensee [50] did a theoretical analysis of the case wherein, for a given market price, the unit cost of producing a good with quality level x is the same for all sellers and can be represented by

$$c = f(x).$$

The function was assumed to be nonlinear and to contain a parameter that indicated the degree to which low-quality brands enjoy a unit cost advantage. Schmalensee then assessed the relationship between advertising and product quality.

Demand, Sales, and Consumption

The quantity sold has been assumed to equal the quantity desired. However, unless every store has the product in stock, demand d will be greater than sales q.[5] This effect is modeled by introducing a variable called availability (av). One operational definition of availability might be the fraction of outlets, weighted by sales volume, handling a product. Then a representation of the relationship between demand and sales could be

$$q = d \times \mathrm{av}$$

where demand (and consequently sales) is a function of the usual managerial decision variables and environmental decision variables. If impulse buying constitutes a material proportion of product sales, then availability is also an argument of the demand and sales functions.

In the middle "stages" of the product life cycle, retail availability does not vary much; that is, it has a low coefficient of variation. Consequently, it is treated as part of the constant intercept in a model. However, when the product is in the introduction or decline phases of the product life cycle, retail availability must appear as a separate variable. Moreover, retail availability is itself a function of what is happening in the marketplace. This function would represent the behavior of the retail sector. For instance, one study [40] found that

$$\mathrm{av} = f(a, \mathrm{av}_{-1})$$

during the introduction of a new frequently purchased grocery item. The difference between demand and sales, assuming a constant advertising rate of \$400,000 per bimonth, is illustrated in Figure 1. Sales climb as retail availability is achieved.

Sales is also not the same as consumption. Winer [62] argues that consumption is the appropriate response variable when examining advertising effects on family behavior because large gaps occurring between purchase

---

[5]Wecker [60] discussed the prediction of demand from sales data in the presence of stockouts.

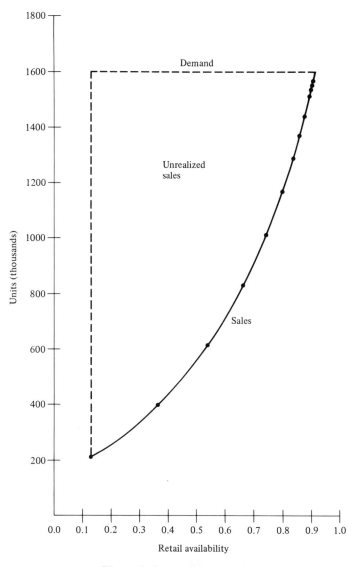

Figure 1. Demand versus sales.

occasions due to stockpiling and the heterogeneity of consumption patterns would distort the measurement of the effects. He views advertising as having transitory effects in that it influences consumption behavior for the concurrent week only as well as having a more permanent impact in the form of an upward shift in the family's mean consumption rate.

The market mechanism, then, can consist of a variety of relationships that describe the behavior of the firm, its distributors, its customers, its competition, and its environment. Our focus will be on the structure of the relationship between the marketing mix for a brand and the resultant sales.

Shape of the Sales Response Function

The shape of sales response to a particular marketing instrument,[6] with the remainder of the marketing mix held constant, is generally concave. Sales always increase with increases in marketing effort, but exhibit diminishing return to scale. Sometimes the sales response function might be S-shaped.[7] Initially sales may exhibit increasing returns to scale and then diminishing returns to higher levels of marketing effort. These two basic shapes are shown in Figure 2. The shape of the response function might be different depending on whether marketing effort is increasing or decreasing. The sales response function might change in response to changes in the environment.

Concave Functions

The preponderance of empirical evidence favors the strictly concave case. This is especially true for mass media advertising of frequently purchased goods. For instance, Lambin [28, p. 95], after doing an analysis of 107 individual brands from 16 product classes and 8 different countries of Western Europe, concluded "evidence [is] that the shape of the advertising response curve is concave downward, i.e., that there is no S-curve and no increasing returns in advertising a given brand by a given firm." Earlier, Simon [54, pp. 8–22] had surveyed the evidence then available on the shape of the response function and found that "both sales and psychological [nonsales measures of behavior] suggest that the shape of the advertising-response function is invariably concave downward, i.e., that there is no S-curve...."

There are several reasons to expect diminishing returns for increased advertising expenditures [22]. For one, the fraction of unreached prospects is progressively reduced as advertising increases. Consequently, most of the impact of additional advertising messages at high levels of advertising takes place by means of increased frequency. Moreover, after a small number of exposures, perhaps as few as three, increased frequency has very limited marginal effectiveness.

---

[6]Price as a marketing instrument might be expressed as the reciprocal of price.
[7]Our concern is not whether the function is S-shaped with time, but rather whether it is S-shaped with effort.

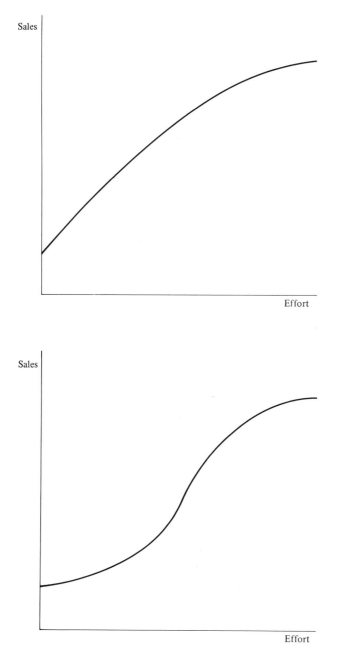

Figure 2. Concave and S-shaped functions.

S-Shaped Functions

An S-shaped sales response to advertising has long been conjectured [66]. However, this proposition has not been tested explicitly. Two studies explored the proposition that the relationship between market share and advertising is S-shaped. Johansson [23] found for women's hair spray that the advertising effect was concave rather than the proposed S-shape. Rao and Miller [48] adopted an ad hoc procedure to develop S-shaped response functions for five Lever brands. The work of Miller and Rao seems suspect, however, since they discarded markets that were "out of line." This meant that for the two brands they discussed in detail, 27% and 20%, respectively, of the markets were omitted! This work, unfortunately, is the only published support for an S-shaped response function.

The lack of evidence for an S-shaped curve has an important implication for the timing of advertising expenditures. An advertiser must choose between two alternative policies, a constant spending rate per period or a pulsed expenditure. Rao [46, p. 55] defines a pulsing policy as a pattern of advertising where periods with high advertising intensity alternate with periods with very little or no advertising. A sufficient condition [47, p. 5] for adopting a pulsing policy would be that the sales response function be S-shaped and the budget constraint be binding. The budget constraint has to require that the alternative constant rate policy be in the region of increasing returns to scale. But most empirical evidence says that the typical brand has a concave sales response function; consequently, the S-shape cannot be used to justify a pulsing policy.[8]

The relationship between market share and share of retail outlets in a market area seems to be S-shaped. Cardwell [11] reported that in marketing gasoline incremental new outlets were substantially below average in gallonage until a certain share of market was achieved. Above this critical market share, performance improved markedly. Lilien and Rao [31] also postulated an S-shaped relationship between share of market and share of outlets. Neither study provides empirical evidence supporting their claims. Naert and Bultez [38] did an analysis of the effect on market share of the distribution network of a major brand of gasoline in Italy. Their results support the S-shape hypothesis at the market share level. However, when the hypothesis was tested at the aggregate brand-switching level, it was rejected. In any event, the relationship between market share and share of outlets may be simply an expression of the difference between demand and sales dicussed previously.

---

[8]Simon [55] further undermines the argument for pulsing.

Threshold, Saturation, and Supersaturation

Three phenomena might also be present in a sales response function. They are threshold, saturation, and supersaturation. These phenomena for an S-shaped curve are illustrated in Figure 3. A threshold occurs when some positive amount of marketing effort is necessary before any sales impact can be detected. The expenditure of only a thousand dollars in a highly competitive mass market is unlikely to show a sales effect. Saturation means that no matter how much marketing effort is expended, there is a finite upper limit to the sales that can be achieved. Buyers become insensitive to the marketing stimulus or find themselves purchasing at their capacities or capabilities. Supersaturation results when too much marketing effort causes a negative response; for example, a buyer might feel that an excessive number of visits by a salesperson is intolerable.

Figure 3. Threshold, saturation, and supersaturation.

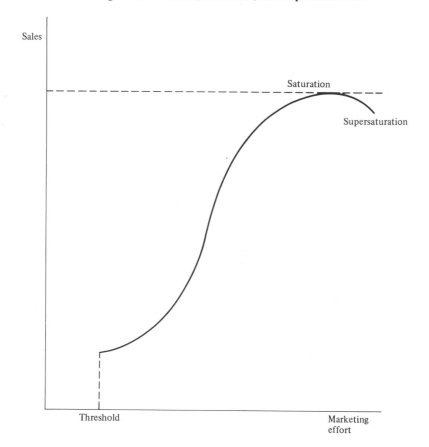

If support for S-shaped sales response functions is weak, even less support exists for a threshold effect. Indeed, Simon [54, p. 22], in the survey mentioned previously, expresses the opinion that "threshold effects...constitute a monstrous myth." Even though the argument might be made at the individual level that a prospect might be unaware of a brand or unwilling to buy it until several advertising messages have been received, this threshold phenomenon has not been found in aggregate sales response functions.

The existence of a saturation level is universally accepted. Nonetheless, the saturation level is rarely explicitly modeled and measured. The usual procedure is to represent response by a function that allows any given level to be surpassed, but requires increasing difficulty to exceed each higher level. This approach is probably adequate for use in decision models focusing on short-run marketing tactics; however, when interest is in long-term strategy, the saturation ceiling should be estimated.

The notion of a supersaturation effect has been promulgated by Ackoff and his colleagues [1, 46, 59] and is being incorporated into marketing theory [15]. Nonetheless, the argument for supersaturation is unconvincing. The only empirical evidence even tangentially bearing on the existence of such an effect comes from Ackoff's Budweiser study. While previous research, such as that of Parsons and Bass [43], has shown that reducing advertising expenditures may increase profits even though sales are lost, the Budweiser study is the only research in which reducing advertising not only increases profits but also increases sales. Haley [20] did report on another beer test in which those areas where advertising was stopped showed better results than the remaining areas. However, subsequent investigation revealed that local distributors, upon finding their advertising support dropped, invested their own funds in advertising. Their efforts more than offset cuts made by the manufacturer. Participants in the Budweiser study have asserted that adequate controls were maintained in their work. Consequently, their results remain an anomaly.[9] Even if supersaturation does exist, it is well outside the usual operating ranges for marketing instruments, since management has little incentive to operate even at saturation.

Although the shape of the sales response is almost surely concave, one should be alert to the possibility of other shapes.[10] Johansson [24] has

---

[9] The result might also be an artifact of the analysis procedures. Sales were defined as actual sales divided by predicted sales where predicted sales were based on an exponential growth model. This peculiar operational definition of sales combined with the limited scope of the analysis technique (analysis of variance) undermines the credibility of the conclusions of the study. A reanalysis of the data using econometric techniques might prove fruitful.

[10] The fit of a concave sales response function should be examined to see if there are any systematic variations between predicted and actual results.

suggested one approach for identifying whether or not a relationship under analysis is S-shaped. In general, one should not think in terms of a single aggregate response function. Specific response functions should be constructed for specific situations.

Asymmetry in Response

The magnitude of sales response to a change in a marketing instrument might be different depending on whether the change is upward or downward. This effect is beyond any that might be explained by the nonlinearity of the sales response function. Little [34] reviews some literature that suggests that sales of packaged goods rise quickly under increased advertising but decline slowly when the advertising is removed. Indeed, Little believes that in some circumstances sales might increase with increased advertising and stay there after withdrawal of advertising.

Parsons [42] gave this explanation of the phenomenon.[11] Higher advertising expenditures create more new customers through greater reach as well as greater frequency. Under the customer holdover effects paradigm, these new customers subsequently repurchase the product. Thus, if advertising is cut back, sales will fall by less than would be the case in the absence of this carry-over effect.

Haley [20] reported on some experiments that showed an immediate sales response to increased advertising. In addition, these experiments indicated that even though the advertising was maintained at the new and higher levels, the magnitude of response gradually became less and less. Little [34] offered two explanations for this. One is that advertising causes prospects to try a product. Only a portion of these new triers became regular purchasers. Consequently, sales taper off from their initial gain to a lower level. The second explanation is that the advertising copy is wearing out. Another possible explanation would be competitive reaction.

Moran [37] provides a summary of some price research that has been conducted in a variety of consumer product categories. He argues that the only way to analyze a price elasticity is in terms of relative price.[12] Relative price expresses a brand's price relative to the average price for the product category in which it competes. One of his major findings is that a brand's upside demand elasticity and downside elasticity can differ. He conjectures that one reason these elasticities might differ is that consumer segments are

---

[11]Parsons also showed how these phenomena might be represented through the use of a rachet model.

[12]This implies that primary demand for the products studied has not been affected by changes in the absolute price levels. Simon [53] reports a similar result.

not equally informed about what is going on. For instance, an unad-vertised price change is more likely to be noticed by current customers.[13]

Systematic Variation

The effectiveness of each controllable marketing instrument is frequently treated as having the same value over time. However, market response to managerial decision variables might change because of the impact of marketing actions by either our company or our competitors or because of shifts in the environment.

One source of systematic parameter variation is the interaction of managerial decision variables with each other. Advertising expenditures often influence the magnitude of price elasticity [37, 57]. Conventional wisdom is that advertising decreases price sensitivity. Schultz and Vanhonacker [51] provide some empirical support for this proposition, yet Wittink [64] gives some evidence that relative price becomes more elastic as advertising share increases. The implication is that advertising tends to increase the price competitiveness of the brand investigated. This supports earlier findings [16, 17] that a high advertising effort yields a higher price elasticity than a low advertising effort. Farris and Albion [18] suggest that the concept of vertical market structures might reconcile what appears to be conflicting evidence. They posit that the relationship between advertis-ing and price depends on whether price is measured at the factory level or at the consumer level.

Moreover, many secondary dimensions of marketing variables are only operative when the primary dimension of the variable is present. If no advertising expenditure is made, the advertising copy can have no impact on sales. Samples and handouts are distributed in conjunction with a sales call. Parsons and Vanden Abeele [45] demonstrated that the effectiveness of the calls made by the sales force of a pharmaceutical manufacturer for an established ethical drug varied systematically as a function of collateral material such as samples used.

Another source of systematic variation in marketing is the product life cycle. Marketing theory states that the demand elasticities of managerial decision variables change over the product life cycle. The theory has been interpreted to say that the advertising elasticity is highest at the growth stage of a product due to the need to create increased product awareness, and lowest during maturity, with elasticities increasing slightly through saturation and decline stages of the product life cycle [35]. The theory supposedly conjectures that the price elasticity increases over the first three

---

[13]Schultz and Vanhonacker [51] speculated that a person who was more brand loyal would be less price sensitive than a new customer. To their surprise, their results indicated that loyalty increases price sensitivity.

stages—introduction, growth, and maturity—and decreases during the decline stage [53].

Empirical evidence on changes in the efficiency of various marketing instruments at different stages of the product life cycle is sparse. Indications are that advertising elasticities generally fall as products pass through their life cycles [2, 41]. Price elasticities seem to decrease markedly during the introduction and growth stages, reaching a minimum in the maturity stage, after which they experience an increase during the decline stage [53]. These results seem inconsistent with current marketing theory.

Systematic variation might occur over individuals or territories rather than over time. Moran [37] found that the price elasticities for a brand varied from market to market and from segment to segment. Wittink [65] tested one brand to evaluate whether demographic variables explained differences in the estimated parameters of the sales response functions for various territories. They did not. Elrod and Winer [14] had only somewhat better luck in relating household characteristics to the estimated parameters in purchasing response functions for different individual households.

Micro Modeling

An alternative to developing an aggregate sales response function directly is to build sales response functions for individual buyers and then to aggregate over these buyers [7, 58]. For example, Verma [58] sought to model competition. His individual model postulates that consumers seek to maximize their utilities subject to constraints. Two important assumptions were made. First, the model is static, and so there are no carry-over effects of advertising. Second, the household production function must exhibit constant returns to scale. He derived an aggregate model that is linear in the first differences of logarithms of the variables. Furthermore, he was able to deduce that the marginal revenue from advertising is greater for "experience" products than for "search" products.

The greatest potential payoff from the aggregation of micro functions to construct a macro function may be in the understanding of carry-over effects of marketing instruments. Although Bultez and Naert [10] argue that increased sophistication in modeling advertising dynamics does not make much difference in terms of profits, they do note that the optimal advertising budget is relatively more sensitive to misspecification of the lag structure. Parsons and Schultz [44] in their chapter on the measurement of carry-over effects conclude,

> Notwithstanding the inherent plausibility of concepts such as the cumulative effects of advertising, distributed lag models in marketing have little or no *theoretical* foundation. In particular, in none of the marketing models has the form of the lag structure been derived as an implication of a given set of behavioral propositions.

Thus micro modeling might provide not only a better appreciation of carry-over effects, but also a scientific basis for testing theories about the nature of the carry-over.

Blattberg and Jeuland [7] attempted to capture the carry-over effects of advertising for a consumer nondurable. Their basic relationship for the individual assumed that advertising insertions influence "brand recall," an unobservable variable, which in turn influences choice probability. Key assumptions include the following: The product is a nondurable in which no new products have recently been introduced; the size of the market is stable; advertising affects only brand choice, not category choice; repeat buying occurs; purchase rate is independent of brand choice; competition has a nonsystematic impact and can be treated as random shocks. This last assumption seems to be the most unrealistic one.

Their key submodel specifies that the probability of recall decreases exponentially as time from last exposure increases. Everyone is assumed to experience the same decay rate for recall. Exposure is random (Bernoulli) and everyone has the same probability of exposure, which is independent of past behavior and constant over time. Finally, the consumer has total awareness after seeing just one advertisement. These assumptions seem unduly restrictive and we hope they will be relaxed in future research.

Blattberg and Jeuland then derived the appropriate aggregate model. They found a nonlinear response to the number of insertions. Moreover, the aggregate sales response function did not have the same functional form as the individual sales response functions.

Market mechanisms can be constructed either at the micro level or at higher levels of aggregation. Higher levels are achieved by aggregating entities, territories, and/or time intervals. Hanssens [21] stresses that the number of structural relationships among variables in a system is a decreasing function of the level of aggregation used to study the system; that is, some detail is lost in the aggregation process.

Sometimes disaggregate and aggregate models can be constructed independently rather than built up from the disaggregate to the aggregate model. Then the issue is whether or not the inferences drawn between the micro and macro models tend to be different. Winer [62] argues that aggregate information may suffice for budget setting, but that a disaggregate approach may be necessary for a more detailed view of the operation of marketing policies.

This chapter has attempted to cover in broad strokes the salient features that a model of a market mechanism might encompass. The emphasis has been on recent literature. Details about how to model specific features, as well as coverage of earlier research, can be found in Kotler [27], Parsons and Schultz [44], and Naert and Leeflang [39]. Some case histories describing managerial applications of the analytical results from econometric studies on marketing relationships can be found in Bass [5].

Future Directions

Knowledge about the nature of the market mechanism has increased appreciably in the last decade or so. Not too long ago managers had little but their own subjective impression of the effectiveness of their advertising. Today managers of heavily advertised brands can measure the effect with reasonable accuracy. Even managers of industrial products have at least a benchmark against which to evaluate their advertising effort [30, 32, 33]. Our task now is to understand the more subtle variations in advertising's impact.

Advertising has been investigated more than the other managerial decision variables in the marketing mix. A better grasp of other marketing instruments, such as a price and sales force effort, is needed. For example, marketing managers would like to know when and to what degree excessive price promotion changes customers' perceptions of the normal price of a product and of its quality. For another, managers would like to know how to assess the impact of a salesperson's effort, especially since empirical evidence has indicated that territory workload and potential are significant determinants in sales differences among territories, whereas sales effort has little, if any, effect.

Some empirical results, such as those involving the product life cycle, seem to be in conflict with marketing theory. Other empirical results, such as those for the price–advertising interaction, have been contradictory. Consider, for example, the relationship between the demand elasticity and relative price. Moran [37] states that the farther a brand's price is from the category average in either direction, the lower its demand elasticity is. Meanwhile, Simon [53] says that the magnitude of price elasticity increases for increasing positive and negative deviations of a brand's price from the average price of brands competing with it.

There are two ways to resolve these disagreements. One way is to acquire more information. Too many marketing studies focus on the same data base, such as the Lydia Pinkham data, of which Winer [63] is but the most recent example. Others use previously examined data bases without acknowledging their heritage. The question arises whether we are learning something new or merely fitting random noise. The scientific approach requires that new models be tested on *new* data.

Our interest is in objective data obtained from natural or planned experiments. Subjective data are very suspect, but sometimes useful on an interim basis until hard data can be obtained. Chakravarti, Mitchell, and Staelin [12] point out the dangers of relying on management judgment to predict parameters in decision-calculus models, particularly when the sales response function is nonlinear. The coupling of universal product code data with split cable television panels seems to hold much promise for making systematic inquiries about consumer products.

The second approach is to recognize that we may obtain different results in different situations. Basmann [3] stresses the importance of specifying the background and initial conditions underlying a statistical test of any model. A test cannot be conclusive unless the background and initial conditions allegedly appropriate for application of a model are actually fulfilled for the time period under examination. One wonders if this requirement is met by some of those doing the research on the supersaturation effect. Also, we have already noted that the different results in the price–advertising interaction literature might be due to different definitions of price. Perhaps the controversy about the shape of the sales response curve is sterile. Conceivably the shape of the sales response function is generally concave while the resultant market share response curves are S-shaped. The bottom line is that we must be very careful about the conditions under which we would expect our model of the market mechanism to hold true.

As we become more scientific in our research (and less expedient), the so-called econometric approach advocated by Parsons and Schultz [44, pp. 17–18] becomes even more appealing. They recommend

1. developing a theory of marketing behavior,
2. expressing the theory as a set of mathematical relationships—a model,
3. designing a rigorous test of the model,
4. choosing an appropriate test of statistical hypotheses,
5. confronting the model with data,
6. testing the conjunction of the model with the data,
7. estimating the parameters of the model, and
8. evaluating the usefulness of the model.

Unlike many decision-calculus models, which are unverified simulations, their approach is just as appropriate for pushing back the frontiers of marketing knowledge as it is for developing marketing decision models.

References

1. Ackoff, Russell, and Emshoff, James R. "Advertising Research at Anheuser Busch, Inc. (1963–1968)," *Sloan Management Review* 16 (Spring), 1–15 (1975).
2. Arora, Rajinder. "How Promotion Elasticities Change," *Journal of Advertising Research* 19 (June), 57–62 (1979).
3. Basmann, Robert L. "The Role of the Economic Historian in Predictive Testing of Proffered 'Economic Laws,'" *Explorations in Entrepreneurial History/Second Series* 2 (Spring/Summer), 159–186 (1965).
4. Bass, Frank M. "The Relationship Between Diffusion Rates, Experience Curves, and Demand Elasticities for Consumer Durable Technological Innovation," Institute Paper No. 660, Krannert Graduate School of Management, Purdue University, March 1978.

5. _____. "Advertising Spending Levels and Promotion Policies: Profit Potential for the Application of Management Science," Institute Paper No. 691, Krannert Graduate School of Management, Purdue University, April 1979.

6. _____, and Bultez, Alain V. "Optimal Strategic Pricing Policies With Learning," Institute Paper No. 736, Krannert Graduate School of Management, Purdue University, September 1979.

7. Blattberg, Robert, and Jeuland, Abel. "A Macro Modeling Approach to Determine the Advertising-Sales Relationship," Working Paper, Graduate School of Business, University of Chicago, 1979.

8. Boston Consulting Group, *Perspectives on Experience*. Boston: Boston Consulting Group, 1972.

9. Bultez, Alain. "Econometric Specification and Estimation of Market Share Models: The State of the Art," in E. Topritzhofer (ed.), *Marketing: Neue Ergebnisse Aus forschung Und Praxis*. Weisbaden: Betriebswirtschaftlicher Verlag Dr. Th. Gabler K. G., 239–263 (1978).

10. _____, and Naert, Philippe A. "Does Lag Structure Really Matter in Optimizing Advertising Expenditures?," *Management Science* 25 (May), 454–465 (1979).

11. Cardwell, John J. "Marketing and Management Science—A Marriage on the Rocks?" *California Management Review* 10 (Summer), 3–12 (1968).

12. Chakravarti, Dipankar, Mitchell, Andrew, and Staelin, Richard. "Judgment Based Marketing Decision Models: An Experimental Investigation of the Decision Calculus Approach," *Management Science* 25 (March), 251–263 (1979).

13. Doraiswamy, Krishna, McGuire, Timothy W., and Staelin, Richard. "An Analysis of Alternative Advertising Strategies," in Neil Beckwith et al. (eds.), *Proceedings*. Chicago, Illinois: American Marketing Association, pp. 463–467 (1979).

14. Elrod, Terry, and Winer, Russell L. "Estimating the Effects of Advertising on Individual Household Purchasing Behavior," in Neil Beckwith et al. (eds.), *Proceedings*. Chicago, Illinois: American Marketing Association, 83–89 (1979).

15. Enis, Ben M., and Mokwa, Michael P. "The Marketing Management Matrix: A Taxonomy for Strategy Comprehension," in O. C. Ferrell, Stephen W. Brown, and Charles W. Lamb (eds.), *Conceptual and Theoretical Developments in Marketing*. Chicago, Illinois: American Marketing Association, 1979, pp. 485–500.

16. Eskin, Gerald J. "A Case for Test Market Experiments," *Journal of Advertising Research* 15 (April), 27–33 (1975).

17. _____, and Baron, Penny H. "Effect of Price and Advertising in Test-Market Experiments," *Journal of Marketing Research* 14 (November), 499–508 (1977).

18. Farris, Paul W., and Albion, Mark S. "The Impact of Advertising on the Price of Consumer Products," *Journal of Marketing* 44 (Summer), 17–35 (1980).

19. Frank, Ronald E., and Massy, William F. *An Econometric Approach to a Marketing Decision Model*. Cambridge, Massachusetts: MIT Press, 1971.

20. Haley, Russell I. "Sales Effects of Media Weight," *Journal of Advertising* 18 (June), 9–18 (1978).

21. Hanssens, Dominque M. "Market Response, Competitive Behavior, and Time-Series Analysis," Working Paper No. 74, Center for Marketing Studies, Graduate School of Management, University of California at Los Angeles, June 1979.
22. Jagpal, Harsharanjeet S., Sudit, Ephraim F., and Vinod, Hrishikesh D. "A Model of Sales Response to Advertising Interactions," *Journal of Advertising Research* 19 (June), 41–47 (1979).
23. Johansson, Johny K. "A Generalized Logistic Function with an Application to the Effect of Advertising," *Journal of the American Statistical Association* 68 (December), 824–827 (1973).
24. _____. "Advertising and the S-Curve: A New Approach," *Journal of Marketing Research* 16 (August), 346–354 (1979).
25. Klein, Roger W., Rafsky, Lawrence C., Sibley, David S., and Willig, Robert D. "Decisions With Estimation Uncertainty," *Econometrica* 46 (November), 1363–1387 (1978).
26. Koehler, Gary L., and Wildt, Albert R. "Characterization and Estimation of Admissable Logically Consistent Parameters for Constrained Linear Models," Research Report No. 78-6, Industrial and Systems Engineering Department, University of Florida, May 1978.
27. Kotler, Philip. *Marketing Decision Making: A Model Building Approach*. New York: Holt, Rinehart and Winston, 1971.
28. Lambin, Jean-Jacques. *Advertising, Competition, and Market Conduct in Oligopoly over Time*. Amsterdam: North-Holland, 1976.
29. _____, Naert, Philippe, and Bultez, Alain, "Optimal Marketing Behavior in Oligopoly," *European Economic Review* 6, 105–128 (1975).
30. Lilien, Gary L. "ADVISOR 2: Modeling the Marketing Mix Decisions for Industrial Products," *Management Science* 25 (February), 191–204 (1979).
31. _____, and Rao, Ambar G. "A Model for Allocating Retail Outlet Building Resources Across Market Areas," *Operations Research* 24 (January–February), 1–14 (1976).
32. _____, and Api Ruzdic, A. "Market Response in Industrial Markets: Models, Estimation, and Application," Working Paper No. 1068-79, Sloan School of Management, MIT, May 1979.
33. _____. "Analyzing National Experiments in Industrial Markets," Working Paper No. 1980-79, Sloan School of Management, MIT, October 1979.
34. Little, John D. C. "Aggregate Advertising Models: The State of the Art," *Operations Research* 27 (July–August), 629–667 (1979).
35. Mahajan, Vijay, Bretschneider, Stuart I., and Bradford, John W. "The Feedback Approaches to Modeling Structural Shifts in Market Response," *Journal of Marketing* 44 (Winter), 71–80 (1980).
36. Metwally, M. M. "Escalation Tendencies of Advertising," *Oxford Bulletin of Economics and Statistics* 40 (May), 153–163 (1978).
37. Moran, William T. "Insights from Pricing Research," in Earl L. Bailey (ed.), *Pricing Practices and Strategies*. New York: The Conference Board, 1978, pp. 7–13.
38. Naert, Philippe A., and Bultez, Alain V. "A Model of a Distribution Network Aggregate Performance," *Management Science* 21 (June), 1102–1112 (1975).

39. _____, and Leeflang, Peter. *Building Implementable Marketing Models.* Leiden: Martinus Nijhoff Social Sciences Division, 1978.
40. Parsons, Leonard J. "An Econometric Analysis of Advertising, Retail Availability, and Sales of a New Brand," *Management Science* 20 (February), 938–947 (1974).
41. _____. "The Product Life Cycle and Time-Varying Advertising Elasticities," *Journal of Marketing Research* 12 (November), 476–480 (1975).
42. _____. "A Rachet Model of Advertising Carryover Effects," *Journal of Marketing Research* 13 (February), 49–55 (1976).
43. _____, and Bass, Frank, M. "Optimal Advertising Expenditure Implications of a Simultaneous-Equation Regression Analysis," *Operations Research* 19 (May–June), 822–831 (1971).
44. _____, and Schultz, Randall L. *Marketing Models and Econometric Research.* New York: North-Holland, 1976.
45. _____, and Vanden Abeele, Piet. "Measurement of Sales Call Effectiveness," *Journal of Marketing Research* 18 (February 1981).
46. Rao, Ambar G. *Quantitative Theories in Advertising.* New York: Wiley, 1970.
47. _____. "Advertising Response Functions—A Survey," Working Paper No. 79–58, Graduate School of Business Administration, New York University, July 1979.
48. _____, and Miller, Peter B. "Advertising/Sales Response Functions," *Journal of Advertising Research* 15 (April), 7–15 (1975).
49. Robinson, Bruce, and Lakhani, Chet. "Dynamic Price Models for New-Product Planning," *Management Science* 21 (June), 1113–1122 (1975).
50. Schmalensee, Richard. "A Model of Advertising and Product Quality," *Journal of Political Economy* 86 (June), 485–502 (1978).
51. Schultz, Randall L., and Vanhonacker, Wilfried R. "A Study of Promotion and Price Elasticity," Institute Paper No. 657, Krannert Graduate School of Management, Purdue University, March 1978.
52. _____, and Wittink, Dick R. "The Measurement of Industry Advertising Effects," *Journal of Marketing Research* 13 (February), 71–75 (1976).
53. Simon, Hermann. "Dynamics of Price Elasticity and Brand Life Cycles: An Empirical Study," *Journal of Marketing Research* 16 (November), 439–452 (1979).
54. Simon, Julian L. *Issues in the Economics of Advertising.* Urbana: University of Illinois Press, 1970.
55. _____. "What Do Zielske's Real Data Really Show About Pulsing?," *Journal of Marketing Research* 16 (August), 415–420 (1970).
56. Steiner, Robert L. "Marketing Productivity in Consumer Goods Industries—A Vertical Perspective," *Journal of Marketing* 42 (January), 60–70 (1978).
57. Sunoo, Don, and Lin, Lynn Y. S. "Sales Effects of Promotion and Advertising," *Journal of Advertising Research* 18 (October), 37–40 (1978).
58. Verma, Vinod K. "A Price Theoretic Approach to the Specification and Estimation of the Sales-Advertising Function," *Journal of Business* 53 (July), S115–S137 (1980).
59. Wald, Clark, Clark, Donald F., and Ackoff, Russell L. "Allocation of Sales Effort in the Lamp Division of the General Electric Company," *Operations Research* 4 (December), 629–647 (1956).

60. Wecker, William E. "Predicting Demand from Sales Data in the Presence of Stockouts," *Management Science* 24 (June), 1043–1054 (1978).
61. Wildt, Albert R. "Multifirm Analysis of Competitive Decision Variables," *Journal of Marketing Research* 11 (February), 50–62 (1974).
62. Winer, Russell S. "On Family Versus Firm Level Analysis of the Effects of Advertising: Implications for Model Building," *Decision Sciences* 10 (October), 547–561 (1979).
63. _____. "An Analysis of the Time-varying Effects of Advertising: The Case of Lydia Pinkham," *Journal of Business* 52 (October), 563–576 (1979).
64. Wittink, Dick R. "Advertising Increases Sensitivity to Price," *Journal of Advertising Research* 17 (April), 39–42 (1977).
65. _____. "Exploring Territorial Differences in the Relationship Between Marketing Variables," *Journal of Marketing Research* 14 (May), 145–155 (1977).
66. Zentler, A. P., and Ryde, Dorothy. "An Optimal Geographical Distribution of Publicity Expenditure in a Private Organization," *Management Science* 4 (July), 337–352 (1956).

5

Subjective Versus Empirical
Decision Models

Philippe A. Naert and Marcel Weverbergh

By empirical decision models we understand models the parameters of which are estimated on the basis of data observed in the marketplace. In this sense empirical models are sometimes called objective. In Bayesian terminology the parameter estimates are based on sample information only.

Estimates of parameters in subjective decision models are arrived at on the basis of quantification of managerial judgment; or to put it in Bayesian language, they are obtained using prior information only.

In this chapter we will first clarify the distinction between the empirical and subjective approaches, and illustrate with examples from marketing. We will see that subjective and empirical data are often combined but in an ad hoc way rather than in the formal context of statistical (Bayesian) decision theory.

The second section examines reasons put forward in the literature for parameter estimation on the basis of judgment only. Next subjective curve fitting as typically found in the marketing literature is linked to the prior parameter and predictive distributions of Bayesian analysis. Whether knowledge of the predictive distribution is necessary is our final subject.

The Empirical Versus the Subjective Approach

The Empirical Approach

As indicated in the introduction, the empirical approach is characterized by the fact that observed objective data form the basis for parameterization. In a marketing context these data will often be of a time series nature. For example, to estimate the effect of advertising on sales, one will typically make use of a number of monthly or quarterly observations of sales and of advertising expenditures in these same periods. The important implication is that if the estimated relation is applied for prediction or optimization, it will essentially be based on the effect advertising had on sales in the past, and the stability of the parameters and of the model structure has to be reasonable to make such extrapolation meaningful. Market data will in other cases be cross sectional. For example, awareness levels in a number of test markets are related to an appropriate measure of advertising pressure in these markets. If this information is to be an input in a new product model, parameter and model structure stability over time is less an issue since the time period of observation will be short and close to the moment of decision.[1]

Econometric methods will typically be applied to estimate parameters of empirical decision models. That is, a functional relation between dependent and explanatory variables will first be postulated based on theoretical knowledge or on common sense. As such, an S-shaped relation between sales (or market share) and advertising corresponds to the common belief that sales first show increasing marginal returns to advertising, then decreasing returns. Since sales are finite, it is further expected that they will asymptotically approach a finite upper limit. Mathematically this can be expressed as follows:[2]

$$q_{jt} = \alpha + (\beta - \alpha) \frac{a_{jt}^{\delta}}{\gamma + a_{jt}^{\delta}} + \varepsilon_{jt} \tag{1}$$

where

q_{jt} represents sales of brand j in period t,

a_{jt} stands for advertising expenditures for brand j in period t,

ε_{jt} is a random disturbance term, and

α, β, γ are model parameters.

For reasons of ease of fit one will often deviate from the theoretical knowledge and retain only decreasing returns to scale as an explicit characteristic of the specification. Multiplicative and semilogarithmic equations such as (2) and (3) satisfy this requirement:

$$q_{jt} = \alpha a_{jt}^{\beta} e^{\varepsilon_{jt}}, \tag{2}$$

$$q_{jt} = \alpha + \beta \ln a_{jt} + \varepsilon_{jt}. \tag{3}$$

---

[1] Of course, the cross-sectional data must be representative, so that extrapolation, for example, from test markets to the national market, is justified. At issue then is cross-sectional stability as opposed to time stability in time series models.

[2] Note that if the additive error term ε_{jt} is, for example, normally distributed, q_{jt} has — at least theoretically — no finite upper limit. But the expected value of (1) does.

The argument for saying that (2) and (3) are as acceptable as representations of the advertising–sales relation as (1) is based on the often observed fact that no data are available for small or for very large values of a_{jt}. Since the specification out of the range of observations does not affect the statistical fit, and since predictions to the left and to the right of that range will be unreliable, appropriateness of specification is in essence only relevant over the range of observations of the explanatory variable(s). Even a linear model,

$$q_{jt} = \alpha + \beta a_{jt} + \varepsilon_{jt}, \tag{4}$$

will often produce a good fit. Use of the estimated version of (4), however, to find the optimal (in the sense of profit maximizing) advertising budget yields a value of zero or infinity.[3] Thus the linear model may do fine as far as statistical fit is concerned but is not meaningful in a normative way.

Summarizing, we can say that in an empirical sense and given that data often cover only a small part of the theoretically possible range of variation of the explanatory variables, deviations from the specification that most closely corresponds to what is known about the phenomenon will in many cases have little impact on the descriptive value of the model. Within the range of observations, these different specifications will also produce almost equally good predictions. Outside of that range we know that some specifications are poor representations of reality and therefore will produce unreliable predictions. But even for a theoretically good specification these predictions will be unreliable, since we have no data on the behavior of the dependent variable for these values of the explanatory variable(s). For example, in Equation (1) q_{jt} takes on a value of α for a_{jt} going to zero and a value of β for a_{jt} going to infinity. It should be clear that given a limited range of variation for a_{jt}, the estimates of α and β will be highly unreliable.[4] Finally, since some models, such as the linear one, work well in a descriptive and to a certain extent in a predictive sense, but produce nonsensical normative results, specification should from an empirical point of view be related to the use one intends to make of the model.

Even the empirical approach has a number of subjective elements to it. First, as was shown above, the choice of specification is at least partially subjective. Second, there is the choice of a criterion to obtain a best fit. In econometrics the least squares criterion is most commonly used, that is, the parameter values that minimize $\Sigma_{t=1}^{T} e_{jt}^2$ (where e_{jt} is the estimated disturbance term and T the number of observations) are retained as best

---

[3] Taking uncertainty into account, and assuming risk aversion, even a linear model will produce a finite optimum.

[4] For a further discussion and a numerical example, see Naert [11] and Naert and Leeflang [13, pp. 110–118].

estimates. Other objective functions are possible, however, and choosing to minimize the sum of the squared residuals is again a partly subjective choice. Similarly, the selection of an appropriate significance level for the statistical evaluation of the estimated parameters will to a certain extent be subjective. We should of course be aware that these subjective elements are not specific to the empirical approach but will be equally present in the subjective approach.

The empirical approach is essentially a partial approach. Measures observed in the marketplace or through experimentation are not the sole source of information to the decision maker. He or she also learns about and gains insight into the market phenomenon from experience. His judgment will implicitly take into account a larger number of variables and different (more up-to-date) dynamics than the empirical approach does. It is therefore appropriate for him to combine the empirically derived information with his subjective judgment. The question is whether this should be done in a formal way or not. Lambin [4], for example, prefers an informal approach. He puts forward two main arguments.[5] First, informal updating is technically simpler. Second, and this is most important when one has implementation in mind, the informal procedure permits the decision maker to be more directly involved. Lambin therefore first obtains empirical estimates, which are then given to the decision maker, who thus has objective measures with which to start. He feels that this is justified because

> it seems very unrealistic, indeed, to expect judgmental estimates of the different response coefficients from the decision maker, even if he is very well informed, without giving him some *organized* prior information or reference values [4, p. 126].[6]

It is indeed true that direct subjective estimation of response parameters is in many cases an impossible task for the decision maker, since he does not typically think in terms of response coefficients. But as will be seen subsequently, the parameter estimates can be arrived at indirectly by asking the decision maker for information on the predictive distribution, for example, the distribution of sales corresponding to different levels of advertising.

Lambin's procedure consists of adjusting the empirically determined coefficients by multiplying them by subjectively estimated indices whose

---

[5]The discussion closely follows Naert and Leeflang [13, pp. 276–277].

[6]What Lambin calls *organized prior information* or *reference values* is in our terminology *sample information*, whereas we have reserved the term *prior information* for the quantified judgmental information.

reference value is 1. In his study of the marketing mix for a major gasoline brand, Lambin [4] proposed three such indices:

1. an advertising creativity and communication value index (ACC),
2. a retail network productivity index (RNP), and
3. a point-of-sales promotion index (PSP).

Lambin's experience was that these indices are most helpful at the implementation stage. He mentions, for example, that the advertising manager had been somewhat reluctant to cooperate because of his main concern with creativity and qualitative aspects of advertising, whereas the empirical estimate only measures an average value of advertising effectiveness. The introduction of the ACC index gave him the opportunity to express his personal view and thus to become an active participant in the decision-making process.

We should observe that this example goes beyond the mere combination of objective and subjective estimates. It also concerns the inability of the empirical specification (or the lack of appropriate historical data) to model the phenomenon in as much detail as the decision maker would like. In aggregate response models, advertising is typically measured in dollars and no adjustment is made for qualitative and creative effects. The ACC index is thus in the first place a means to resolve this shortcoming rather than an adjustment of the average advertising effect on the basis of subjective judgment.

We could also present the aforementioned combination of data and judgment as follows. Advertising effectiveness has two components: average effectiveness and quality. Sample information is available for estimating average advertising effectiveness, and prior information on that component is considered irrelevant (noninformative) by the decision maker. As to the quality component, no sample information is at hand; only prior information is available.

One of the disadvantages of informal updating should now be referred to. The ultimate value of the parameter will depend on the empirical estimate, the decision maker's judgment, and the confidence he has in his judgment. It will not, however, depend much on the quality, that is, on the (lack of) variance of the empirical estimate. Whether that variance is large or small, relative to the confidence he has in his own judgment, will not affect the adjustment much, if at all. There is perhaps an educative role here for the model builder, who should teach the decision maker to relate his confidence in an empirical estimate to its estimated variance.

Summing up, we note that in the empirical approach sample information is at the core of the analysis. Judgmental information is often not incorporated, and if it is, then an ad hoc adjustment is more common than a formal one.

The Subjective Approach

The subjective approach to marketing decision models owes its popularity to a large extent to John Little's pioneering article introducing the notion of a decision calculus [5]. He defines a decision calculus as "a model-based set of procedures for processing data and judgments to assist a manager in his decision making" [5, p. B470].

Proponents or followers of this approach have in general put much stronger emphasis on the subjective component than on the empirical or data component of the definition. Central to the approach is the subjective estimation of the model's parameters. The estimation does not, however, take place through direct assessment of these parameters, but in an indirect way on the basis of a few simple questions put to the decision maker. The main virtue of the method is that the questions are understandable to the decision maker because they are phrased in his normal language, not in strange mathematical symbols, and try to correspond to his way of thinking about the problem. Although there is no direct reference at all to the response coefficients, estimates can be derived from the answers given by the decision maker. This will now be illustrated for Equation (1), which is also the one Little uses in [5], but with sales q_{jt} replaced by the brand's share m_{jt}. It should be obvious that we should not get very far if we were to ask the decision maker, "What do you think the values of α, β, γ, and δ are?" But if we ask him what he thinks market share will become if advertising is reduced to zero, it is likely that he will have a meaningful answer.[7] That answer provides us with an estimate of the lower limit of market share α. Similarly, the decision maker's opinion may be asked concerning the market share he expects if advertising is increased to saturation. His answer gives us an estimate of β. Next we ask him for the level of advertising expenditures a_{jc} that will maintain current share m_{jc}. Finally we could ask what market share to expect (m_{jc+}) when advertising expenditures are increased 50% over the current level $(a_j = 1.5a_{jc})$. Plugging the answers to the last two questions into Equation (1), we obtain

$$m_{jc} = \alpha + (\beta - \alpha)\frac{a_{jc}^{\delta}}{\gamma + a_{jc}^{\delta}} \tag{5}$$

and

$$m_{jc+} = \alpha + (\beta - \alpha)\frac{(1.5a_{jc})^{\delta}}{\gamma + (1.5a_{jc})^{\delta}}. \tag{6}$$

Since estimates of α and β were already obtained, (5) and (6) form a system of two equations in two unknowns, from which estimates of γ and δ

---

[7]For simplicity of exposition we leave out all dynamic considerations.

can easily be derived. It should be made clear immediately that Little's procedure is not the same as the prior probability assessment of (a set of points on) a response function, since there is nothing stochastic about it. The procedures are, however, related, as will be explained in Section 3.

Since Little's original article, many others have developed decision-calculus models, and most of them have applied subjective estimation procedures of the kind proposed by Little and illustrated above. In a number of these applications empirical data are not considered at all and empirical estimation procedures are even looked upon by some with a little disdain as something acceptable in the sixties but not in the seventies! It should be emphasized, however, that the originator of the decision-calculus approach never claimed that data are useless. In [5, p. B472], for example, he states that a linear regression could perhaps be used to estimate m_{jc+}, whereas the extreme values α and β could be assessed subjectively. He is also aware that more complicated approaches such as Bayesian analysis or adaptive control are possible, but formal updating procedures are not retained—at least not from the start—because Little considers the intellectual cost of such complications to be too high [5, p. B473]. But he believes that even more sophisticated approaches could probably be translated into operational terms.

It is instructive to consider how Little deals with the use of empirical data and of empirical data estimation procedures in another paper, where his marketing mix model BRANDAID is developed [6, 7]. The underlying model structure is intrinsically nonlinear, that is, no transformations can be found that make the model linear in the parameters. In the past, empirical estimation of such model structures would have been troublesome. Nowadays, however, computer packages for nonlinear estimation, or adapted versions of packages for nonlinear programming, are easily available to make intrinsic nonlinearity much less of an issue.[8]

Little [7, p. 661] recommends starting with judgmental numbers in order to "prevent people from over-interpreting historical analyses, which invariably are based on a limited time period and a limited set of variables. Statistical results sometimes take on an air of authority because of their seeming objectivity." One can of course turn the argument around and say that the subjective estimation approach illustrated above also takes on a perhaps unwarranted air of authority, since it may produce the impression that giving answers to just a few simple questions suffices for the model builder to derive what look like exact values of the parameters. The method indeed allows for no variance in the estimators, a point we will come back to.

---

[8]As a result, ease-of-fit considerations are much less constraining in model specification than they were ten years ago.

In decision-calculus applications subjective estimates are sometimes adjusted according to the following pattern.[9] Historical data—for example, sales or market share—are compared with values of the same variables arrived at by putting the original subjective estimates into the model, and this for the whole period covered by the data. The parameters are then adjusted to produce a better match (read statistical fit) between the two time series. But that is exactly what the econometric procedures try to accomplish, and if this adjustment procedure is followed, the subjective approach may in the end also put much emphasis on the historical data (perhaps a lot more than it intended to). This conclusion should, however, be somewhat qualified as follows. Given that the decision makers are themselves doing the adjustment, they are well placed to take into account any events that should make subjectively estimated sales or shares deviate from the historical ones. Furthermore, the very fact of being closely involved in the parameterization process makes the end result much more believable to the potential user. The process is therefore at least very valuable from an implementation point of view.

To summarize, the subjective approach puts primary emphasis on the quantification of managerial judgment, but will sometimes adjust for sample information in an ad hoc way.

The Bayesian Approach

We have seen that subjective adjustments to empirical estimates, or adjustments of subjective estimates on the basis of empirically derived information, are carried out in an ad hoc way. Yet the combination of subjective (prior) and empirical (sample) information can be performed in a formal way through Bayesian analysis. The combination procedure leads to final or posterior estimates (see Figure 1), as is illustrated by the following example. A company is evaluating a potential new product. One of the important parameters in the decision to launch or not to launch the product is the trial rate θ. If the firm has prior experience within the same product class, it will be possible and meaningful to extract a probability assessment from the people who have that experience. This probability assessment is then summarized under the form of a prior distribution $f(\theta)$. The company may have planned one or more test markets, the trial sales in which yield sample information ζ. This sample evidence is summarized in the likelihood $l(\zeta|\theta)$. The posterior distribution $f(\theta|\zeta)$ can then be seen as the adjustment of the prior information on the basis of the empirical evidence.

$$f(\theta|\zeta) = f(\theta)l(\zeta|\theta)/\int f(\theta)l(\zeta|\theta)\,d\theta. \tag{7}$$

---

[9]Calibration is the term used by Little to refer to subjective parameter adjustment.

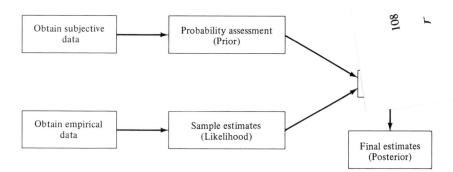

Figure 1. General framework for Bayesian analysis.

Pure empirical estimation can then be considered the limiting case of (7) where no prior information is available, or where the prior information is uninformative, whereas pure subjective estimation would be the special case where no sample information is at hand.[10]

Since formal updating procedures exist, one could consider the introduction of informal or ad hoc procedures such as those discussed earlier as a step backward. We should keep in mind, however, that some strong arguments were presented against the formal approach, and in particular to the technical difficulties involved and to the growing concern with implementation. We will study this point in more depth by examining the link between Little's subjective estimation procedure and the assessment of prior probability in Bayesian inference, and by pointing to some of the technical difficulties involved. Before that, we want to examine some of the reasons often found in the literature for rejecting or at least seriously questioning the econometric approach.

Questioning the Econometric Approach

The literature contains a number of reasons for rejecting or questioning the econometric approach to parameter estimation. The main ones are the following: Econometric estimation requires good data, the approach is essentially static, specifications are often nonrobust, only a small number of variables can be handled, and parameter estimates are unreliable. We will examine each of these points in turn, and each time check whether or not subjective estimation is more promising.

---

[10] In the classical econometric approach an estimated parameter is a random drawing from a distribution that has the true value as its (unknown) mean, whereas in the Bayesian approach the true value of the parameter is random.

.conometric Estimation Requires Good Data

As indicated in [12], to be adjudged "good," data must meet certain standards of availability, quality, variability, and quantity. Data concerning some variables will not be easy to secure. For example, suppose product availability is to be measured by a weighted number of stores, where the weights are proportional to store size. The number of stores may be easy to obtain, but store size (except in a very rough form) will be much harder to get at. Other data, such as sales of competing brands, are available from firms carrying out retail store audits, but at a cost, an element that also should enter the picture.

Quality of the data may refer to a number of characteristics. First is the question whether a variable measures what it is supposed to measure. For example, advertising expenditures should not be charged to the periods in which the advertising bills are paid, but to the periods in which the advertisements appear in the media. Or, if we buy competitive advertising data from advertising audience agencies, we must be assured that all media are included (press, radio, television, billboard, etc.).

Variability is essential to the econometric approach since it tries to explain variation in the dependent variable on the basis of variation in the independent or explanatory variables. If, then, an explanatory variable does not vary, or shows only limited variability, its effect on the dependent variable cannot be assessed.

Finally, quantity is important, since the number of observations directly relates to the statistical quality of the estimates.

It should be clear that in some cases data will not exist (for example, if no historical records have been kept), or that data will be available in insufficient quantity (for example, in new product situations). It is also true that lack of variability, for example, in (real) price data, will often plague the statistical analyst. Quality of data is often problematic, since lack of quality means errors in variables and has, certainly as far as marketing is concerned, not received the attention it deserves.[11]

Subjective estimation, however, also requires good data. If one wants to have an informative prior distribution, the assessor—that is, the person providing subjective estimates—must have considerable knowledge and experience regarding the phenomenon. Also, even if the assessor is knowledgeable, extracting the information must be done with great care. To make probability assessment comprehensible and operational is no trivial matter.[12]

---

[11]A notable exception is Vanden Abeele's doctoral dissertation [18].
[12]See, for example, Winkler [19, 20] and Hogarth [3].

The Econometric Approach Is Essentially Static

The econometric approach can no doubt handle the dynamic effect of various marketing instruments by the introduction of lag structures. It is, however, fair to say that in many empirical studies very simple and often unrealistic distributed lag structures have been assumed. The numerous models assuming a geometric lag structure provide good evidence to that effect. Also it is often (implicitly) assumed that different variables have the same lag structure and lag parameter. Letting lag structure and/or lag parameters differ across variables normally results in more complex intrinsically nonlinear specifications, which one often tries to avoid in empirical work, as a quick survey of econometric applications in marketing can easily show. Once again, however, more complex specifications can be handled, but must be estimated by other than the most commonly used linear estimation methods. An example was given in our discussion of the subjective approach, where it was said that Little estimated BRANDAID not only by quantifying judgment, but also by fitting the same model structure to three years of monthly data by way of a nonlinear estimation procedure.

This by no means implies that econometrics can handle any type of dynamics. For example, a model such as Urban's new product model SPRINTER [16, 17], where fractions of the potential market move from and to the different states of triers, repeaters, and loyals, does not lend itself to simple econometric analysis.[13]

The static nature of the models lies perhaps more in the fact that with time series as the data base there is an assumption of time stability in both model structure and parameters (see also the discussion of the empirical approach in Section 1). Subjective estimates do not have this disadvantage, since they yield parameter assessments relevant for the time the assessment is made. But even with time series, the assumption of parameter stability can be relaxed. The literature contains a number of approaches which allow parameters to vary over time.[14]

Econometric Specifications Are Not Robust

Little calls a model robust if the user finds it difficult to make the model give bad answers [5, p. B470]. He suggests that robustness can be obtained by selecting a model structure that inherently constrains answers to a

---

[13] This is of course not to say that no empirical data analysis is possible in estimating such models.
[14] For an introductory survey of some of these approaches see Maddala [9, Chapter 17]. Applications in a marketing context are presented by Bultez [1] and Parsons [14].

meaningful range of values.[15] According to Little [7, p. 661], most statistical models are not robust. We have already indicated that this is indeed the case in a large number of, if not most, empirical studies. Yet if logical consistency is considered a primary characteristic of a good model, then the model builder experiences no serious problems in providing such a structure. The resulting model will typically be intrinsically nonlinear, but as has been pointed out before, appropriate estimation procedures are now generally available, and ease of fit is therefore no longer a reason for avoiding nonlinearity in the parameters.

It remains true, of course, that the often limited range of observations for the available data concerning the different explanatory variables may lead to unreliable estimates of some or all of the parameters. In other words, the data do not justify the complexity of structure one believes to be present in the real phenomenon.

One may of course wonder whether subjective estimation will perform significantly better on that score. In some situations at least, the answer is negative. If the firm, for example, has no experience with a product's performance outside of a certain range of values for the different explanatory variables, it is likely that subjective estimates of the parameters will be no more reliable than their empirically based counterparts. Take, for example, Equation (1). If the firm has never had a very low (but neither has it had a very high) advertising budget, econometric estimates of α and β will have large estimated variances, but the subjective prior distributions of these same parameters will show equally large variances.

The Econometric Approach Can Only Handle a Small Number of Variables

Reliability of the parameter estimates depends on the number of degrees of freedom in estimation, that is, on the difference between the number of observations and the number of parameters. That the observations are often scarce puts a limit on the number of parameters, and therefore on the number of variables that can be handled. This is particularly true in single-equation models. It is well known that systems of equations—for example, those appropriate for modeling a national economy—can handle hundreds of variables.

A second reason why the number of variables in an econometric model will typically be small is related to the structure of the data. Often, and particularly with time series data, one variable or a set of variables will be strongly correlated with one or a linear combination of other explanatory variables. That is, the data base will be plagued by multicollinearity. The

---

[15] Other authors prefer the label "logical consistency" to avoid confusion with the notion of robustness in statistics.

trouble with this is that the estimated parameter variances grow larger as a data matrix shows more severe multicollinearity. In empirical work some variables will often be dropped from an equation, not because they are considered irrelevant to the phenomenon under study, but because they are too strongly correlated with other variables.

But handling a large number of variables may also be problematic in subjective estimation. Let us illustrate this with an example from Little [6]. The basic equation of his BRANDAID model is

$$q_t = q_0 \prod_{i=1}^{I} e_{it},$$ (8)

where

q_0 is the reference brand sales rate,
e_{it} is the effect on brand sales of the ith sales influence (an index), and
I is the number of influences on brand sales.

Thus, we obtained sales in period t by multiplying a reference value by a set of effect indices. Subjectively estimating the joint effects, including possibly complex interactions, of a number of influences on sales will in general be very difficult to do. Given the multiplicative structure of (8), subjective estimation is much simplified, since each index e_{it} can be subjectively assessed independently of the values the other e_{jt} ($j \neq i$) take on. With a more complex interaction structure, subjective estimation would be much less trivial.[16]

Subjective Curve Fitting

First we must extend the notion of the prior parameter distribution to the case of a response function. Let us again take the market share function of Equation (5). For clarity of the subsequent discussion all stochastic variables are indicated with a tilde, and for simplicity of notation the indices j and t are dropped:

$$\tilde{m} = \tilde{\alpha} + (\tilde{\beta} - \tilde{\alpha}) \frac{a^{\tilde{\delta}}}{\tilde{\gamma} + a^{\tilde{\delta}}} + \tilde{\varepsilon},$$ (9)

or more generally written

$$\tilde{m} = \tilde{m}(a, \tilde{\theta}, \tilde{\varepsilon}),$$ (10)

where $\tilde{\theta} = (\tilde{\alpha}, \tilde{\beta}, \tilde{\gamma}, \tilde{\delta})$. Subjective estimation would then in the first place mean that one tries to obtain the prior distribution $f(\tilde{\theta})$ of the parameter

---

[16]See, for example, Tydeman and Mitchell [15].

vector $\tilde{\theta}$. Alternatively, one can try to obtain the predictive distribution directly. That is, for each value of a, the distribution $f(\tilde{m}(a, \tilde{\varepsilon}))$ is obtained. The relation with (10) is as follows:

$$\tilde{m}(a, \tilde{\varepsilon}) = \int \tilde{m}(a, \tilde{\theta}, \tilde{\varepsilon}) f(\tilde{\theta}) \, d\tilde{\theta}. \tag{11}$$

However, we recall from the discussion of Little's estimation procedure that there is no question of anything being stochastic at all. Let us therefore examine his procedure in more detail and link it to the stochastic elements that have just been introduced. It should be recalled that Little proposes to estimate a four-parameter curve on the basis of four observations. In the context of the terminology of the beginning of this section, these four observations represent a central tendency value from each of four predictive distributions (that is, the predictive distributions corresponding to four different values of a). From these four values and the corresponding values of a, the four parameters are derived simply by solving a system of nonlinear equations. The basis of the approach to estimation is then that one generates the smallest possible number of observations—smallest in the sense that if there were one less, insufficient information would be available to get estimates for all the parameters. This concern for minimizing the number of subjective data points is explained by Little as follows:

> It is doubtful that, as of today, we could specify a sales response curve in any greater detail than represented by a smooth curve through four appropriately chosen points [5, p. B472].

This seems to be the prevailing opinion among authors applying a decision-calculus approach. Lodish [8], for example, uses the same functional form as (9), again in its deterministic version, to relate the number of sales calls to the expected sales to a given account.[17]

Typical, then, for most of the estimation procedures commonly applied in decision-calculus models is that they do not involve a criterion for goodness of fit. There is indeed no need to specify an objective function such as "minimizing the sum of the squared residuals" or something similar, and the procedure therefore seems straightforward and intuitively appealing. Some of the most fervent proponents of the approach are said to believe that subjectively estimated parameters are definitely better than econometrically determined ones, since the latter often show large variances, whereas the approach outlined above yields a perfect fit to the data.

---

[17]In some cases even simpler procedures are applied. In Urban [17], Montgomery, Silk, and Zaragoza [10], and Little [7], a response curve is arrived at by simple linking of a few estimated points by linear segments. This and the following quotation from John D. C. Little are reprinted by permission from "Models and Managers: The Concept of Decision Calculus," *Management Science* 16, No. 8 (April 1970). Copyright 1970 by The Institute of Management Sciences.

Unfortunately, things are not really all that simple. Suppose that instead of the S-shaped specification (9), we had taken the following mathematical representation:

$$m = \alpha + \beta a + \gamma a^2 + \delta a^3 + \tilde{\varepsilon}; \qquad\qquad (12)$$

we would also have obtained a perfect fit, since (12) is also a four-parameter curve.[18] This results from the fact that when the number of parameters equals the number of observations, no degrees of freedom are available for estimating the error variance. Thus, although technically speaking a perfect fit is obtained, in an econometric sense nothing can be said about the goodness of fit, since we have no information at all with which to do so. The consequence is that even totally meaningless specifications will give the impression of being appropriate because of the perfect fit of the estimated response curve to the data. Little [5, p. B472], however, does not consider this problem a substantive one when, concerning the specification of the response function, he states:

> Actually, I am willing to use anything. The curve could go down or up or loop the loop for all I care. It should be changed when and if a product manager wants it changed. Meanwhile, he can give four numbers, each of which has operational meaning to him and which together will specify a curve.

There is, however, more. It should be obvious that in the mind of the decision maker there is much uncertainty as to the response of market share to advertising. Suppose we obtain a pessimistic, optimistic, and most likely (modal) estimate rather than just one point estimate. Pessimistic, for example, means that there is only a 5% chance that market share will be lower, whereas optimistic implies a 5% chance that market share will be higher. In most situations the difference between the optimistic and pessimistic estimates will be substantial, as is illustrated in Figures 2 and 3. In the case of Figure 3, uncertainty is more limited for values of advertising expenditures within than outside the range of historical advertising expenditure levels. This varying level of uncertainty in the subjective estimates is to be expected, since managers will be less confident about points on the response curve where the firm has never been.

If instead only one point estimate is obtained for each advertising expenditure level considered, we are likely to get a modal or other central tendency value. If we want to be sure of what the answers mean, the questions should be unambiguously stated. For example, if we are interested in modal values, questions like "What do you think market share will be if advertising is reduced to zero?" should be replaced by something like

---

[18] In this case, saturation advertising should not be one of the inputs.

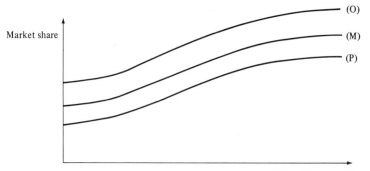

Figure 2. Optimistic (O), pessimistic (P), and modal (M) market share: advertising
response curves (constant uncertainty).

"What do you think the most likely value of market share will be if
advertising is reduced to zero?"

A final word about the estimated parameters: If they are derived from
the expected values of the predictive distributions, then they are not the
expected values of $\tilde{\alpha}, \tilde{\beta}, \tilde{\gamma}, \tilde{\delta}$, the reason being the nonlinearity of (9), which
causes $E(\tilde{m}(a, \tilde{\varepsilon}))$ to differ from $E(\tilde{m}(a, E(\tilde{\theta}), \tilde{\varepsilon}))$.

Let us now turn to what the econometrician has to add to the debate. He
will in any event feel extremely unhappy and uncomfortable with the
fitting procedure discussed above. He wants not only estimates but also
information about their quality to enable him to test certain hypotheses.
This goal requires the availability of information about the variance of the
estimators, and since these variances depend on the error variance, the
latter must be estimated as well. For this he must have more observations

Figure 3. Optimistic (O), pessimistic (P), and modal (M) market share: advertising
response curves (varying uncertainty).

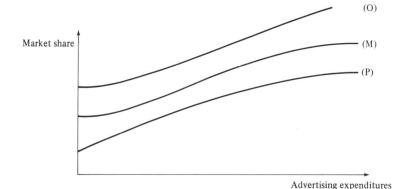

than parameters. Since in addition the variances of the estimators depend on the number of observations, the econometrician wants the difference between the number of observations and the number of parameters to be as large as possible.

Suppose for a moment that in the subjective assessment 10 or 15 inputs are used instead of just 4. That is, the decision maker or assessor is asked his market share expectations for advertising expenditures equal to the current budget, the current budget plus 10%, plus 20%,..., minus 10%, minus 20%, and so on. This yields a scatter of points through which a market share function can be fitted. It is obvious that no perfect fit will result. Yet the estimated error variance thus obtained will by no means be an approximation of the error variance of the subjective response function. The basis for the econometric estimation is indeed a set of point estimates each of which is the subjective estimate of the *expected value* of a predictive distribution. In other words, they are all estimates of the *expected response curve*.

Why then does the expected response curve not fit the data perfectly? There are several possible explanations. First, the assessor may be inconsistent in giving his estimates.[19] This might be controlled to a certain extent by pointing inconsistencies out to him, so that appropriate corrections can be made. Second, the assessor may be uncertain about the mean of his subjective distribution, which brings us into the philosophical issue of probabilities of probabilities. We will not get into this here but refer the interested reader to De Finetti [2]. Both of these reasons are likely to be joined by a third one, namely, that the assumed response function does not really correspond to that of the assessor. The mathematical form is to a certain extent forced upon him, but of course he will generally not be able to tell the model builder which form to use. He can only give a rough idea of the graphical representation.

In this section we have seen that the estimation procedures typical of the decision-calculus approach are very simple and not very demanding for the assessor. They do, however, have the disadvantage of providing only partial information about the parameters and the corresponding response curve. If more complete information is desired, it is, at least in theory, advisable to increase substantially the number of input values of the explanatory variables (for example, 10 or 15 values for the level of advertising expenditures), and to assess the predictive distributions corresponding to each of them. Winkler [19] discusses several techniques for assessing an entire probability distribution on the basis of a limited number of points from that distribution. For example, for a given level of

---

[19] This may be less of a problem when obtaining central tendency estimates, but will often be an issue when an entire distribution is subjectively assessed, the main reason being that people are not very experienced in thinking in probabilistic terms.

advertising expenditures a, the five fractiles .01, .25, .50, .75, and .99 can be assessed by asking the following question: "What is your assessment of market share m such that there is a probability x that m is less than the assessment?" In this question x subsequently takes on the value of each of the different fractiles. We should be aware that many people will have difficulty in making such probability assessments since, as we already observed in footnote 19, people do not typically think in terms of probabilities. In addition, with 15 values for a and 5 fractiles to be assessed for each value, a total of 75 assessments has to be made, as compared to 4 in Little's example. The whole procedure thus becomes very tedious and involved, and questions of cooperation and respondent's fatigue and their impact on the quality of the assessments become relevant. We should therefore wonder whether this extensive effort is worthwhile. In other words, we must ask ourselves why we want to know the predictive distributions and the prior parameter distributions rather than just their first moments. This will be further examined in the following section.

Is Knowledge of the Predictive Distribution or of the Prior Parameter Distribution Necessary?

In this section we will examine whether knowledge of the prior distribution, or at least of more than just its first moment, is necessary. In a positive sense we could ask what use is actually made of more complete descriptions of a response than just a central tendency value. This will be done in the first subsection. In the remainder we discuss the question in a decision-theoretic framework.

In a Classical Econometric Framework

In classical econometric analysis, the true parameters are assumed nonstochastic, whereas their estimates are random. With normally distributed error terms, satisfying the assumption of the basic linear model, estimators also follow a normal distribution with the true parameters as their expected values and with a variance–covariance matrix that is a function of the error variance. The estimation output then contains a drawing from the multivariate normal distribution of the estimator vector and an estimated variance–covariance matrix. In most marketing decision models, with econometrics as the estimation method, predictions from the estimated model are assumed to yield expected values of the dependent variable. Uncertainty about these predictions seldom enters the analysis explicitly, particularly in optimization applications. Most explicit consideration of uncertainty enters in the model building stage, where estimator variance will be looked at in going from original to final specification. In prediction and optimization it will at a minimum provide the decision maker with a feeling for the confidence he can put in the results derived from the model.

We conclude that in the classical framework a formal integrated treatment of uncertainty is not directly available, which may lead to some neglect of the importance of uncertainty. This framework is provided in the decision-theoretic approach, which we now describe.

In a Decision-Theoretic Framework

It should be clear that when one wishes to combine sample and prior information in a formal way, knowledge of the prior distribution of the parameters is needed.

Even when combining sample and prior information in an ad hoc way, one should at least have an idea of the variance of the prior parameters. Without this, there is no way to evaluate the relative confidence one can have in each set of estimates.

Suppose now that no sample information is at hand or that for reasons explained on page 108 it is considered irrelevant. Subjective information is then the only kind of usable information, and posterior and prior distributions are the same. How much we need to know about the predictive or prior distributions then depends on the intended use of the model. We will distinguish more specifically between prediction and optimization. In the first case the model must be able to answer "what if" type questions. For example, what profit is to be expected if the advertising budget is set equal to a_0? Optimization, on the other hand, refers to issues such as finding the advertising budget that yields an optimal level of profit. Formally the latter can be defined as the advertising budget that maximizes the decision maker's utility, and we therefore must know (or assume) the form of his utility function. Let us first consider a nonlinear utility function, more specifically, one that is quadratic in profit π:

$$U = u_0 + u_1\pi + u_2\pi^2. \tag{13}$$

Let profit be

$$\pi = (p-c)Qm - a, \tag{14}$$

where $p-c$ is unit margin and Q is industry sales. For the sake of simplicity of exposition we assume $(p-c)Q = p'$ to be constant. Let us further assume that

$$m = \alpha + \beta a + \varepsilon. \tag{15}$$

We know from the first section that with a linear utility function the solution would be unbounded. This is no longer the case with the quadratic utility function (13).

Under certainty, that is, not taking ε into account, and assuming α and β to be nonstochastic, we obtain by substituting (14) into (13)

$$U = u_0 + u_1[\, p'\alpha + (p'\beta - 1)a\,] + u_2[\, p'\alpha + (p'\beta - 1)a\,]^2, \tag{16}$$

which reaches a maximum for $a = a^*$,[20]

$$a^* = -\frac{u_1 + 2u_2 p'\alpha}{2u_2(p'\beta - 1)}. \tag{17}$$

Next we consider two cases of uncertainty. First only ε is stochastic and has mean zero and variance σ_ε^2. The utility function now becomes

$$U = u_0 + u_1[\, p'\alpha + (p'\beta - 1)a + p'\varepsilon\,] + u_2[\, p'\alpha + (p'\beta - 1)a + p'\varepsilon\,]^2 \tag{18}$$

and we will now maximize expected utility

$$E(U) = u_0 + u_1[\, p'\alpha + (p'\beta - 1)a\,] + u_2[\, p'\alpha + (p'\beta - 1)a\,]^2$$
$$+ u_2 p'^2 \sigma_\varepsilon^2. \tag{19}$$

Since only the last term in (19) differs from (16) and since it does not depend on a, the optimal level of the advertising budget is again given by (17).

The example illustrates that not uncertainty, but uncertainty about the instrument effectiveness, is important. This can be seen by making α and β stochastic. Let their expected values and variances, respectively, be μ_α, μ_β and σ_α^2, σ_β^2 and their covariance $\sigma_{\alpha\beta}$.[21] Equation (15) can then also be written

$$m = \mu_\alpha + \mu_\beta a + u \tag{20}$$

where u has a zero mean and variance σ_u^2, and with u and ε related as follows:

$$u = \alpha - \mu_\alpha + (\beta - \mu_\beta)a + \varepsilon \tag{21}$$

and

$$\sigma_u^2 = \sigma_\alpha^2 + \sigma_\beta^2 a^2 + 2\sigma_{\alpha\beta}a + \sigma_\varepsilon^2. \tag{22}$$

Using (21) we can rewrite (18)

$$U = u_0 + u_1[\, p'\mu_\alpha + (p'\mu_\beta - 1)a + p'u\,] + u_2[\, p'\mu_\alpha + (p'\mu_\beta - 1)a + p'u\,]^2. \tag{23}$$

---

[20] Depending on the values of u_1, u_2, p', α, and β, a^* could of course be negative. That is due to the nonrobustness of the market share function, the limited range of π for which a quadratic utility function is appropriate, and the assumed certainty. We will not worry much about the first two problems here, since the choice of specification of the market share and utility functions was deliberately kept simple for the sake of clarity of exposition and not for their realism.

[21] And assuming $\sigma_{\alpha u} = \sigma_{\beta u} = 0$.

The expected value of (23) is

$$E(U) = u_0 + u_1 \left[p'\mu_\alpha + (p'\mu_\beta - 1)a \right] + u_2 \left[p'\mu_\alpha + (p'\mu_\beta - 1)a \right]^2$$
$$+ u_2 p'^2 \left(\sigma_\alpha^2 + \sigma_\beta^2 a^2 + 2\sigma_{\alpha\beta} a + \sigma_\varepsilon^2 \right) \qquad (24)$$

and the value of a that maximizes $E(U)$ now becomes

$$a^* = -\frac{(p'\mu_\beta - 1)(u_1 + 2u_2 p'\mu_\alpha) + 2u_2 p'^2 \sigma_{\alpha\beta}}{2u_2 \left[(p'\mu_\beta - 1)^2 + p'^2 \sigma_\beta^2 \right]}, \qquad (25)$$

an expression that contains not only the first moments μ_α and μ_β but also the second moments σ_β^2 and $\sigma_{\alpha\beta}$. Thus with a quadratic utility function, or for most other nonlinear utility functions for that matter, maximizing utility will normally require knowledge of higher moments of the distribution of the parameters.

In most normative applications found in the marketing literature, profit rather than utility is maximized, which means that, at least implicitly, the decision maker's utility is assumed to be linear in profit. If in Equation (14) m is the only stochastic component, and it is linear in the stochastic parameters and error term, knowledge of these expected values is sufficient to determine an optimal budget. Unfortunately, if m is nonlinear in the stochastic parameters, then its expected value will not be a function of just the expected value of the parameters but of higher moments as well. Thus in Equation (9) $\tilde{m}$ is nonlinear in $\tilde{\theta}$, and $E(\tilde{m}(a, \tilde{\varepsilon}))$ will not be only a function of $E(\tilde{\theta})$. Moreover, $m(a, E(\tilde{\theta}), E(\tilde{\varepsilon}))$ will only be an approximation of the expected value of market share. How good the approximation will be is hard to tell without information on the distribution of $\tilde{\theta}$.

There is a growing tendency among model builders to avoid putting optimization routines into their models, even when optimization poses no insurmountable analytical or numerical problems. There are several reasons for this tendency.[22] First is the desire to avoid a "push-button" approach, where the model tells the decision maker what he ought to do. Too much dependency on model results may gradually lead the decision maker to lose touch with what really goes on in the market, and get him into difficulty when he must handle discrepancies between real and model-predicted results. In other cases, decision makers may simply resent models that tell them what to do, and as such normative models are harder to implement. In addition, models often look at only a partial reality, without taking the broader picture (for example, decisions concerning other products) into account. Finally, it is well known that deriving utility functions for individuals or groups of individuals is a nontrivial affair. As a result of these various considerations, models are now often of a predictive kind.

---

[22] The discussion follows Naert and Leeflang [13, p. 42].

With them we can try out a variety of possible decisions and use their implicit utility function to make the best choice.

Prediction or optimization does not make too much difference as far as information need is concerned. The main difference is that in predictive models the information is not always used in as explicit a way. But just as large estimated variances cause skepticism among users of econometric results, so should large variances in prior parameters of predictive distributions induce people to be cautious when working with subjective estimates.

Predictive Versus Prior Parameter Distributions

As pointed out in the section describing the subjective approach, in most cases it is highly unrealistic to expect decision makers to be capable of assessing prior parameter distribution directly. The assessment of predictive distributions will usually be easier. Yet a look at Equation (25) suggests that knowledge of (some of) the moments of the prior parameter distribution may be required. In fact, however, we can easily envisage an alternative way for obtaining a value for a^* based on knowledge of the predictive distributions only. From (13) and (14) it follows that

$$U = u_0 + u_1(p'\tilde{m} - a) + u_2(p'\tilde{m} - a)^2. \tag{26}$$

Using (20) we can write the expected utility as

$$E(U) = u_0 + u_1 p' E(\tilde{m}(a)) - u_1 a + u_2 p'^2 \left[\sigma_u^2(a) + E(\tilde{m}(a))^2 \right]$$
$$- 2a u_2 p' E(\tilde{m}(a)) + u_2 a^2. \tag{27}$$

This expression is only a function of a and of the first two moments of the predictive distributions.

Since (27) shows that the expected utility can be calculated without knowledge of the moments of the prior parameter distribution, one may well wonder whether knowledge of the latter distribution is of any use. We should first recall that if sample information on the parameters is available, prior information is necessary in calculating the posterior distribution. Second, working with the predictive distributions only is not very convenient. For example, in (27) $E(\tilde{m}(a))$ is itself a function of a, and so could be $\sigma_u^2(a)$. Maximization of $E(U)$ will then require some kind of iterative process. For a number of values of a, the predictive distributions and hence their first two moments are assessed. For each a, $E(U)$ can then be calculated. Comparing these different values will determine the range of values for a within which $E(U)$ will reach a maximum, but will not yet tell us what the optimal value of a is. For each iteration, new subjective assessments will be necessary, a very cumbersome procedure indeed.

Even if we are only interested in prediction, lack of knowledge about the parameters makes things very difficult. Each time a level of a is considered for which no previous assessment has been made, a new predictive distribution must be assessed.

Thus on the one hand we would like to know the prior parameter distribution, but on the other hand we prefer to assess predictive distributions, since we do not believe in direct assessment of the prior parameters. Therefore a link between these distributions remains to be established. Relating to the example from the classical econometric framework the equivalence goes as follows:

$$E(\tilde{m}) = \mu_\alpha + \mu_\beta a,$$
$$\sigma_{\tilde{m}}^2 = \sigma_u^2 = \sigma_\alpha^2 + \sigma_\beta^2 a^2 + 2\sigma_{\alpha\beta} a + \sigma_\varepsilon^2. \tag{28}$$

A formal and operational procedure linking predictive and prior parameter distribution is, for a linear model, given by Winkler.[23] It should of course be added immediately that things will become significantly more complicated at a technical level when response functions are nonlinear.

Conclusions

Theoretically speaking, decision models should be developed in such a way that the full decision-theoretic approach can be applied. That is, they should contain a module for eliciting prior distributions, a module for handling sample information, the technical procedure for combining both types of information, and finally, a module for evaluating the consequences of decisions considered in the light of the model obtained. That should enable the user to take whatever he likes or considers most appropriate for his decision situation. For example, in some cases he may judge sample information to be irrelevant, therefore limiting himself to prior information only; and in the case of prior information only, he may in a particular situation consider knowledge of the expected value of the predictive distributions to be sufficient for his purposes. In other cases both prior and sample information will be available and the decision maker may want to make use of both.

Unfortunately the operational possibilities of the approach are more limited than the theoretical ones. There is first the technical handicap of combining sample and prior information. In most real cases the results will not be at all trivial to derive. Second, eliciting probability distributions is operationally quite demanding and it is not at all clear that man is capable of performing probability assessments. For example, Hogarth has argued in a review article [3, p. 271] that "since man is a selective, sequential

---

[23] Various shortcuts to Winkler's procedure are possible, depending on the knowledge one can assume. For example, the number of assessments to be made will be substantially reduced if σ_u^2 and σ_ε^2 can be assumed to be constant.

information processing system with limited capacity, he is ill-suited for assessing probability distributions." In addition, nothing has been said here about the problems of combining prior distributions when several actors are involved in the decision-making process.[24]

Given these constraints, it is not surprising to find that, at a time when implementation is given priority status in model building, preference is given to approaches that are operational rather than to theoretically attractive ones.

References

1. Bultez, A. V. "Competitive Strategy for Interrelated Markets," Ph.D. dissertation, Catholic University of Louvain, 1975.
2. De Finetti, B. "Probabilities of Probabilities: A Real Problem or a Misunderstanding," in A. Aykac and C. Brumat (eds.), *New Developments in the Applications of Bayesian Methods*. Amsterdam: North-Holland, 1977.
3. Hogarth, R. M. "Cognitive Processes and the Assessment of Subjective Probability Distributions," *Journal of the American Statistical Association* 70, 271–294 (1975).
4. Lambin, J. J. "A Computer On-Line Marketing Mix Model," *Journal of Marketing Research* 9, 119–126 (1972).
5. Little, J. D. C. "Models and Managers: The Concept of a Decision Calculus," *Management Science* 16, B466–B485 (1970).
6. _____. "BRANDAID: A Marketing Mix Model, Part I: Structure," *Operations Research* 23, 628–655 (1975).
7. _____. "BRANDAID: A Marketing Mix Model, Part II: Implementation, Calibration and Case Study," *Operations Research* 23, 656–673 (1975).
8. Lodish, L. M., "CALLPLAN: An Interactive Salesman's Call Planning System," *Management Science* 18, B25–B40 (1971).
9. Maddala, G. S. *Econometrics*. New York: McGraw-Hill, 1977.
10. Montgomery, D. B., Silk, A. J., and Zaragoza, C. E. "A Multiple Product Sales Force Allocation Model," *Management Science* 18, P3–P24 (1971).
11. Naert, Ph. A. "Should Marketing Models Be Robust?" Paper presented at IBM Conference on the Implementation of Marketing Models, Ottignies, Belgium.
12. _____. "The Validation of Macro Models," *Proceedings ESOMAR Seminar on Market Modelling, Part II*, Noordwijk-aan-Zee, The Netherlands, pp. 17–30 (1975).
13. _____ and Leeflang, P. S. H. *Building Implementable Marketing Models*. Leiden: Martinus Nijhoff Social Sciences Division, 1978.
14. Parsons, L. J. "The Product Life Cycle and Time-Varying Advertising Elasticities," *Journal of Marketing Research* 12, 476–480 (1975).
15. Tydeman, J., and Mitchell, R. B. "Subjective Information Modelling," *Operational Research Quarterly* 28, 1–19 (1977).

---

[24]For a short survey of group assessment see Naert and Leeflang [13, pp. 266–274].

16. Urban, G. L. "SPRINTER Mod. I: A Basic New Product Analysis Model," *Proceedings of the National Conference of the American Marketing Association* pp. 139–150 (1969).

17. _____. "SPRINTER Mod III: A Model for the Analysis of New Frequently Purchased Consumer Products," *Operations Research* 18, 805–854 (1970).

18. Vanden Abeele, P. "An Investigation of Errors in the Variables on the Estimation of Linear Models in a Marketing Context," unpublished Ph.D. dissertation, Stanford University, 1975.

19. Winkler, R. L. "The Assessment of Prior Distributions in Bayesian Analysis," *Journal of the American Statistical Association* 62, 1105–1120 (1967).

20. _____. "The Consensus of Subjective Probability Distributions," *Management Science* 15, B61–B75 (1968).

21. _____. "Prior Distributions and Model Building in Regression Analysis," in A. Aykac and C. Brumat (eds.), *New Developments in the Applications of Bayesian Methods*. Amsterdam: North-Holland, 1977, pp. 233–242.

6

New Product Models

Gert Assmus

The introduction of a new product is usually preceded by the following steps:

1. the creation and design of new product concepts,
2. the evaluation of alternative concepts,
3. the development of a prototype, and
4. test marketing.

At each step, another commitment of corporate resources is required, and management has to decide whether or not to proceed toward market introduction. This go–no go decision is based on an analysis of the future profitability of the product and requires an assessment of the market that the product would capture once launched.

The new product models to be reviewed in this chapter are designed to aid the marketing manager in estimating sales and/or market share for a new product before it is introduced into the market. The specific features of any given model are shaped by the purpose it is supposed to serve, and this purpose is likely to vary with the stage of the new product development process where the model is applied. For example, at an early stage, management is often interested in the appeal of various product attributes relative to the attributes of existing products. Thus, an appropriate new product model has to incorporate such attributes and be able to relate them to market share predictions. On the other hand, once a product has been designed, management may be interested in the impact of alternative marketing mixes on expected sales. In order to be useful at this point, therefore, a new product model has to include such variables as advertising, price, and promotion.

New product models take basically two alternative approaches toward the projection of sales:

1. *Trial–repeat models* break total sales down into sales from trial purchases and sales from repeat purchases;
2. *Competitive share models* estimate the market share that the new product will capture within a well-defined market.

As a rule, competitive share models are more likely to be applied at the early stages of new product development, whereas trial–repeat models are more appropriate for decisions at a later development stage. Yet trial–repeat models are also used successfully at an earlier stage, even before an actual product has been designed.

This chapter first reviews a few selected models in each of these two categories. No attempt is made to provide a complete survey of all the new product models that have ever been published.[1] Then the application of new product models is discussed. This is followed by a brief discussion of emerging trends and future research in the new product area.

Trial–Repeat Models

In trial–repeat models total sales are composed of sales from trial purchases and sales from repeat purchases. In any one period after the introduction, sales are [21, pp. 552–53]

$$S_t = s_{Ft} N_{Ft} + s_{Rt} N_{Rt},$$

where

S_t is total sales in period t,
s_{Ft} is the average purchase volume per period per first-time buyer,
N_{Ft} is the number of first-time buyers in period t,
s_{Rt} is the average purchase volume per period per repeat buyer, and
N_{Rt} is the number of repeat buyers in period t.

The number of first-time buyers in any period t is given by the trial rate and the number of potential buyers in the target population:

$$N_{Ft} = f_t B,$$

where

f_t is the proportion of all buyers in the target population who are trying the new product for the first time in period t, that is, the trial rate, and
B is the number of potential buyers in the target group.

---

[1]Comprehensive surveys of trial–repeat models are given by Cannon [10] and Midgley [28].

The number of repeat buyers in period t is defined by the repeat purchase rate and the number of persons who have tried the product at least once during the preceding periods:

$$N_{Rt} = r_t F_t B,$$

where r_t is the repeat purchase rate in period t and

$$F_t = \sum_{i=1}^{t-1} f_i$$

is the cumulative trial rate. The ultimate, or steady-state, sales level for a new product can be computed as follows:

$$S = TRIB,$$

where

S   is the ultimate sales level,
T   is the ultimate cumulative trial rate for the new product,
R   is the ultimate repeat purchase rate,
I   is the average purchase quantity, and
B   is the number of potential buyers.

Trial and repeat purchases will now be discussed in more detail.

Trial Purchases

Triers are those persons who buy a new product or new brand at least once. If they are not expected to repeat the purchase within the planning horizon, a new product model deals only with trial purchases and does not incorporate any repeat purchases. For example, a short-term model for predicting sales of a consumer or industrial durable is only concerned with the first purchase of the product.

New product models can be classified on the basis of the variables that are included for explaining why a specific cumulative trial rate, or trial level, will be achieved after a certain number of periods.

1. *Macroanalytical* models explain trial purchases with the help of certain exogenous uncontrollable variables.
2. *Behavioral* models explicitly deal with various stages of buyer readiness that may result in a trial purchase.
3. *Managerial* models introduce variables that can be controlled by a company.

These three categories are not exclusive of each other. For example, managerial models often contain behavioral variables as well as macroanalytical parameters. Yet these categories represent three distinctive approaches that have been taken by model builders in the past. The following discussion examines models in each of these three categories.

Macroanalytical Models. These models of trial purchases predict sales for a new product by modeling the diffusion process. Only a few macroparameters, such as the population size, the propensity to innovate, and the propensity to imitate, are used to explain the first purchases of a new product through time.

One of the earliest applications of the diffusion concept to the introduction of a new product was proposed by Fourt and Woodlock [16]. They postulated that the number of new triers in any period is equal to a given percentage of those customers who have not tried the product yet, but are expected to become triers now or in future periods:

$$Q_t = r\overline{Q}(1-r)^{t-1},$$

where

Q_t represents incremental triers as a fraction of potential sales in period t,

r is the rate of penetration of untapped potential, and

$\overline{Q}$ is the potential sales as a fraction of all buyers.

Since the penetration rate r is considered constant, the diffusion process reflects how fast buyers learn about the new product and seek to purchase it. Market penetration is greatest in the first period and declines exponentially in subsequent periods.

Other diffusion models employ alternative curves to represent the trial process. For example, based on Rogers's diffusion theory, the number of new triers is assumed to be normally distributed over time [35]. This leads to an S-shaped market penetration curve. In this case, trial is assumed to be a function of a social process where a few innovators will adopt the product first and lead the way for the imitators who constitute the majority of the total market.

Bass [4] proposed a model that includes a coefficient of innovation as well as a coefficient of imitation.[2] The innovators are not influenced by the number of persons who have already tried the product. The number of imitators, on the other hand, is considered a function of cumulative trial at any point in time:

$$Q_t = (p + rQ_T/\overline{Q})(\overline{Q} - Q_T),$$

where

Q_t is the number of new triers in period t,

Q_T is the cumulative number of triers until period t,

$\overline{Q}$ is the total number of potential triers,

---

[2] Nevers [29] tested the Bass model with data from several product introductions and compared it with a model proposed by Mansfield [26].

r is the effect of each trier on each nontrier, and
p is the individual conversion rate in the absence of earlier triers' influence.

Bernhardt and MacKenzie [6] suggest more comprehensive diffusion models allowing for entry and exit of potential triers over time. Dodson and Muller [14] elaborate further and not only incorporate the influence of external information sources such as advertising into their diffusion model but also extend their model by considering repeat purchases.

Behavioral Models. In these models various stages of buyer readiness leading to a trial purchase are explictly represented. These stages are at the cognitive or the affective level, or at both.

The most commonly modeled variable at the cognitive level is awareness. It is assumed that a person has to be aware of a new product before a trial purchase will be made. Urban [43] divides the awareness stage into four levels: (a) awareness of the brand, (b) of its advertisements, (c) of specific product appeals, and (d) of word-of-mouth recommendations. A person is assumed to move through these awareness levels sequentially, and each higher level is associated with a higher trial probability.

Perhaps the most comprehensive behavioral model was developed by Amstutz [2]. His computer simulation model traces awareness and attitude for a consumer population of any desired number. Persons in this simulated population respond to promotional communications from producers and retailers as well as to word-of-mouth communications from other consumers. These communications are specified in terms of product and brand awareness and attitudes that may result in a purchase of the new product. Amstutz's model has been a significant attempt to present virtually all the variables that might possibly affect consumer choice in an all-encompassing framework. Its value for predicting sales or market share in an applied situation, however, has been questioned [22].

Managerial Models. These models introduce controllable variables for explaining the trial rate. These variables are related to the trial rate directly, or they are assumed to affect some intermediate variables that, in turn, impact on a person's trial probability. Product sampling programs, distribution level, price, and product positioning are examples of controllable variables that are directly related to trial rates in new product models.

In the packaged goods industry, trial is often induced by distributing free samples of the new product. The trial rate for this product due to sampling can then be defined by the probability that a person will receive a free sample multiplied by the probability that the person who receives the sample will actually use it [41]. In some models, the trial of a product due to sampling is distinguished from a trial due to purchase, since a "sample trier" is less likely to purchase the product in future periods than is a "purchase trier," who was sufficiently interested in the new product to spend his own money in order to familiarize himself with it [3].

The distribution level is another variable that may affect the trial rate for packaged consumer goods. In new product models, this variable is usually defined as the proportion of retail outlets that carry the new product weighted by their sales volume in the product category. It is assumed that the buyer is more likely to try the new product if it is conveniently available to him. In their ASSESSOR model, Silk and Urban [41] compute the trial rate, if no sampling takes place, as the product of three probabilities: (1) the probability of a consumer making a trial purchase given awareness and availability; (2) the probability that the consumer will be aware; and (3) the probability that the new brand will be available, which is measured by the distribution level.

The relative price of the newly introduced brand may also directly affect trial. In the TRACKER model, incremental trial from one period to the next is adjusted by a relative price term [8]:

$$\Delta T_t^* = \bar{P}_t^{\gamma} \Delta T_t,$$

where

ΔT_t^* is the adjusted incremental trial,

$\bar{P}_t$ is the price of the new brand at time t divided by the average price of the product category in period t,

γ is a parameter, and

ΔT_t is the incremental trial if $\bar{P}_t = 1$.

If $\bar{P}_t < 1$, then the price of the new brand is below that of the product category, and expected trial is increased by a certain percentage. If $\bar{P}_t > 1$, expected trial is reduced accordingly. For $\gamma > 1$, the effect of price differences across products will be accentuated. If $\gamma < 1$, the difference will be less pronounced.

Advertising is an example of a controllable variable that is often related to trial through another variable. It is usually assumed that advertising affects trial indirectly by creating awareness first [3, 23, 43, 46]. Advertising may be expressed in terms of absolute dollars or in terms of gross rating points (GRPs). In the AYER model, the advertising copy quality is recognized by an additional multiplicative variable [12].

As awareness increases, it becomes more difficult to reach nonaware buyers through advertising. Therefore, diminishing returns to advertising are assumed. Blattberg and Golanty [8] suggest the following mathematical relationship between awareness and gross rating points:

$$\ln \frac{1-A_t}{1-A_{t-1}} = \alpha - \beta \text{GRP},$$

where A_t is the brand's total awareness in period t, GRP is the number of gross rating points delivered for the brand in period t, and α and β are parameters of the model. If α is positive, then awareness declines when there is no advertising. If α is negative, awareness increases even without advertising. Parameter β represents the responsiveness of awareness to advertising. This functional form shows diminishing returns to advertising. It also allows the awareness to decline from the previous period's level if the number of GRPs falls below a certain threshold.

In the AYER model [12] advertising recall (AR), or awareness, is related not only to media impressions (AHI) and copy execution (CE), but also to product positioning (PP), consumer promotions containing advertising messages (CP*), and category interest (CI):

$$AR = a_1 + b_{11}(PP) + b_{12}(\sqrt{AHI \times CE}) + b_{13}(CP^*) + b_{14}(CI).$$

This expression implies diminishing returns for advertising, whereas awareness is assumed to be a linear function with respect to the other variables. This model predicts awareness at a specific point in time and does not capture the dynamics of increasing or diminishing awareness over time.

If an awareness variable is introduced into a new product model, it has to be related to trial. In the DEMON [23] as well as in the NEWPROD model [3], the number of persons becoming triers in any one period is assumed to constitute a constant proportion of those who are aware of the new product but have not yet tried it. In the TRACKER model [8], the authors distinguish two potential trier groups. One group consists of buyers who become aware in the present period. The other group consists of those persons who were aware in the previous periods, but have not yet tried the product. The newly aware potential triers are assumed to have a higher probability of trial than persons in the latter group.

In the AYER model [12], the initial purchase (IP) is related not only to awareness (AR), but also to retail distribution factors (DN), packaging characteristics (PK), a known or family brand name (FB), the amount and type of consumer promotion (CP), the extent of consumer satisfaction with the product if it has been sampled (PS), and the level of usage of the product category (CU):

$$IP = a_2 + b_{21}(AR) + b_{22}(DN \times PK) + b_{23}(FB) + b_{24}(CP)$$

$$+ b_{25}(PS) + b_{26}(CU).$$

The AYER model considers the first revenue purchase in a shopping context as the dependent variable. Actual trial could have occurred earlier if the consumer received a free sample. The more satisfied the consumer is with a sampled product, the more likely he is to purchase this product on his own.

Repeat Purchases

Repeat purchases become an important ingredient in the prediction of sales or market share if the buyer can be expected to repeat the purchase during the planning horizon. The accurate prediction of repeat purchases is therefore crucial for forecasting sales of frequently purchased goods.

The definition of a repeat purchase depends on the definition of trial and varies between models accordingly. If only the first purchase is counted as a trial, then the first repeat purchase takes place when a buyer buys a product for the second time. On the other hand, if the consumption of a free sample is considered a trial, then the first actual purchase is counted as a repeat purchase.

Analogous to the above discussion of the trial rate, the approach to the modeling of repeat purchases can be classified as either macroanalytical, behavioral, or managerial.

Macroanalytical Models. In these models the prediction of repeat purchases is based on exogenous parameters, such as repeat ratios or brand-switching probabilities. Fourt and Woodlock [16] introduce the concept of repeat ratios. The first repeat ratio is the fraction of initial buyers who make a second purchase. It can also be interpreted as the probability that a first-time buyer will buy the product for a second time [15, 27]. The second repeat ratio would then be the fraction of the number of first repeaters who buy the product for a third time. These ratios tend to grow larger as a group of hard-core loyal buyers eventually evolves.

In the PERCEPTOR and later in the ASSESSOR models, the repeat rate S is derived as the equilibrium share of a first-order two-state Markov process [41, 45]:

$$S = p_{21}/(1 + p_{21} - p_{11}),$$

where, for those who have tried the new brand, p_{ij} is the probability of purchase of brand j at the next purchase opportunity when brand i was purchased last, $0 \leqslant p_{ij} \leqslant 1$. Obviously, this equation computes the ultimate repeat purchase rate, and it does not show how this rate evolves over time.

Behavioral Models. Repeat purchases are explained in terms of internal behavioral variables in these models. A comprehensive framework is again presented by the SPRINTER III model [44]. Once a consumer has tried a product he is placed in the "preference class." Based on their trial use experience, people in the preference class are further classified by their awareness of specific product and advertising appeals. Advertising can increase this awareness. Given their purchase frequencies, some consumers are then classified as being ready for a purchase and their awareness is translated into intent or predisposition to repurchase. Whether or not they actually end up buying the company's brand again depends on a number of intervening variables, including the in-store price, displays, and facings. Once a buyer has repeated a purchase, displays and facings are assumed to be of no importance, but relative price changes could cause a buyer to switch to another brand.

Managerial Models. Although the repeat purchase rate is admittedly a crucial input to the computation of market share for frequently purchased goods, only a surprisingly small number of new product models attempt to relate it explicitly to managerially controllable variables. The AYER model, the NEWPROD model, and the TRACKER model are exceptions. These managerial models also incorporate a product satisfaction variable for explaining repeat purchases.

In the AYER model, the relative price of the brand is introduced as one of the determinants of repeat purchase [12]. Specifically, the model implies that repeat purchase levels will depend primarily on the extent of consumer knowledge, the level of initial trials, satisfaction with prior purchases, the frequency of purchase for products in the category, and the price of the product relative to other products in the category. The functional relationship between repeat purchases and these variables is not revealed.

The NEWPROD model postulates that a repeat purchase is more likely to occur if the expectations that were raised by the company's advertising are met by the consumption experience when the buyer tries the new product [3]. First, an advertising copy test determines which attributes of the product were communicated through the ad copy. Then these attributes are rated by the persons who tried the product in a consumer use test. These ratings, in turn, are related to the repeat rate. Thus, a change in the advertising copy, emphasizing different product attributes, could bring about a change in the repeat rate.

The TRACKER model also assumes that a trier will be a repeat user if he has had a positive experience with the product and expresses an intention to repurchase it [8].

Competitive Share Models

In the recent past a number of new product models have evolved that do not focus on trial and repeat rates in predicting market share, although some of their variables may be related to these concepts. Instead, these models emphasize the competitive structure of the market in which the new product is to be launched. An equilibrium market share is determined either by analyzing the buyers' choice from a set of competing products or by relying on an analysis of the market structure. The first type of competitive share models will be classified as buyer behavior models, the second type as market structure models.

Buyer Behavior Models

The prediction of market share in buyer behavior models always involves the identification of the relevant product market and the prediction of brand choice. If the model incorporates product attributes, a product space is revealed and preferences are predicted based on the ratings of those attributes.[3]

Identification of the Market. The identification of the relevant market for a new product in buyer behavior models is based on customer perception and behavior [13, 19, 34]. This is usually done by first determining the size and composition of the customers' evoked sets for a specific product class [17, 41, 45]. "Evoked" is defined as brands last used, ever used, on hand, or not considered for use. The product market would thus be given by all those products that were elicited from some prespecified minimum proportion of respondents under some broad market definition, such as health care services or deodorants. Day and Shocker [13] have suggested that the market should be defined situationally in terms of intended usage. Recent work by Srivastava, Shocker, and Day [42] attempts to create a situational typology from factors that appear to explain specific objective situations. Products judged appropriate for these situations would then define a product market.

Creation of the Product Map. If product choice is related to the attributes of competing products, those attributes which distinguish the product alternatives in the relevant market have to be identified first [1]. Shocker and Srinivasan emphasize that the attributes should not only be meaningful to the customers but should also be related to variables that the marketer knows how to influence or control, such as physical properties, price, promotion frequency, and message [38, 39]. A perceptual product space is now identified by having respondents rate the established as well as the new products on those attributes. Each product occupies a unique position in this space which is to be related to individual (or segment) choice behavior or preference.

Prediction of Preference. Three alternative approaches that have been proposed for predicting preferences for the established and the new products are (1) the ideal point model, (2) the vector model, and (3) utility theory.

1. The ideal point model represents the decision maker by a location within the product space that indicates the "ideal" combination of

---

[3] For an excellent review of the pertinent literature see Shocker and Srinivasan [39].

product attributes. The decision maker's utility for a given product is assumed to be inversely related to its overall Euclidean distance from his ideal point, after weighting the distance for each attribute by the relative importance that the respondent assigns to this product attribute [38, 45].

2. The vector model is a special case of the ideal point model. It is assumed that the ideal levels of any given attribute are either plus or minus infinity. Thus it is only necessary to know what relative importance a decision maker assigns to each attribute in order to compute the expected utility associated with the purchase of a given product [32].

Both ideal point and vector models can be classified as linear compensatory models. Both models have received considerable attention in marketing and have been tested empirically. Generally, they have been credited with possessing predictive ability [36], but some mixed empirical results have also been reported [37, 47]. Even though the empirical evidence is encouraging, the models lack an axiomatic theory for specifying the functional form of combining the attribute measures into a measure of preference or utility [7].

3. Hauser and Urban [17] base their new product model on utility theory as it was developed by von Neumann and Morgenstern. They draw on a deductive theory to derive unique functional forms from fundamental axioms and verifiable assumptions describing how a buyer evaluates alternative products. A utility function is derived whose coefficients reflect the relative importance of relevant product attributes, their interdependencies, and the risk attitude of the decision maker. The utility is a cardinal measure of the goodness of the evaluated product.

Prediction of Brand Choice. In order to estimate market share for a new product, a link has to be established between preference or utility and actual choice behavior. Several models stop with the modeling of preference and do not deal with choice behavior. The assumption is made that a customer would always buy the product for which he displays the highest preference. Yet choice may differ from preference because purchase may be affected by many factors over which the marketer has only limited control [39]. For example, brand availability at any given time, special deals, interpersonal influence, or the desire for variety may keep a buyer from purchasing a brand for which he expressed the highest preference. A stochastic formulation may take such factors into account.

A stochastic choice model, however, may also be justified on the basis of psychological choice axioms. Luce [25, pp. 24–77] has shown that a simple axiom about choice probabilities implies the existence of a ratio scale for the alternatives from which the choice is to be made. According to Luce's choice theorem, preferences and choice probabilities are related in the following way:

$$P_{ij} = V_{ij} \Big/ \sum_{k=1}^{m_i} V_{ik}, \qquad V_{ik} \geqslant 0, \qquad k = 1, \ldots, j, \ldots, m_i,$$

where

P_{ij} is the probability that buyer i will choose product j,
V_{ij} is buyer i's ratio scaled preference for product j, and
m_i is the number of products in respondent i's relevant set of alternatives.

This functional form was modified by Pessemier et al. [33], who introduced an exponent β:

$$P_{ij} = (V_{ij})^{\beta} \Big/ \sum_{k=1}^{m_i} (V_{ik})^{\beta}.$$

A characteristic value of β is expected to be associated with each product class, and it reflects how the intervening forces interact to transform preferences into predicted market share.

In the ASSESSOR model, individual purchase probabilities for the new brand are estimated and then aggregated across individuals to obtain an estimate of the expected market share [41]. The modified Luce model is applied to the estimation of the purchase probabilities. The calculation of market share also takes into account that the new brand will not necessarily be an element of the relevant set of brands from which the consumer is choosing. Therefore,

$$M_j = E_j \sum_{i=1}^{N} P_{ij} \Big/ N,$$

where

M_j is the expected market share for brand j,
E_j is the proportion of consumers who include brand j in their relevant set of alternatives, and
P_{ij} is the predicted probability of purchase brand j by consumer i, with $i = 1, \ldots, N$.

The similarity between this formulation and the trial–repeat model is obvious. Empirical studies show that brands in the relevant set are for the most part accounted for by past usage or "trial." On the other hand, the variable $\sum_j P_{ij}/N$ is a measure of the average repeat purchase [41].

The predictive results from stochastic choice models have been compared with those from single choice models where the most preferred product is always chosen [31, 33]. Generally, the aggregate results were approximately the same. Yet it may be necessary to choose a probabilistic model for "less important" decisions (for example, soft drinks rather than automobiles), since the error component may be larger [39] for such decisions.

Market Structure Models

In a market structure model, the equilibrium market share for a new product is determined from the number of products in the market and their respective shares, and from the consumer preference structure. In the HENDRY model a "par share" for a new entry into a product category is computed for a new brand that meets the standards set by leading products in the category in terms of generic product benefits and values and in terms of advertising copy, packaging, merchandising, and product performance. An effectiveness coefficient accounts for the difference between the expected share performance for a par product and that of the actual new product [18].

The prediction of market share in the HENDRY model is based on the assumption of a heterogeneous population of zero-order consumers [20]. That is, the individual consumer chooses among the brands according to a constant probability vector, which may be different from that for another consumer. If only "directly competing brands" are considered, the expected probability of buying brand h for a consumer who switches out of brand i is proportional to the market share of brand h. A switching constant is introduced into the model as a measure of the actual amount of brand switching in a specific market or, expressed positively, as a measure of brand loyalty [5]. Obviously, the identification of "directly competing brands," that is, the definition of the market, is one of the most important inputs to the analysis. The HENDRY model requires the partitioning of markets into a hierarchy of product set structures.

Once a given product class market has been defined in terms of current market shares and a switching constant, the par share for a new entry can be computed. Markets with many current brands in a single category yield low par shares, whereas markets with only a few brands yield high par shares. If the market is characterized by a relatively large switching propensity, the new brand can capture a larger share than if a high loyalty factor prevailed.

The Application of New Product Models

The successful implementation of a new product model requires a consistent measurement and/or estimation procedure. This procedure is straightforward if the parameters are unambiguously defined and can be observed directly. An example is the implementation of a trial–repeat model with trial and repeat data from a test market. In many cases, however, a new product model contains variables that can be interpreted in several different ways and/or variables that cannot be observed directly. As a consequence, the measurement methodology then becomes an integral part of this new product model.

For example, if a trial–repeat model also includes an awareness variable, the measurement instrument has to be described fully before the model becomes operational. It could be "aided" or "unaided" awareness, and in either case, the measure is likely to vary with the specific research methodology. Thus, it is necessary to specify how the sample is to be selected, whether the data are to be collected through mail surveys or by telephone or personal interviews, and what scaling technique is to be employed when the awareness measure is needed for the model's implementation.

If the variables cannot be observed directly, the model builder has to specify what substitute measures are to be employed. For example, in the ASSESSOR model, which was explicitly developed for the *pre*test market evaluation of packaged goods, the trial rate is established through a laboratory-based experimental procedure as follows [41]: Intercept interviews are conducted with shoppers near a shopping center to recruit a representative sample of customers. The selected respondents are then asked to enter a laboratory facility nearby where they are shown advertising material for the new brand and for the leading established brands. Following the advertising exposure, they are led to a simulated retail store where quantities of the full set of competing brands, including the new one, are displayed and available for purchase. Most of the participants, who are given $2.00 for their cooperation, buy one of the brands. If it is the new brand, the purchase is counted as a trial.

As an alternative to the data-based implementation, the parameters of a new product model can also be based on strictly judgmental inputs. For example, the NEWPROD model is used most often by the product manager in the following way [3]: At an early stage in the product development process, before any market data have been collected, the manager conducts a sensitivity analysis on the model, experimenting with alternative trial and repeat rates for the new product. He thus establishes the critical values for these rates that the product needs to achieve in order to break even or meet some other financial criterion. Based on his experience with similar products in the past, he then decides whether or not it is realistic to assume that these values can be reached when certain advertising, sampling, and couponing programs are employed. If the analysis leads to the conclusion that the product cannot meet the financial criteria, it will be abandoned at this point. If the manager concludes that the product is likely to be a financial success, the product development process is continued, and this includes the market research phase leading to the data-based implementation of the NEWPROD model at a later time.

The judgment-based experimentation with new product models is generally encouraged if two conditions prevail: (1) the manager has easy access to the model, which may be available on an interactive computer system; (2) the manager is thoroughly familiar with the variables of the model and with the measurements for such variables that were collected for comparable products in the past.

Before a new product model is accepted by the user it has to be validated. The validation of a model can take different forms. A model is considered a valid representation of the market response to a new product if it reflects the manager's perception of market reality. If the manager was involved in developing the model, he understands the way it works, and therefore believes that the model's sales projections are correct [3].

Comparing the output from two or more different models is another possible validation test. The "ASSESSOR measurement and model system" calls for the user to implement two models for the pretest market evaluation of new packaged goods: a competitive share model as well as a trial–repeat model [41]. If the two models yield results that are in close agreement, then this can serve to strengthen confidence in the prediction. On the other hand, divergent forecasts trigger a search for possible sources of error or bias that might account for the discrepancy.

A more rigorous, and objective, validation requires a comparison of actual with forecasted market results. Especially when a new product model is supplied to a company as a consulting service from the outside, a successful validation history is most important in gaining the user's confidence. When such comparisons are provided, they are uniformly impressive (see, for example, Silk and Urban [41], Assmus [3]). Thus, a new product model may be widely accepted even though the user does not fully understand how the model arrives at its market projections and what the underlying assumptions are. "Blind faith" in the model's predictions can, of course, be dangerous. Assmus [3] reports about a situation where the failure of the NEWPROD model to predict the correct market share destroyed the blind faith that had been created by an almost flawless validation history. Fortunately, the test was performed on a product history and not a "live" case, and this validation test resulted in wiser future applications of the model.

Emerging Trends and Future Research

New product models have been around for about two decades. The following discussion is an attempt to identify trends in the development of such models and to speculate where the research efforts of the next decade may be focused. New product models will be discussed in the following contexts: (1) product concept testing and market identification, (2) probabilistic forecasts, (3) product portfolios, and (4) ongoing planning and monitoring processes.

Product Concepts and Market Identification

A historical analysis of new product models indicates that the thrust of the research in this area has shifted to the early phases of the product development process. Historically, the first new product models were developed for a systematic analysis of test market data [16, 31]. Thus, the first trial–repeat models were structured around the trial and repeat measures from actual test markets.

The regression study by Claycamp and Liddy in 1969, which linked new product performance to research data that are available before test marketing, has to be considered a real breakthrough. Since then, many more models have been developed that are applicable before test market data are collected. One of the main reasons for this emphasis on the early phases of the product development process is simply that there is a large potential payoff to screening out products with a low success probability and thereby avoiding the costs of a test market whenever possible. More recent research has focused on (1) the evaluation of product concepts and (2) market identification.

1. The study of product concepts represents an immediate application of the marketing concept by developing products in accordance with the customers' desires. The emergence of powerful analytical tools, such as multidimensional scaling and conjoint analysis, has made it possible for the researcher to identify relevant market attributes and to predict how customers will react to new product entries.
2. Any new product model requires a definition of the market where the new product will be competing with existing products. In trial–repeat models, the market for a new product is commonly defined in terms of a target group of potential buyers who are the current buyers of competing products in the same category [3, 41]. A new product, however, does not always fit into any predefined product category, especially if it does not replace a product with very similar characteristics. The development of competitive share models has been particularly significant in forcing the researcher to identify explicitly those products that will be in direct competition with the new product, and the definition of the relevant market often poses considerable difficulty. Yet, any sales or market share projection is extremely suspect if it is not based on a sound market definition.

The thrust of future research in the new product area can be expected to continue to be at the early stages of product development. Aside from concept evaluation and market identification, idea generation and technological forecasting may attract increased attention.

Probabilistic Forecasts

The majority of new product models generates a deterministic forecast even though no model is able to predict sales for a new product with absolute certainty. Shoemaker and Staelin [40] demonstrate this point by implementing the Parfitt–Collins trial–repeat model with purchase panel data from 2000 households covering three new product introductions, and from 1000 households for one product introduction. They found that the predictions for sales or market shares could vary widely due to sampling error alone. The average coefficient of variation was 27%. This implies that there would be a 32% chance of predicting a market share below 7.3% or above 12.7% when the true market share is 10%. There would be a 5% chance that the forecast share would be below 4.6% or above 15.7%. Their findings are especially disturbing in light of the following considerations: (a) The sampling error is only one of several sources of uncertainty about the "true" trial and repeat rates for the market introduction of the new product. As a matter of fact, it may not even be the most significant contributor to variations in the prediction of sales. Nonsampling errors caused by the chosen data collection method may be substantial and, compared to sampling errors, far more difficult to assess. (b) Purchase panel data provide direct measures of trial and repeat under fairly realistic conditions, whereas any other data seem to be farther removed from these crucial variables.

A few new product models have addressed the problem of uncertainty explicitly (for example, Charnes et al. [11], Urban [44], Hauser and Urban [17]). Future research is needed to link the generation of an explicit probability distribution of sales or market share to the measurement methodology for the implementation of the model.

Product Portfolios

Recent research into product portfolios has demonstrated that it would be unwise to optimize the performance of any one product without considering the side effects of this product on the performance of other products that the company is marketing. For example, the application of financial portfolio theory to the product portfolio suggests that a company may be able to add new products to its portfolio and thereby reduce the risk of achieving a certain rate of return on investment, or the product introduction may lead to an increase of the rate of return while leaving the risk level unchanged [9, 48]. The portfolio approach by the Boston Consulting Group recommends a balanced portfolio of cash-generating and cash-needing products. A new product may offset such a balance if its market introduction requires large amounts of cash but there are no "cash cows" in the current portfolio.

Future research is needed to identify the criteria other than sales and market share that characterize a successful addition of a product to an existing product portfolio.

Planning and Monitoring

Planning a new product introduction is an ongoing process throughout the various phases of the development process, and it does not stop once the product has been launched into the market. The marketing plan has to be constantly adjusted to take advantage of new information about the market response. By projecting sales and/or market share, new product models are providing benchmarks against which the actual market performance can be measured. If there are any significant deviations of the actual results from the forecast, it can be concluded that the sales projection was based on faulty assumptions. A correction of those assumptions leads to a revised forecast and possibly to a redesign of the marketing mix in future periods.

Given its role in this monitoring process, a new product model can be especially useful if it contains variables that are assumed to be causally related to sales. For example, "by relating advertising expenditures, price, and perceptions of performance/acceptability of the product to sales, the TRACKER model indicates how an unsuccessful product can be redesigned or the marketing mix changed to make possible a successful introduction" [8, p. 192]. Aside from carefully choosing such causal variables, future research into new product models is likely to pay more attention to the selection of control variables whose performance will provide valuable clues about the true market response. For example, tracking attitudinal variables may help to signal potential problems with future repeat rates.

The selection of such variables, of course, has to be coordinated with the choice of an information system that will produce the appropriate measurements. The designer of new product models has to specify what measurements should be taken during the product introduction if the models are to be integrated into the planning process. The designers of the TRACKER model, for example, specify that the implementation of the model calls for three waves of 500–1000 questionnaires every four weeks after introduction. In addition to information about product usage and awareness (that is, variables that are included in the model), data about product satisfaction and repeat purchase intentions are collected. This information is of diagnostic value, since the answers to these questions may indicate why a new product is failing or why it is successful [8].

Conclusions

Most new product models demonstrate how management science can be successfully applied to a marketing problem. These models are likely to meet the following two criteria:

1. They have been developed according to the decision-calculus approach; that is, the models are simple, robust, adaptive, and complete, and are easy to communicate with and control [24]. Several successful new product models met those criteria even before John D. C. Little specified them in his well-known article. Later, the explicit application of the criteria helped in the development of new product models.
2. The development and implementation of successful new product models has been relatively inexpensive. This is likely to be true if the model has a simple structure with few variables, and if it does not require extensive data gathering procedures. This would be the case if the models were developed around existing data bases. The development cost of the NEWPROD model was roughly $5000. The total cost of using the TRACKER model, including data collection, has been stated to be around $15,000. These are comparatively small amounts, considering the potential payoffs from a more accurate and credible sales forecast.

References

1. Alpert, Mark I. "Definition of Determinant Attributes: A Comparison of Methods," *Journal of Marketing Research* 8 (May), 184–191 (1971).
2. Amstutz, Arnold E. *Computer Simulation of Competitive Market Response.* Cambridge, Massachusetts: The MIT Press, 1967.
3. Assmus, Gert. "NEWPROD: The Design and Implementation of a New Product Model," *Journal of Marketing* 39 (January), 16–23 (1975).
4. Bass, Frank M. "A New Product Growth Model for Consumer Durables," *Management Science* 15 (January), 215–227 (1969).
5. _____. "The Theory of Stochastic Preference and Brand Switching," *Journal of Marketing Research* 11 (February), 1–20 (1974).
6. Bernhardt, Irwin, and MacKenzie, Kenneth D. "Some Problems in Using Diffusion Models for New Products," *Management Science* 19 (October), 187–200 (1972).
7. Bettman, James R. "The Structure of Consumer Choice Processes," *Journal of Marketing Research* 8 (November), 465–471 (1971).
8. Blattberg, Robert, and Golanty, John. "Tracker: An Early Test Market Forecasting and Diagnostic Model for New Product Planning," *Journal of Marketing Research* 15 (May), 192–202 (1978).

9. Burger, Philip C. "A Marketing Model for Selecting among Interdependent New Product Candidates," paper presented at the Fall Conference of the American Marketing Association, 1975.

10. Cannon, Tom. "New Product Development," *European Journal of Marketing* 12, 215–248 (1978).

11. Charnes, A., DeVoe, J. K., and Learner, D. B. "DEMON: Decision Mapping via Optimum Go–No Networks—A Model for Marketing New Products," *Management Science* 12 (July), 865–877 (1966).

12. Claycamp, H. J., and Liddy, L. E. "Prediction of New Product Performance: An Analytical Approach," *Journal of Marketing Research* 6 (November), 414–420 (1969).

13. Day, George S., and Shocker, Allan D. "Analytical Approaches to Identifying Competitive Product-Market Boundaries," Working Paper 76-112. Cambridge, Massachusetts: Marketing Science Institute, 1976.

14. Dodson, Joe A., Jr., and Muller, Eitan. "Models of New Product Diffusion through Advertising and Word-of-Mouth," *Management Science* 24 (November), 1568–1578 (1978).

15. Eskin, G. J. "Dynamic Forecasts of New Product Demand Using a Depth Repeat Model," *Journal of Marketing Research* 10 (May), 115–129 (1973).

16. Fourt, L. A., and Woodlock, J. W. "Early Prediction of Market Success for New Grocery Products," *Journal of Marketing* 24 (October), 31–38 (1960).

17. Hauser, John R., and Urban, Glen L. "A Normative Methodology for Modeling Consumer Response to Innovations," *Operations Research* 25 (July–August), 579–619 (1977).

18. *HendroDynamics: Fundamental Laws of Consumer Dynamics*. Hendry Corporation, 1970–1971, Chapters 1 and 2.

19. Johnson, Richard M. "Market Segmentation: A Strategic Management Tool," *Journal of Marketing Research* 8 (February), 13–18 (1971).

20. Kalwani, Manohar U., and Morrison, Donald G. "A Parsimonious Description of the Hendry System," *Management Science* 23 (January), 467–477 (1977).

21. Kotler, Philip. *Marketing Decision Making: A Model Building Approach*. New York: Holt, Rinehart and Winston, 1971.

22. Larréché, Jean-Claude, and Montgomery, David B. "A Framework for the Comparison of Marketing Models: A Delphi Study," *Journal of Marketing Research* 14 (November), 487–498 (1977).

23. Learner, D. B. "Profit Maximization through New Product Marketing Planning and Control" in F. M. Bass, C. W. King, and E. A. Pessemier (eds.), *Applications of the Sciences in Marketing Management*. New York: Wiley, 1968, pp. 151–167.

24. Little, John D. C. "Models and Managers: The Concept of a Decision Calculus," *Management Science* 16 (April), B466–B485 (1970).

25. Luce, R. Duncan. *Individual Choice Behavior*. New York: Wiley, 1959.

26. Mansfield, Edwin. "Technical Change and the Rate of Imitation," *Econometrica* 29 (October), 741–766 (1961).

27. Massy, W. F. "Stochastic Models for Monitoring New Product Introduction," in F. M. Bass, C. W. King, and E. A. Pessemier (eds.), *Applications of the Sciences in Marketing Management*. New York: Wiley, 1968, pp. 85–111.

28. Midgley, David F. *Innovation and New Product Marketing*. New York: Wiley, 1977.
29. Nevers, John V. "Extensions of a New Product Growth Model," *Sloan Management Review* 13 (Winter), 77–91 (1972).
30. Parker, Barnett R., and Srinivasan, V. "A Consumer Preference Approach to the Planning of Rural Primary Health Care Facilities," *Operations Research* 24 (September–October), 991–1025 (1976).
31. Parfitt, J. H., and Collins, B. J. K. "Use of Consumer Panels for Brand-Share Prediction," *Journal of Marketing Research* 5 (May), 131–145 (1968).
32. Pessemier, Edgar A., and Root, H. Paul. "The Dimensions of New Product Planning," *Journal of Marketing* 27 (January), 10–18 (1973).
33. _____, Burger, Philip, Teach, Richard, and Tigert, Douglas. "Using Laboratory Preference Scales to Predict Consumer Brand Preferences," *Management Science* 17 (February), 371–385 (1971).
34. Rao, Vithala R., and Soutar, Geoffrey N. "Subjective Evaluations for Product Design Decisions," *Decision Sciences* 6 (January), 120–134 (1975).
35. Rogers, Everett M. *Diffusion of Innovations*. New York: The Free Press, 1962.
36. Ryan, Michael J., and Bonfield, Edward H. "The Fishbein Extended Model and Consumer Behavior," *Journal of Consumer Research* 2 (September), 118–136 (1975).
37. Sheth, Jagdish N., and Talarzyk, W. W. "Perceived Instrumentality and Value Importance as Determinants of Attitudes," *Journal of Marketing Research* 9 (February), 6–9 (1972).
38. Shocker, Allan D., and Srinivasan, V. "A Consumer-Based Methodology for the Identification of New Product Ideas," *Management Science* 20 (February), 921–937 (1974).
39. _____. "Multiattribute Approaches for Product Concept Evaluation and Generation: A Critical Review," *Journal of Marketing Research* 16 (May), 159–180 (1979).
40. Shoemaker, Robert, and Staelin, Richard. "The Effects of Sampling Variation on Sales Forecasts for New Consumer Products," *Journal of Marketing Research* 13 (May), 138–143 (1976).
41. Silk, Alvin J., and Urban, Glen L. "Pre-Test Market Evaluation of New Packaged Goods: A Model and Measurement Methodology," *Journal of Marketing Research* 15 (May), 171–191 (1978).
42. Srivastava, Rajendra, Shocker, Allan D., and Day, George. "An Exploratory Study of Situational Effects on Product-Market Definition," Working Paper, Graduate School of Business, University of Pittsburgh, 1977.
43. Urban, Glen L. "Market Response Models for the Analysis of New Products," in Robert L. King (ed.), *1968 Fall Conference Proceedings*. Chicago, Illinois: American Marketing Association, 1969, pp. 105–111.
44. _____."Sprinter Mod III: A Model for the Analysis of New Frequently Purchased Consumer Products," *Operations Research* 18 (September-October), 805–854 (1970).
45. _____."PERCEPTOR: A Model for Product Positioning," *Management Science* 21 (April), 858–871 (1975).
46. Wachsler, Robert A., Pringle, Lewis G., and Brody, Edward I. "NEWS: A

Systematic Methodology for Diagnosing New Product Marketing Plans and Developing Actionable Recommendations." Unpublished paper, Research Department, Batten, Barton, Durstine and Osborn, Inc., New York, 1972.

47. Wilkie, William L., and Pessemier, Edgar A. "Issues in Marketing's Use of Multi-Attribute Attitude Models," *Journal of Marketing Research* 10 (November), 428–441 (1973).

48. Wind, Yoram. "Product Portfolio Analysis: A New Approach to the Product Mix Decision," in Ronald C. Curhan (ed.), *1974 Combined Proceedings*. Chicago, Illinois: American Marketing Association, 1975, pp. 460–464.

7

A Model for Product Management*

Edgar A. Pessemier

This chapter describes a model and computer program that can help a manager develop an effective marketing program for an established product. PLANOPT, the interactive program, uses the author's optimization approach to developing a marketing strategy [5]. It has been programmed by Thomas L. Pilon and is available from the Marketing Science Institute. The modeling philosophy that it employs is related to a number of earlier analytical schemes, such as Little's BRANDAID model. These models use subjective and objective inputs to guide a manager's evaluation of various marketing budgets and budget allocations. Furthermore, some structural properties of the model are similar to those proposed by Kotler [2], Urban [7], and Kuehn and Weiss [3]. The current version of the PLANOPT model differs from the above-mentioned approaches in one or more prominent ways. The detailed presentation that follows will highlight these differences.

The Problem

The management of an existing product has two basic aspects. The first concerns the product's design and price. These elements define the product's intrinsic value to users. The second concerns the remaining elements in the marketing mix, most notably advertising, personal selling, distribution support, and sales promotion. In the case of many mature products,

---

*The PLANOPT program that was used in the following analysis was written by Thomas L. Pilon. An improved version of the program is available from the Marketing Science Institute, 14 Story Street, Cambridge, Massachusetts 02138. For additional details, see the *Journal of Marketing Research* (November), 564 (1979).

design changes occur infrequently and are driven by technological or competitive factors largely out of the control of the marketing manager. Furthermore, price changes for many mature products may be more a matter of responding to market forces than the result of a conscious planning process. For these reasons and to simplify the presentation, issues of product design and price making will be assigned a secondary role.

The central marketing management problems that will be explored in some detail are the decisions about how many dollars to devote to marketing for an established product during the next planning period, say one year, and how to allocate these funds to the nonproduct elements of the marketing mix. Since much of the data needed to solve these problems necessarily involve managerial judgments, the model employs convenient input formats and makes use of the manager's particular point of view and expertise.

Some Philosophical and Theoretical Considerations

In thinking about the benefits that a firm delivers to buyers and users, the effect of the product's features and price are easily recognized. Delivered value can be enhanced by more efficient production methods that lower price, and thoughtful design changes can improve product performance. These kinds of moves should be actively explored by a product manager even though implementation may be in the hands of personnel outside of the marketing organization.

A variety of methods are available for appraising design and pricing opportunities (see Pessemier [5], especially Chapter 5). When applied to the problem at hand, these market mapping procedures can help forecast changes in market shares that are due to price and design features. The easiest way to think of these forecasts is to consider them estimates of the probability of product purchase in the face of full information and a complete assortment. In the following discussion, these estimated purchase probabilities will be labeled $PP(i)$ for brand i.

The effect of marketing mix expenditures on the value received by buyers and users is less direct but nonetheless real. Each element in the mix increases appreciation of the product's potential benefits, of its convenient availability, or of other aspects of the offer that make purchase and use more appealing. To the extent that marketing funds fail to accomplish these purposes, money is wasted that could be used to lower costs and prices, improve product designs, or otherwise establish a favorable competitive position. Therefore, it is reasonable to expect that firms with favorable competitive positions not only offer useful products at reasonable prices but that they also support these products with marketing expenditures and marketing mixes that offer more value to buyers and users than the costs they incur. If this were not the case, competitors would develop more acceptable, lower-priced offerings. The fact that diverse price, product design, and marketing support programs find important buyer and user support simply testifies to the differences between different market segments. Some customers want high quality and a reassuring advertising image and are willing to pay the price. Others may be price conscious and are willing to travel long distances to buy for less. These and similar differences must be recognized in establishing a product's total marketing strategy.

Structure of the Model and Organization of the Computer Program

In the model that is described below, the problem of finding the best level of marketing expenditures and their allocation to different types of marketing effort can be divided into two parts, the effects of the firm's action on product class demand and the effect of its actions on the share of product class demand that is received by its product offering. The product class unconditional total unit sales (UTUS) equation is

$$UTUS_t = BU_t \times PQ_t$$

$\quad$ = unconditional total unit sales from a segment or market in
$\quad\quad$ period t, $\hspace{6cm}$ (1)

where

$\quad BU_t$ $\quad$ is the number of buying units in the segment or market during period t, and

$\quad PQ_t$ $\quad$ is the average purchase quantity per buying unit in the segment or market during period t.

The above unit sales estimate is unconditional in the sense that marketing variables are at their standard levels in some initial period o, before consideration is given to the conditions that may prevail during period t. The conditional total unit sales (CTUS) are assumed to be functions of the expected average unit price and total marketing effort in relation to these same variables during the base period.

$$CTUS_t = UTUS_t(TM_t/TM_o)^{\alpha}(APU_o/APU_t)^{\beta}$$
$\hspace{10cm}$ (2)

where

$\quad TM_t$ $\quad$ is the product class marketing expenditure during t,

$\quad TM_o$ $\quad$ is the product class marketing expenditure during o,

$\quad APU_t$ $\quad$ is the average product class unit price during t,

$\quad APU_o$ $\quad$ is the average product class unit price during o,

$\quad \alpha$ $\qquad$ is a marketing elasticity parameter, $\alpha \geqslant 0$,

$\quad \beta$ $\qquad$ is a price elasticity parameter, $\beta \geqslant 0$.

The above estimate of product class sales during planning period t must be divided among competing firms. The division will reflect the relative effectiveness of each firm's handling of each element of the marketing mix. In that sense, each element contributes a part worth to the bundle of benefits offered by each product. The part worth (PW) expression for all elements except the price–design element takes the form of the Luce choice theorem [4] or the Bell, Keeney, and Little market share theorem [1]. In the present case, effective values are determined by dollar expenditures and the time-period subscript has been dropped.

$$PW(i, k) = W(k) \times REX(i, k)$$

$ =$ the part worth of product i contributed by marketing mix element $k, k = 1, \ldots, K$.

$W(k) =$ the relative importance weight for marketing mix element k.

$REX(i, k) =$ the relative expenditures on behalf of product i for (3) marketing mix element k.

$ =$ $EX(i, k)/TEX(k)$ and $REX(i, K) = PP(i, K)$.

$EX(i, k) =$ the expenditure on behalf of product i for marketing mix element k.

$TEX(k) =$ total product class expenditures for marketing mix element k.

The sum of the relative expenditures across the i brands is equal to 1, and the sum of the importance weights across the k elements is equal to 1. Therefore, the sum of the part worth measures across all elements of the marketing mix and the sum of the worth contributed by all products fully account for the total value delivered by the product class.

The final part worth element is $PP(i, K)$, a measure of the probability of choosing a product purely on the basis of its intrinsic design/price value. As noted earlier, this is a separate measure of relative effect that does not depend on the specific marketing expenditures that will be optimized in the present model. In that sense, design and price are taken as data. They are not subject to optimization on any given application of the model. For four nonproduct elements and one product element, the conditional market share of primary demand received by product i is

$$CMS(i) = W(1) \times REX(i, 1) + W(2) \times REX(i, 2) + \cdots + W(5) \times PP(i, 5).$$

$$(4)$$

Therefore the estimated conditional unit sales for product i in period t are

$$CUS(i)_t = CTUS_t \times CMS(i)_t. \tag{5}$$

Before leaving the additive part worth model, two points should be made. First, it would be desirable, at least in principle, to use part worth components that are based on strict consumer effects instead of the functional cost categories such as advertising or personal selling. Relative levels of consumer effects such as favorable product image, widespread product recognition, and convenient product availability should be the part worth components. Unfortunately, measures of these effects are seldom available in a form that facilitates model building. For this reason, the readily available expenditure data on mix components must be used.

Second, it is easy to make a case for more complex model forms, say a multiplicative model (see Pessemier and Wilkie [6]). Although the introduction of interaction effects among mix elements may be appealing, these more sophisticated forms are rejected for practical reasons. They are harder to understand and make it more difficult for managers to provide appropriate subjective inputs. Furthermore, little empirical evidence can be found to strongly support these alternative formulations. As experience and understanding increase, greater attention should be directed to finding the best model for the particular problem at hand.

Given the above structure of demand, attention must be paid to how unit sales influence unit cost. The model provides two ways to introduce unit cost, as a direct estimate or as a set of inputs to a volume-dependent experience curve. The model also accepts various constraints on the ranges of marketing mix variables. These and several other important inputs must be provided by the user. An initial set of importance weights are significant parts of the required data. Since the historical share of product class spending on each element in the marketing mix is an approximate guide, the program uses these data to help the user develop an initial set of values. In turn, the program helps the user modify the initial elements so that they become accurate predictors of the product's current market share. These steps can be traced in the illustrative applications that appear later in this chapter.

Optimizing the Marketing Program

Once a suitable set of importance weights are in hand, the model specification phase of the analysis is complete and optimization can proceed. This part of the analysis sequentially examines how many dollars must be added to each marketing mix element to increase the product's market share by some fixed increment, say 0.001. If one or more elements can be found that produce larger gains than the costs that must be incurred, the most efficient change is made in one element. Then the data are updated and the process is repeated. Increased expenditures will be made in this incremental fashion until no profitable increases can be located.

After a search for an efficient increase in market share has been made, then a search for an efficient reduction in market share is made and associated dollar reductions in each element are examined to see if one or more reductions will save more than is lost by way of the reduced market share. When reduction is attractive, the element offering the best net saving is chosen. When the reduction has been made, the data are updated and the process repeated until no additional favorable reductions can be made. These steps will be illustrated in a later section.

The basic value equation for a market share (MS) is

$$V(\text{MS}) = \text{CMS} \times \text{CTUS} \times (\text{UP} - \text{UC}) \tag{6}$$

where UP is the unit price and UC the variable unit cost. Therefore, the value V of a change in market share of size ΔMS is

$$\Delta V(\text{MS} + \Delta \text{MS}) = \left[(\text{CMS} + \Delta \text{MS})\text{CTUS}(\text{UP} - \text{UC}) \right] - V(\text{MS}). \tag{7}$$

The amount by which each marketing mix element must be adjusted to get the ΔMS change in market share is computed by adding an appropriate amount $X(i, k)$ to the current expenditure. From Equations (3) and (4),

$$\text{PW}(i, k) + \Delta \text{MS} = W(k) \frac{\text{EX}(i, k) + X(i, k)}{\text{TEX}(k) + X(i, k)}. \tag{8}$$

Solving for the required change in expenditures for element i yields

$$X(i, k) = \frac{\left[\text{PW}(i, k) + \Delta \text{MS} \right] \text{TEX}(k) - W(k) \times \text{EX}(i, k)}{W(k) - \left[\text{PW}(i, k) + \Delta \text{MS} \right]}. \tag{9}$$

The $X(i, k)$ that achieves the desired result at the smallest cost is selected, the expenditure on this mix element is increased, total marketing expenditures are increased, and the demand and costs components of the value equation are modified. As noted earlier, a similar procedure is employed to test the advisability of reducing a product's market share.

Note that changes in the value of a new strategy involve changes in primary demand, market share, and unit cost. In the above steps, costs are automatically adjusted. If alternative unit prices are employed, the value of the design–price element in Equation (4) must be replaced with a suitable new value, the new average price must be accounted for in Equation (2) when computing primary demand, and the new unit sales, unit cost, and price data enter Equations (6) and (7). Although these factors complicate the computer algorithm, little extra effort is required on the part of a manager when examining alternative prices and feasible increases or decreases in the marketing budget.

Some Issues in the Use of Manager–Computer Systems

As the above discussion and the examples appearing below point out, the manager must supply a good deal of quantitative data. In the case of many established products, analyses of historical data may be very helpful. The behavior of unit cost and the sensitivity of primary demand to changing levels of price and marketing support illustrate potentially productive areas for supporting analytical work. On the other hand, it is easy to overstate the value of historical analyses, particularly when marketing conditions are changing in ways that make them misleading. Furthermore, analyses of historical evidence are time consuming and costly. For these reasons, the manager should carefully examine the potential value of these analyses before they are undertaken.

In the example covered in this section, an effort has been made to ask for managerial judgments in a simple form and to let the computer algorithm assume the burden of manipulation and analysis. Clearly, managers will be uncertain about some of the subjective estimates that they provide. In a decision-theoretical spirit, the manager should be encouraged to perform sensitivity analyses on some of the more important judgmental elements. Doing so will build further appreciation of the model's properties and the degree to which selected inputs affect the computed "optimal" strategy.

The PLANOPT program is divided into two subprograms; PLANNR develops the consistent model used by OPTIM to compute an optimum (nonproduct) marketing budget and its distribution to the respective marketing mix elements. Before starting the main sections of PLANNR, the analyst can change both the step size (PCH) by which the search for consistent importance weights $W(k)$ is made and the tolerable (TOL) market share prediction error.

PLANNR—A MODEL USED TO FORECAST THE EFFECTS OF MARKETING STRATEGIES ON BEHALF OF AN ESTABLISHED BRAND

DO YOU WANT TO CHANGE PLANNR PARAMETERS? 1 = YES; 2 = NO
: 1

DO YOU WANT TO CHANGE PCH FROM ITS CURRENT VALUE OF .030? 1 = YES; 2 = NO
: 2

DO YOU WANT TO CHANGE TOL FROM ITS CURRENT VALUE OF .010? 1 = YES; 2 = NO
: 2

The first two main steps of the PLANNR subprogram develop the data and compute product class conditional unit sales (CUS) [see Equations (1) and (2)].

STEP 1—ESTIMATING THE UNCONDITIONAL TOTAL UNIT SALES DURING A STANDARD OR TYPICAL PERIOD FOR THE PRODUCT CLASS. THE FORECAST DEPENDS ONLY ON MARKET AND PRODUCT CLASS CHARACTERISTICS.

ENTER YOUR BEST ESTIMATE OF THE TOTAL NUMBER OF BUYING UNITS IN THOUSANDS OF UNITS THAT WILL BE ACTIVE DURING THE PERIOD
: 140

ENTER YOUR BEST ESTIMATE OF THE AVERAGE PURCHASE QUANTITY PER ACTIVE BUYING UNIT DURING THE PERIOD
: 50

BASED ON THE INFORMATION YOU HAVE PROVIDED, THE UNCONDITIONAL FORECAST OF TOTAL UNIT SALES DURING A STANDARD OR TYPICAL PERIOD FOR THE PRODUCT CLASS IS   7000.0

STEP 2—ESTIMATING THE PRODUCT CLASS CONDITIONAL TOTAL UNIT SALES, GIVEN THE EXPECTED TOTAL PRODUCT CLASS MARKETING EXPENDITURES AND THE AVERAGE PRICE PER UNIT.

ENTER THE TOTAL PRODUCT CLASS MARKETING EXPENDITURES IN THOUSANDS OF DOLLARS DURING THE STANDARD OR TYPICAL PERIOD THAT WAS ASSUMED IN STEP 1
: 1000
NOW ENTER THE TOTAL PRODUCT CLASS MARKETING EXPENDITURES IN THOUSANDS OF DOLLARS THAT YOU BELIEVE WILL ACTUALLY OCCUR DURING THE NEXT PERIOD
: 1100
BASED ON YOUR ESTIMATE, THE RELATIVE MARKETING PRESSURE ON TOTAL UNIT SALES DURING THE NEXT PERIOD IS   1.10

NOW SUPPOSE THAT THE ABOVE RELATIVE MARKETING PRESSURE DECREASED BY 5 PERCENT. ENTER THE PERCENTAGE DECREASE IN TOTAL UNIT SALES YOU BELIEVE WOULD RESULT FROM THE CHANGE

(NOTE: ALL PERCENTAGES ARE TO BE ENTERED WITHOUT A DECIMAL POINT. FOR EXAMPLE, TO INDICATE FIVE PERCENT SIMPLY ENTER "5".)
: 5

ENTER THE PRODUCT CLASS AVERAGE PRICE PER UNIT DURING THE STANDARD OR TYPICAL PERIOD THAT WAS ASSUMED IN STEP 1
: 3
NOW ENTER THE PRODUCT CLASS AVERAGE PRICE PER UNIT THAT IS EXPECTED TO ACTUALLY OCCUR DURING THE NEXT PERIOD
: 3.15
BASED ON YOUR ESTIMATES, THE RELATIVE PRICE EFFECT ON TOTAL UNIT SALES IS   .95

NOW SUPPOSE THAT THE ABOVE RELATIVE PRICE EFFECT DECREASED BY 5 PERCENT. ENTER THE PERCENTAGE DECREASE IN TOTAL UNIT SALES YOU BELIEVE WOULD RESULT FROM THE CHANGE
: 10

BASED ON ALL THE ESTIMATES YOU HAVE PROVIDED SO FAR, THE PRODUCT CLASS CONDITIONAL TOTAL UNIT SALES FOR THE NEXT PERIOD IS   6984.1

The third step is concerned with developing the data and parameters needed to complete the initial computations of the firm's market share [see Equations (3) and (4)]. Note that the value of $PP(i,5)$, the product's relative value, is developed by alternative approaches before a final subjective estimation is entered. Initial aid is also provided in making and adjusting the importance weights $W(k)$.

STEP 3—ESTIMATING YOUR BRAND'S SHARE OF CONDITIONAL TOTAL UNIT SALES DURING THE NEXT PERIOD.

FOR THE FOLLOWING LIST OF MARKETING MIX ELEMENTS ENTER THE AMOUNT IN THOUSANDS OF DOLLARS CURRENTLY BUDGETED TO YOUR BRAND FOR THE NEXT PERIOD. IF NO EXPENDITURES ARE PLANNED ENTER 0

ADVERTISING
 : 75
SALES PROMOTION
 : 125
PERSONAL SELLING
 : 150
DISTRIBUTION SUPPORT
 : 200

THE TOTAL PLANNED MARKETING EXPENDITURE FOR YOUR BRAND DURING THE NEXT PERIOD ARE   550.

THE PERCENTAGE OF ALL MARKETING DOLLARS ALLOCATED TO EACH ELEMENT IN THE MARKETING MIX FOR YOUR BRAND DURING THE NEXT PERIOD IS

	PERCENT OF TOTAL
ADVERTISING	.14
SALES PROMOTION	.23
PERSONAL SELLING	.27
DISTRIBUTION SUPPORT	.36

NEXT, FOR THE FOLLOWING LIST OF MARKETING MIX ELEMENTS, ENTER THE AMOUNT IN THOUSANDS OF DOLLARS YOU EXPECT ALL COMPETITORS, INCLUDING YOUR BRAND, WILL ACTUALLY SPEND IN THE NEXT PERIOD

ADVERTISING
 : 750
SALES PROMOTION
 : 1250
PERSONAL SELLING
 : 2000
DISTRIBUTION SUPPORT
 : 1500

PLANNED MARKETING EXPENDITURES FOR THE PRODUCT CLASS DURING THE NEXT PERIOD ARE   5500.

THE PERCENTAGE OF ALL MARKETING DOLLARS ALLOCATED TO EACH
ELEMENT IN THE MARKETING MIX FOR THE PRODUCT CLASS DURING THE NEXT
PERIOD IS

	PERCENT OF TOTAL
ADVERTISING	.14
SALES PROMOTION	.23
PERSONAL SELLING	.36
DISTRIBUTION SUPPORT	.27

FOR EACH ELEMENT IN YOUR MARKETING PROGRAM, YOUR EXPENDITURE
RATIOS (YOUR PLANNED EXPENDITURES AS A PERCENTAGE OF TOTAL
PRODUCT CLASS EXPENDITURES) DURING THE NEXT PERIOD ARE

	PERCENT OF PRODUCT CLASS
ADVERTISING	.10
SALES PROMOTION	.10
PERSONAL SELLING	.07
DISTRIBUTION SUPPORT	.13

ONE ELEMENT OF THE MARKETING MIX THAT REMAINS TO BE CONSIDERED IS
THE BRAND'S BASIC APPEAL. A BRAND'S APPEAL OR RELATIVE WORTH IS BASED
ONLY ON PRICE, DESIGN, AND PRODUCT PERCEPTIONS. IT IS MEASURED AS A
PERCENTAGE OF THE COMBINED APPEAL OR WORTH OF ALL THE BRANDS IN
THE PRODUCT CLASS.

HAVE YOU ESTIMATED YOUR BRAND'S RELATIVE WORTH BY MAPPING OR
SCALING METHODS? 1 = YES; 2 = NO
: 2

THINK OF PLACING YOUR BRAND AND ALL SIGNIFICANT COMPETING BRANDS
IN EXTENDED USE TESTS WITH A REPRESENTATIVE GROUP OF CONSUMERS.
AFTER THE TEST ALL CONSUMERS ARE GIVEN MONEY. PART OF THIS MONEY
MUST BE USED TO PURCHASE ONE OF THE PRODUCTS. A MEASURE OF THE
RELATIVE WORTH OF YOUR BRAND IS THE PROPORTION OF THE SUBJECTS WHO
CHOOSE TO BUY YOUR PRODUCT.
ENTER THE PERCENTAGE OF THE SUBJECTS THAT YOU EXPECT TO BUY YOUR
BRAND INSTEAD OF THE BRANDS OF YOUR SIGNIFICANT COMPETITORS
: 12

ANOTHER WAY OF DETERMINING YOUR BRAND'S RELATIVE WORTH IS AS
FOLLOWS. ESTIMATE THE TYPICAL FULL ALLOCATED COST OF DEVELOPING
AND PRODUCING A UNIT OF YOUR BRAND. THIS IS EQUIVALENT TO THE UNIT
PRICE LESS THE UNIT COST OF MARKETING AND THE UNIT PROFIT. STATED
ANOTHER WAY, IT IS THE SUM OF ALL RELEVANT UNIT PRODUCT COSTS. ENTER
THIS VALUE
: 1.5
NOW ESTIMATE THE EQUIVALENT AVERAGE UNIT COST FOR ALL OF THE
BRANDS IN THE PRODUCT CLASS, INCLUDING YOURS
: 2

FINALLY, ESTIMATE YOUR BRAND'S SHARE OF LAST YEAR'S PRODUCT CLASS
UNIT SALES
: 12

YOU HAVE NOW ESTIMATED THE RELATIVE WORTH OF YOUR BRAND BY TWO
DIFFERENT PROCEDURES. THE ESTIMATES ARE

	PERCENT RELATIVE WORTH
EXTENDED USE PROCEDURE	12.0
UNIT COST–UNIT SALES PROCEDURE	9.0

BASED ON THESE TWO ESTIMATES, WHAT IS YOUR FINAL ESTIMATE OF THE RELATIVE WORTH OF YOUR BRAND?
: 11

THE RELATIVE IMPORTANCE OF THE BRAND'S DESIGN AND PRICE TO BUYERS MUST ALSO BE ASSESSED. ONE SIMPLE INITIAL ESTIMATE IS TO SET IT EQUAL TO PRODUCT EXPENDITURES AS A PROPORTION OF PRODUCT PLUS MARKETING EXPENDITURES. TO PROVIDE THE ADDITIONAL ESTIMATE NEEDED TO COMPLETE THIS COMPUTATION, ENTER THE AVERAGE INDUSTRY BEFORE TAX PROFIT PER UNIT
: .85

THE INITIAL APPROXIMATIONS OF THE IMPORTANCE OF EACH MARKETING MIX ELEMENT IN PROVIDING WORTH TO BUYERS ARE

	RELATIVE IMPORTANCE
ADVERTISING	.050
SALES PROMOTION	.083
PERSONAL SELLING	.100
DISTRIBUTION SUPPORT	.133
PRODUCT APPEAL	.635

DO YOU WANT TO ALTER THE SET OF RELATIVE IMPORTANCE WEIGHTS? 1 = YES; 2 = NO
: 1

THE INITIAL APPROXIMATIONS OF THE RELATIVE IMPORTANCE WEIGHTS WERE BASED ON INDUSTRY AVERAGES. LARGE CHANGES IN THESE WEIGHTS SHOULD BE MADE ONLY ON THE ASSUMPTION THAT YOUR BRAND'S PRODUCT APPEAL AND/OR MARKETING MIX EFFECTIVENESS DIFFER SIGNIFICANTLY FROM MOST OTHER BRANDS IN THE INDUSTRY.
ENTER IN DECIMAL FORM THE NEW SET OF RELATIVE IMPORTANCE WEIGHTS (THESE WEIGHTS SHOULD SUM TO 1.0)

ADVERTISING
 : .05
SALES PROMOTION
 : .083
PERSONAL SELLING
 : .1
DISTRIBUTION SUPPORT
 : .133
PRODUCT APPEAL
 : .635

THE NEW SET OF INITIAL APPROXIMATIONS OF THE IMPORTANCE OF EACH MARKETING MIX ELEMENT IN PROVIDING WORTH TO BUYERS ARE (THE WEIGHTS MAY HAVE BEEN RESCALED TO SUM TO 1.0)

RELATIVE IMPORTANCE

ADVERTISING	.050
SALES PROMOTION	.083
PERSONAL SELLING	.100
DISTRIBUTION SUPPORT	.133
PRODUCT APPEAL	.634

THE SET OF RELATIVE IMPORTANCE WEIGHTS IMPLIES A SPECIFIC MARKET SHARE FOR YOUR BRAND. TO EVALUATE THE COMPUTED MARKET SHARE, ENTER THE MARKET SHARE YOU EXPECT TO RECEIVE IN THE NEXT PERIOD (ASSUMING YOUR PLANNED MARKET EXPENDITURES)
: 9.74

THE COMPUTED MARKET SHARE USING THE RELATIVE IMPORTANCE WEIGHTS DISPLAYED ABOVE IS   10.83 PERCENT

SINCE THE COMPUTED MARKET SHARE EXCEEDS THE ESTIMATED MARKET SHARE, THE EFFECT OF THE IMPORTANCE WEIGHTS MUST BE ADJUSTED TO REDUCE THE COMPUTED MARKET SHARE. THE EFFECT OF A 3.0 PERCENT REDUCTION OF EACH IMPORTANCE WEIGHT ON THE COMPUTED MARKET SHARE IS SHOWN BELOW

LINE NO.	DESCRIPTION	EFFECT ON THE COMPUTED MARKET SHARE OF A 3.0 PERCENT REDUCTION
1	ADVERTISING	− .00015
2	SALES PROMOTION	− .00025
3	PERSONAL SELLING	− .00022
4	DISTRIBUTION SUPPORT	− .00053
5	PRODUCT APPEAL	− .00209

CHOOSE AN IMPORTANCE WEIGHT THAT, WHEN ADJUSTED DOWNWARD, WILL HAVE A RELATIVELY LARGE EFFECT AND WILL IMPROVE THE SET OF IMPORTANCE WEIGHTS. ENTER THE LINE NUMBER CORRESPONDING TO THE CHOSEN MARKETING ELEMENT IN THE ABOVE TABLE
: 5

THE REVISED RELATIVE IMPORTANCE WEIGHTS FOR EACH MARKET MIX ELEMENT ARE

RELATIVE IMPORTANCE

ADVERTISING	.050
SALES PROMOTION	.083
PERSONAL SELLING	.119
DISTRIBUTION SUPPORT	.133
PRODUCT APPEAL	.615

THE COMPUTED MARKET SHARE USING THE RELATIVE IMPORTANCE WEIGHTS DISPLAYED ABOVE IS   10.76 PERCENT

SINCE THE COMPUTED MARKET SHARE EXCEEDS THE ESTIMATED MARKET
SHARE, THE EFFECT OF THE IMPORTANCE WEIGHTS MUST BE ADJUSTED TO
REDUCE THE COMPUTED MARKET SHARE. THE EFFECT OF A 3.0 PERCENT
REDUCTION OF EACH IMPORTANCE WEIGHT ON THE COMPUTED MARKET SHARE
IS SHOWN BELOW

LINE NO.	DESCRIPTION	EFFECT ON THE COMPUTED MARKET SHARE OF A 3.0 PERCENT REDUCTION
1	ADVERTISING	− .00015
2	SALES PROMOTION	− .00025
3	PERSONAL SELLING	− .00027
4	DISTRIBUTION SUPPORT	− .00053
5	PRODUCT APPEAL	− .00203

CHOOSE AN IMPORTANCE WEIGHT THAT, WHEN ADJUSTED DOWNWARD, WILL
HAVE A RELATIVELY LARGE EFFECT AND WILL IMPROVE THE SET OF
IMPORTANCE WEIGHTS. ENTER THE LINE NUMBER CORRESPONDING TO THE
CHOSEN MARKETING ELEMENT IN THE ABOVE TABLE
: 5

THE REVISED RELATIVE IMPORTANCE WEIGHTS FOR EACH MARKET MIX
ELEMENT ARE

	RELATIVE IMPORTANCE
ADVERTISING	.050
SALES PROMOTION	.083
PERSONAL SELLING	.137
DISTRIBUTION SUPPORT	.133
PRODUCT APPEAL	.597

THE COMPUTED MARKET SHARE USING THE RELATIVE IMPORTANCE WEIGHTS
DISPLAYED ABOVE IS   10.70 PERCENT

DO YOU WANT TO RUN PLANNR AGAIN? 1 = YES; 2 = NO
: 2

At this point all the data have been adjusted and checked to complete
Equation (5).

In adjusting the salience weights to obtain a consistent model, an
infeasible solution may be encountered for several reasons. First, a budget
that is too large or too small may have been chosen as input in relation to
the expected market share input. Second, the market share input that the
budget was expected to produce may be unreasonably high or low. Third,
the marketing mix expenditures input may be so allocated to mix elements
that appropriate weights cannot be found. If an infeasibly low share is
input, it could be made feasible by reducing the computed weights so that
they sum to less than one and by treating one less this sum as a loss in
marketing inefficiency. Conversely, for infeasibly high share input, the
computed weights could be increased to a feasible level by allowing their
sum to exceed one, treating the excess as superior marketing efficiency.

Neither of the latter alternatives is attractive. When an infeasible set of input data is encountered, the three sources of difficulty noted above should be carefully considered and the input data should be revised as necessary. In particular, the manager should be satisfied that the final set of importance weights and the input expenditures are well within reasonable limits and closely match his best judgments about the realities of the marketplace. At this point, a transition can be made from the PLANNR submodel to the OPTIM submodel.

The second part of the PLANOPT is OPTIM, the optimizing phase. First, the analyst can change several model controls: DCMS, which is the change in market share in Equations (7)–(9), and NPRINT, which provides a trace of the optimization procedure when set equal to 1. Next, allowable limits are placed on expenditures for each marketing mix element. Then the data needed to test alternative product prices can be entered. Finally, appropriate cost data are provided before the program starts the analysis sequence. The results of this sequence are listed in an appropriate format. Further analyses can be completed by returning to the start of the PLANNR or OPTIM subprograms.

OPTIM—AN OPTIMIZATION PROCEDURE USED TO OPTIMIZE THE SIZE AND ALLOCATION OF MARKETING MIX EXPENDITURES FROM PLANNR

DO YOU WANT TO CHANGE OPTIM PARAMETERS? 1 = YES; 2 = NO
: 1

DO YOU WANT TO CHANGE DCMS FROM ITS CURRENT VALUE OF   .005? 1 = YES; 2 = NO
: 2

DO YOU WANT TO CHANGE NPRINT FROM ITS CURRENT VALUE OF 1? 1 = YES; 2 = NO
: 2

TO COMPLETE THE "OPTIMIZATION" OF YOUR MARKETING BUDGET, THE FOLLOWING DATA ARE REQUIRED:

YOUR PLANNED EXPENDITURES (THOUSANDS OF DOLLARS) FOR ADVERTISING ARE   75.
THE MINIMUM ALLOWABLE EXPENDITURE IS
: 10
**   THE MAXIMUM ALLOWABLE EXPENDITURE IS**
: 400

YOUR PLANNED EXPENDITURES (THOUSANDS OF DOLLARS) FOR SALES PROMOTION ARE   125.
THE MINIMUM ALLOWABLE EXPENDITURE IS
: 10

THE MAXIMUM ALLOWABLE EXPENDITURE IS
: 400

YOUR PLANNED EXPENDITURES (THOUSANDS OF DOLLARS) FOR PERSONAL
SELLING ARE   150.
THE MINIMUM ALLOWABLE EXPENDITURE IS
: 10
THE MAXIMUM ALLOWABLE EXPENDITURE IS
: 400

YOUR PLANNED EXPENDITURES (THOUSANDS OF DOLLARS) FOR DIS-
TRIBUTION SUPPORT ARE   200.
THE MINIMUM ALLOWABLE EXPENDITURE IS
: 10
THE MAXIMUM ALLOWABLE EXPENDITURE IS
: 400

WHEN YOUR BRAND'S RELATIVE WORTH WAS ESTIMATED TO BE 11 CHOICES
OUT OF 100, YOUR ASSUMED UNIT PRICE WAS
: 3.15

OTHER UNIT PRICES AND THEIR ASSOCIATED RELATIVE FREQUENCIES OF
CHOICE IN BLIND TESTS WHICH YOU WANT TO TEST ARE

	RELATIVE FREQUENCY OF CHOICE
HIGHER	(TIMES OUT OF 100)
UNIT PRICE	FOLLOWING BLIND USE TESTS
: 4	9

	RELATIVE FREQUENCY OF CHOICE
LOWER	(TIMES OUT OF 100)
UNIT PRICE	FOLLOWING BLIND USE TESTS
: 2.5	13

CAN YOU PROVIDE EXPERIENCE CURVE DATA TO USE IN ESTIMATING UNIT
COSTS? 1 = YES; 2 = NO
: 1

TO COMPUTE UNIT COSTS FROM EXPERIENCE CURVE INFORMATION PROVIDE
THE FOLLOWING DATA:
THE TOTAL NUMBER OF UNITS PRODUCED UP TO THE BEGINNING OF THE
PLANNING PERIOD
: 3000

THE COST OF THE LAST UNIT PRODUCED
: 2

THE NUMBER OF ADDITIONAL UNITS THAT MUST BE PRODUCED TO REDUCE
THE ABOVE UNIT COST BY ONE-TENTH
: 500

OPTIMIZATION TRACE

J: 1 = ORIGINAL PRICE, 2 = HIGHER PRICE, 3 = LOWER PRICE
K: 0 = ORIGINAL BUDGET, 1 = UP BUDGET, 2 = DOWN BUDGET
L: ITERATION NUMBER
UP: UNIT PRICE
UC: UNIT COST
MXME: MARKETING EXPENDITURE FOR MIX ELEMENT ♯
MS: MARKET SHARE
NVMS: NET VALUE MARKET SHARE

J	K	L	UP	UC	MXME ♯1	MXME ♯2	MXME ♯3	MXME ♯4	MS	NVMS
1	0	0	3.15	1.85	75.	125.	150.	200.	.107	421.
1	1	1	3.15	1.85	75.	125.	150.	200.	.107	421.
1	2	1	3.15	1.85	75.	125.	150.	200.	.107	421.
1	2	2	3.15	1.85	75.	47.	150.	200.	.102	460.
1	2	3	3.15	1.86	75.	47.	74.	200.	.097	497.
1	2	4	3.15	1.86	75.	47.	74.	138.	.092	519.
1	2	5	3.15	1.87	75.	47.	74.	80.	.087	534.
1	2	6	3.15	1.88	75.	47.	74.	27.	.082	544.
2	1	1	4.00	1.87	75.	125.	150.	200.	.095	828.
2	2	1	4.00	1.87	75.	125.	150.	200.	.095	828.
2	2	2	4.00	1.87	75.	47.	150.	200.	.090	847.
2	2	3	4.00	1.88	75.	47.	74.	200.	.085	863.
3	1	1	2.50	1.83	75.	125.	150.	200.	.119	20.
3	2	1	2.50	1.83	75.	125.	150.	200.	.119	20.
3	2	2	2.50	1.84	75.	47.	150.	200.	.114	75.
3	2	3	2.50	1.84	75.	47.	74.	200.	.109	127.
3	2	4	2.50	1.85	75.	47.	74.	138.	.104	165.
3	2	5	2.50	1.85	75.	47.	74.	80.	.099	199.
3	2	6	2.50	1.86	75.	47.	74.	27.	.094	227.

NET VALUE OF MARKET SHARE
(000 OF DOLLARS)

	ORIGINAL BUDGET	UP BUDGET	DOWN BUDGET
ORIGINAL PRICE	421.06	421.06	544.28
HIGHER PRICE	828.16	828.16	862.77
LOWER PRICE	20.22	20.22	227.36

ORIGINAL PRICE 3.15

	UNIT COST	MARKETING MIX EXPENDITURES 1	2	3	4	TOTAL BUDGET	MKT SHARE	NET VAL SHARE
ORIGINAL BUDGET	1.85	75.	125.	150.	200.	550.	.107	421.
BEST UP BUDGET	1.85	75.	125.	150.	200.	550.	.107	421.
BEST DOWN BUDGET	1.88	75.	47.	74.	27.	223.	.082	544.

HIGHER PRICE 4.00

	UNIT	MARKETING MIX EXPENDITURES				TOTAL	MKT	NET VAL
	COST	1	2	3	4	BUDGET	SHARE	SHARE
ORIGINAL BUDGET	1.87	75.	125.	150.	200.	550.	.095	828.
BEST UP BUDGET	1.87	75.	125.	150.	200.	550.	.095	828.
BEST DOWN BUDGET	1.88	75.	47.	74.	200.	396.	.085	863.

LOWER PRICE 2.50

	UNIT	MARKETING MIX EXPENDITURES				TOTAL	MKT	NET VAL
	COST	1	2	3	4	BUDGET	SHARE	SHARE
ORIGINAL BUDGET	1.83	75.	125.	150.	200.	550.	.119	20.
BEST UP BUDGET	1.83	75.	125.	150.	200.	550.	.119	20.
BEST DOWN BUDGET	1.86	75.	47.	74.	27.	223.	.094	227.

DO YOU WANT TO RUN OPTIM AGAIN? 1=YES; 2=NO
: 2

DO YOU WANT TO RUN PLANNR AGAIN? 1=YES; 2=NO
: 2

With a total marketing expenditure of $550,000, the net value of the initial strategy $(1,0,0)$ is $421,000. This value is net of the marketing expenditures. At the initial $3.15 price, the best marketing program $(1,2,6)$ allocates $75,000 to advertising, $47,000 to sales promotion, $74,000 to personal selling, and $27,000 to distribution support, for a total expenditure of $223,000 and a net value of $544,000. For the $4.00 price, $396,000 are allocated, $75,000, $47,000, $74,000, and $200,000, respectively, for a net value of $863,000. Finally, at the $2.50 price the best budget and allocation produced a net value of $227,000 and is clearly inferior to the other two pricing alternatives.

The loss in market share $(0.022=0.107-0.085)$ that is suffered to improve the net value of the program for the next period may make the program an unacceptable component of a longer-range strategy. The acceptability of this reduced market share will depend on such matters as the undesirable effects that it may have on the firm's marketing effort for all products, the alternative uses of freed production capacity, and the extent to which shares can be modified as circumstances change. It is equally important to consider responses that competitors may make to any particular strategy adopted on behalf of the firm's product. Although the topic will not be discussed here, the above model can be used to test a series of moves by the firm and countermoves by competitors over a relatively long planning horizon. As a minimum, the effect of a competitor's best move in period $t+1$ should be examined prior to reaching a final decision.

Conclusion

The PLANOPT model and supporting interactive computer program is an easily implemented approach to strategy planning for an established product. Input requirements are modest and computing costs are nominal. The model's output provides explicit evaluations of various price, budget, and marketing mix alternatives, greatly simplifying the final decision process.

For the sake of simplicity, the program does not directly treat several significant issues. These issues concern (1) the strategy planning appropriate to the early growth period in a product's market life, (2) the overall effects of separate strategies employed for different market segments, and (3) the integrated cost, price, and positioning strategies associated with alternative product designs. Each of these problems can be handled in separate analyses. Joining them in a single integrated algorithm would greatly increase the problems encountered by managers, analysts, and computer systems.

References

1. Bell, David, Keeney, Ralph, and Little, John "A Market Share Theorem," *Journal of Marketing Research* 12, 136–41 (1975).
2. Kotler, Philip. *Marketing Decision Making: A Model Building Approach*. New York: Holt, Rinehart and Winston, 1971, pp. 85–112.
3. Kuehn, Alfred, and Weiss, Doyle. "Marketing Analysis Training Exercise," *Behavioral Science* 10, 51–67 (1965).
4. Luce, R. Duncan. *Individual Choice Theory*. New York: Wiley, 1959.
5. Pessemier, Edgar. *Product Management: Strategy and Organization*. New York: Wiley, 1976, especially Chapters 5, 6, and 8.
6. _____ and Wilkie, William. "Multi-attribute Choice Theory—A Review and Analysis," in G. David Hughes and Michael Ray (eds.), *Buyer/Consumer Information Processing*. University of North Carolina Press, Chapel Hill, 1974, pp. 288–330.
7. Urban, Glen. "A New Product Analysis and Decision Model," *Management Science* 14, B-490–B-517 (1968).

8

Experience with Decision-Calculus Models and Decision Support Systems

Leonard M. Lodish

"Do the best you can with what you have."

This statement summarizes my philosophy when building models and decision support systems to aid marketing managers. My criterion for success is whether the system or model usage proves to be a good investment for the firm. The costs of this investment include computer time to develop the model and associated decision support system, outside consulting time that may be needed, and what is very important, the incremental time of all of the people in the firm who are involved in the model building, implementation, and usage activity. The benefits or payoffs from the investment should be demonstrated savings in the costs of implementing marketing activities, or increased sales and profits resulting from new marketing activities that would not have been undertaken without the use of the decision model. This pragmatic orientation changes the criterion for model evaluation from that which typical academics would use.

In this chapter, we will discuss some implemented examples in marketing of decision-calculus models with which this author or his colleagues have had firsthand experience. The examples will be in sales force management, retailing, and consumer goods marketing mix decisions. We will conclude with some comments about the characteristics of the model implementation that did or did not help the return on the model building investment. Before we discuss examples, we should first define a decision-calculus model.

According to John D. C. Little [2],

> A manager tries to put together the various resources under his control into an activity that achieves his objectives. A model of his operation can assist him

but probably will not unless it meets certain requirements. A model that is to be used by a manager should be simple, robust, easy to control, adaptive, as complete as possible, and easy to communicate with. By simple is meant easy to understand; by robust, hard to get absurd answers from; by easy to control, that the user knows what input data would be required to produce desired output answers; adaptive means that the model can be adjusted as new information is acquired; completeness implies that important phenomena will be included even if they require judgmental estimates of their effect; and, finally, easy to communicate with means that the manager can quickly and easily change inputs and obtain and understand the outputs.

Such a model consists of a set of numerical procedures for processing data and judgments to assist managerial decision making and so will be called a decision calculus.[1]

Sales Force Deployment Examples

Since 1971, 25 sales forces have used CALLPLAN [4], a decision-calculus model, to improve the performance of individual salesmen in allocating their time among accounts and prospects. One of the firms, United Airlines, empirically validated the benefits of model use by field experimentation. (See Fudge and Lodish [1] for details on this experiment.) Ten CALLPLAN participants were chosen randomly from ten pairs of salesmen who were individually matched by local management using personal characteristics, territory size, revenue, and account mix. The remaining ten salesmen in the control group were told that they were participating in an experiment and each member manually estimated anticipated sales to compare with the CALLPLAN group. After six months the average CALLPLAN salesperson had 8.1% higher sales than his matched counterpart. The probability that such a large increase could occur by chance is less than 2.5%.

Input into the CALLPLAN model is objective data on travel time, time per call, and account profitability. Judgmental sales response estimates to various call frequencies are also input to the model. These are made by the salesman and his manager for each account. Initial model implementation was made at $1\frac{1}{2}$-day seminars that included the salesmen and their managers and a corporate staff person as the leader. The salesmen and their managers spent most of their time estimating the effects of changes in call frequency policy on sales to accounts. The objective of data on travel time and costs was very straightforward for the salesmen to obtain. There was typically much discussion of the sales response estimates between the salesman and his manager. Questions such as "If you call more frequently

---

[1] Reprinted by permission from John D. C. Little, "Models and Managers: The Concept of Decision Calculus," *Management Science* 16, No. 8 (April 1970). Copyright 1970, The Institute of Management Sciences.

what will you do? Whom will you see? How will your competitors react?" were continually discussed. One of the reasons that the computer users were more successful than their matched counterparts was that the salesmen and their managers explicitly evaluated many more alternative call policies than they typically would in their normal planning cycle. The model and the response function estimates caused the salespeople and their managers to look at many more alternative call policies. Once estimated, all the data were fed directly into a computer by the salesmen at the remote terminals in the seminar room. After the information was entered, within minutes the salesman had a printout of the optimal call policy for his territory. The rest of the seminar time the salesmen and managers spent fine tuning their estimates and doing various sensitivity analyses with call policy alternatives. During the next eight months the salesmen had the opportunity to update their estimates and rerun their optimal call policies on three occasions. This implementation at United was quite typical of most CALLPLAN implementations.

The United salesmen's reaction to the decision-calculus model was typical of most salesmen and sales managers. Before the salesmen got their first results at the computer terminal, their initial reaction to CALLPLAN was one of caution and skepticism. However, experience with the interactive program transformed this attitude into varying levels of enthusiasm as the salesman realized that he was controlling the program, rather than it controlling him. Once the salesman realizes that all the computer and model are doing is a lot of arithmetic and evaluations that the salesman would like to do but could not do because of limitations to his computing power, his attitude toward the model changes very dramatically. The computer is improving the processing of the salesman's and manager's own information. After the salesman has gone through this activity two or three times, his intuition seems to be updated so that he can anticipate what the model will recommend. Thus, the second year of model implementation is probably not as good an investment as the first year because of this phenomenon. Since the experiment in 1975, United Airlines cautiously rolled out the use of CALLPLAN, one sales district at a time until, in 1978, they implemented CALLPLAN on a nationwide basis. Their analysis during the rollout phase showed that CALLPLAN was continuing to provide benefits greater than the cost of providing the system. These costs included two days of salesperson time off the road to begin the system and computer time for analyzing alternative call policies.

Once a district has implemented CALLPLAN, the sales response estimates of each salesman for all of his accounts and prospects can be integrated into a model that can be used for territory realignment and sales force size decision. See Lodish [5, 6] for details. A regional sales manager of a large chemical producer was interested in this aspect of the model when he began using the system. His sales force consisted of seven salespeople covering New York State and New England. One of those salespeople was retiring. Because of cost pressures from management, the sales manager was seriously considering not replacing that salesperson and reallocating his accounts to other people within the district. Salespeople developed their own CALLPLAN analysis for their accounts and prospects. The computer then took all of the CALLPLAN estimates for all of the salespeople and assumed that all of the time resources of all the salespeople were available to call on any of the accounts and prospects. Travel time was assumed to be the current round trip time to each salesperson's geographical subarea.

The output of that analysis is shown in Tables 1 and 2. Table 1 shows the sales and profit (adjusted sales) impact of reallocating the existing seven salespeople to accounts and prospects so that the marginal profit of one hour would be equal across all salespeople. Table 2 shows how much time should be spent in each geographical subarea in the district compared to the amount of time that is presently being spent there. This is a guideline for the sales manager to use in making territory realignment decisions. Note that a 6.71% profit improvement was predicted for this realignment. The most significant number on the output to the manager was the marginal value of one more hour of salesperson time. This marginal value was $700 in profit. Even though this was a highly paid sales force that utilized a great deal of training and travel and entertainment expenses, the marginal cost of having a salesperson in the field was nowhere near $700. It was closer to $50 when all costs were considered. Just looking at that number and realizing how it was calculated, the sales manager changed his decision not to replace the salesperson who was retiring. He then looked at options of adding more people to the regional sales force because of high marginal value per hour. Tables 3 and 4 show the first part of the analysis for adding one person and adding two persons to the sales force. Notice that even after two people are added, the marginal value still remains quite high.

Table 1. Current Size. A Comparison of Results Based upon Reallocating the Accounts and Prospects

	Totals for all territories (×$1000)	(%)
Optimal sales	59,429	
Present sales	55,691	
Improvement	3,737	6.71
Optimal adjusted sales (profit)	15,898	
Present adjusted sales (profit)	14,716	
Improvement	1,182	8.03
Marginal value	0.70	

Table 2. Time Reallocation

Area	Optimal number of half hours in 3 months	Present policy	Optimal number of trips in 3 months	Present policy
WLCT	38	27	3	2
EHCT	23	22	2	2
WTBY	124	83	6	4
NBTN	10	19	1	2
NHCT	203	187	8	6
RT52	22	18	2	1
GRTM	88	56	6	4
PROY	134	110	4	3
HOLL	11	11	1	1
PITT	0	55	0	3
ALBY	0	96	0	4
NEWK	123	142	6	5
JERC	58	62	4	3
PASS	56	62	3	3
PATE	90	134	7	10
PARS	60	100	3	4
DOYE	0	12	0	1
MAMH	147	151	4	3
BRQE	115	87	6	4
LGIS	24	24	2	3

Note: Total number of half hours allocated, 3700.

The manager decided to add one more person to the regional sales staff compared to his prior decision to subtract one person, for a net change of two people. He did not add any more people for the simple reason that there was risk associated with obtaining the model's predicted sales increase. He knew that if he hired another salesperson, it would cost $50,000–$70,000 per year. Because the output of the model was based on subjective estimates, he was not sure whether the model's predicted sales

Table 3. One Salesperson Added

	Totals for all territories	
	($)	(%)
Optimal sales	60,532	
Present sales	55,691	
Improvement	4,841	8.69
Optimal adjusted sales	16,177	
Present adjusted sales	14,716	
Improvement	1,461	9.93
Marginal value	0.50	

Note: Total number of half hours allocated, 4200.

Table 4. Two Salespeople Added

	Totals for all territories	
	($)	(%)
Optimal sales	61,224	
Present sales	55,691	
Improvement	5,533	9.94
Optimal adjusted sales	16,362	
Present adjusted sales	14,716	
Improvement	1,646	11.19
Marginal value	0.31	

Note: Total number of half hours allocated, 4700.

and profit increases would really happen. He compromised by adding one person instead of two or three. This is typical of the way most managers use models. The geographical area breakdowns of time required were used by the manager to manually reallocate the region among the eight people. He now knew what the work load requirements were for each subarea and found it quite easy to assign people to each subarea in order to keep their total work loads within reason, cover all of the accounts with the needed call frequencies, and keep travel time as small as possible.

A basic problem that salespeople and sales managers face in determining the sales response functions at specific accounts is that it is typically difficult and costly, experimentally or empirically, to significantly improve their subjective estimates. They can only track the results of each policy as it is implemented. The next examples show that by beginning with models using subjective estimates, managers are prodded to do empirical analysis to improve those estimates when such empirical analysis is feasible and makes economic sense.

A Retailing Decision Support System

A large mass market retailer felt a need to improve the planning and decision making of its management. Over a period of a little more than one year, a decision support system was built to enable management to improve its marketing planning and decision making. Figure 1 shows all of the system components. For more details see Lodish [7]. The first system component that was developed was the yearly planning and market resource allocation model. As the figure shows, this model takes as input reference conditions, management judgments of sensitivities (sales response changes) to changes in marketing variables, and marketing plan alternatives. The output of this model is of two types:

1. the sales and profits anticipated for the alternative plan according to the judgments of management about the sensitivity of the marketplace to changes in the marketing variables described in the plan;

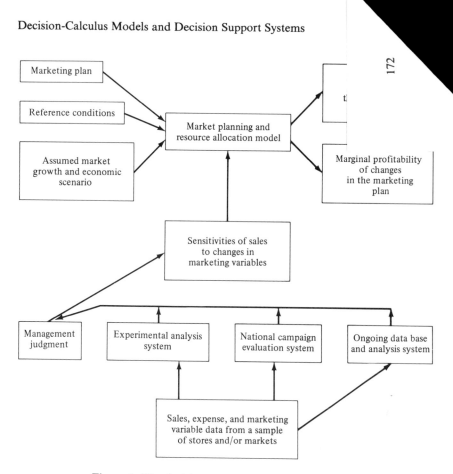

Figure 1. The decision support system—an overview.

2. an evaluation of marginal changes from reference conditions and a printout of the marginal contribution of these marginal changes.

The model is designed modularly so that it can work at different levels of aggregation. For example, it may be run for a specific department, for a group of departments considered either independently or in the aggregate, or for different subgroups of stores considered separately or together.

Once management had some experience with the resource allocation model, they realized that their confidence in their subjective estimates of sensitivities of response to marketing variables was not as high as they would like. They then decided to develop systems to aid them in making judgments about sensitivities. The other three components of the decision support system are different methods for evaluating sensitivities. These systems are (1) an ad hoc national campaign and event evaluation system, (2) a system for designing and analyzing marketing experiments, and (3) an ongoing interactive data base and analysis system.

The national campaign and event evaluation system is designed to get estimates of the sales effectiveness of large national campaigns or events that are run periodically by the retailer. This system takes internal sales data from a sample of stores and looks at sales of the items promoted in their departments before, during, and after a national event occurs. Various measures of sales effectiveness can be utilized, depending on the type of campaign and data availability. Typically, sales growth from the prior year during and after the campaign is compared to growth during the previous period. Sometimes adjustments are needed for prior period campaigns. The results of the national event are broken out by store type, region, market type, and other variables that may cause differences in the effectiveness of a national campaign over different stores or departments. An important feature of this system is the statistical analysis that is done to obtain confidence intervals on effectiveness of the national campaign for the various subgroups of stores, which are analyzed based on the variation across stores. This national campaign system is really almost an experimental analysis system without the luxury of all of the controls that can be put into a well-designed experiment.

In cases where management has had much difficulty in estimating sensitivities, carefully designed marketing experiments to evaluate alternatives are called for. The data input to the marketing experiment module is very similar to that for national campaigns. The store sample may be different because the marketing experiment may be running in different areas than those that are appropriate for national campaign evaluation. The analysis of the marketing experiment will be typically more complex than that for a national campaign because there will be more marketing variables varying simultaneously, and statistical analysis may be necessary to isolate the effects of the experimental variables.

After a few months of utilizing the above modules of the decision support system, management realized that it lacked basic data to use in helping to formulate sensitivities, alternative plans for future marketing activities, and tracking progress toward the plans. The interactive data base and analysis system was developed to give management a continuous picture of how their marketing activities were working. This data base is developed from a sample of stores that are thought to be typical of various types of stores around the country. This data base has been used for statistical analysis to analyze past history for naturally occurring experiments to determine if management's sensitivities need to be revised. The data base has also been used for tracking the effectiveness of past decisions, developing ad hoc management reports to answer various questions that typically arise over time, generating hypotheses for phenomena that may be occurring in the marketplace, and as an early warning system for controlling potential problems.

The marketing experiments, in particular, have had a very significant impact on the profitability of this retailer. Because management was unsure of the sensitivity of various departments to marketing variables, experiments were performed in a number of areas. Particularly significant was a combination price level, percent off for price break, and advertising method experiment. Analysis of this experiment showed that certain combinations of markup policy and price break policy, combined with the correct method of advertising, could improve the profitability of a group of items in the store by orders of magnitude.

The output of another experiment in media strategy for another item in the store is shown in Table 5. The key point here is that the prior management decision (which they were unsure of) was that magazines were the place to spend the majority of their media dollars. Based on this experiment, their media strategy was changed to significantly favor television. The item became one of the most successful in the history of the retailer.

Use of the decision model and the decision support system it has spawned has caused managers of many departments to change their marketing planning procedures to be much more rational. However, because there is no test and control situation, it is difficult to put a precise profitability estimate on the benefits that have been obtained by utilizing the model and decision support system for planning purposes. The groups using the model did improve in sales and profits after beginning to use the model as a planning aid. The top marketing executive in the firm was so impressed with the quality of the planning that he was receiving from people utilizing the model that he himself requested the development of a longer-term version of the model so that he could evaluate strategic planning scenarios over a five-year planning horizon. It is also interesting to note that the documented increase in profitability due to the two above-mentioned experiments was orders of magnitude greater than the expense of building the complete decision support system, including the model, associated data base system, experimental analysis system, and national campaign evaluation system.

Table 5. Implications Based on National Scale-up

Media	Estimated sales per thousand-dollar media expenditure ($)	Lower bound on estimate ($)	Upper bound on estimate ($)
ROP,[a] Circulars	7,252	3,516	10,987
Television	11,741	8,732	14,750
Radio	7,170	−3,072	17,412
Magazines	4,200	−2,741	11,140

[a] Run-of-press (newspapers).

Consumer Goods Marketing

The prototype decision-calculus model is BRANDAID [3], developed by
John D. C. Little. The following example shows how BRANDAID was
implemented in one consumer package goods firm.[2] All the data have been
disguised to protect confidentialities. For concreteness, we have renamed
the product brand Q.

BRANDAID was implemented by a project team consisting of brand
management, marketing research, advertising management, and outside
consultants. The outside consultants provided the computer software for
running the model, data analysis expertise, and help in translating
managerial information into model inputs. The basic objective of the
model building activity was to aid in brand planning and tracking and to
help determine the best levels for advertising, promotion, and price for
brand Q. The team attempted to model monthly sales at the factory of
brand Q for five years. The model methodology tried to break down brand
Q sales into component parts due to elements of the marketing mix. These
component parts are the BRANDAID submodels. The reference year was
arbitrarily chosen as a year in which price and advertising were pretty

Figure 2. How did we get promotional response?

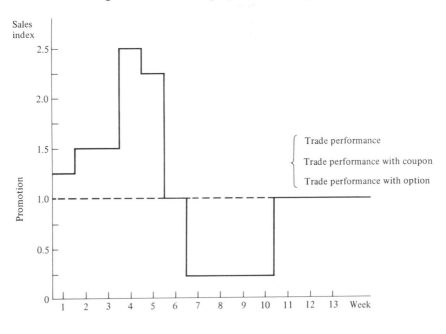

---

[2] The author thanks John D. C. Little for the use of private correspondence upon which
this example is based.

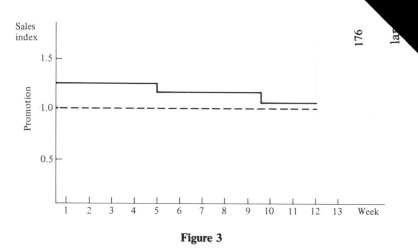

Figure 3

much constant and a full "normal" schedule of promotions was executed. Each of the effect indices discussed below is calculated by one of the BRANDAID submodels compared to the reference year.

Using a combination of subjective analysis modified by empirical analysis of 150 brand Q promotions during the five-year period, the team developed a "promotion template," shown in Figure 2. As can be seen from the graph, all trade promotions behave in a very similar manner. There is a small increase in the first few weeks on the announcement, then a big jump during the shipping period, and a deep trough after the promotion is over, because the trade has loaded up on their inventory during the promotion. Notice that the area under the peak is only slightly

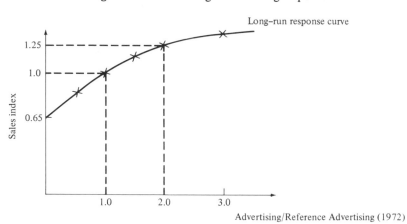

Figure 4. How did we get advertising response?

ger than the area in the valley. The group found that trade promotions provided only a small net increase in sales.

A newspaper coupon promotion causes a different sales effect pattern, as shown on the next graph, Figure 3. The effect of newspaper coupons on sales was felt to be far more gradual than a trade performance promotion.

The advertising submodel was completely estimated subjectively by the brand team. The submodel input is shown in Figures 4 and 5. Using those response curves and actual brand Q advertising expenditures, the BRANDAID advertising submodel calculates the advertising effects as shown in Figure 6. Notice that very little of the monthly fluctuation in sales is caused by advertising. The basic reason for this was that there was very little important fluctuation in the brands advertising strategy over the five-year period; moreover, the brand team felt that advertising effects were fairly gradual. The team concluded that they needed an advertising pressure test so that they could confirm or deny the team's advertising judgments.

Figure 7 shows the team's estimate of price response. The derivation of the price response was based on analysis of three periods of price history. During one period, brand Q's price was consistently above that of its major competitor. During another period brand Q's price actually fell below that of the major competitor. In later periods of the data the price ratio was considerably higher than it had been at any time. Based on two ways of looking at the sales decline that occurred in the most recent periods, two different estimates of price elasticity were obtained and used in the model runs.

Figure 5

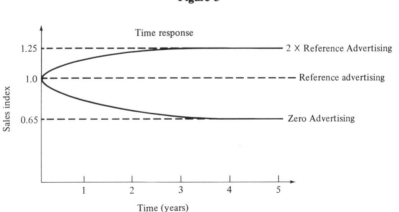

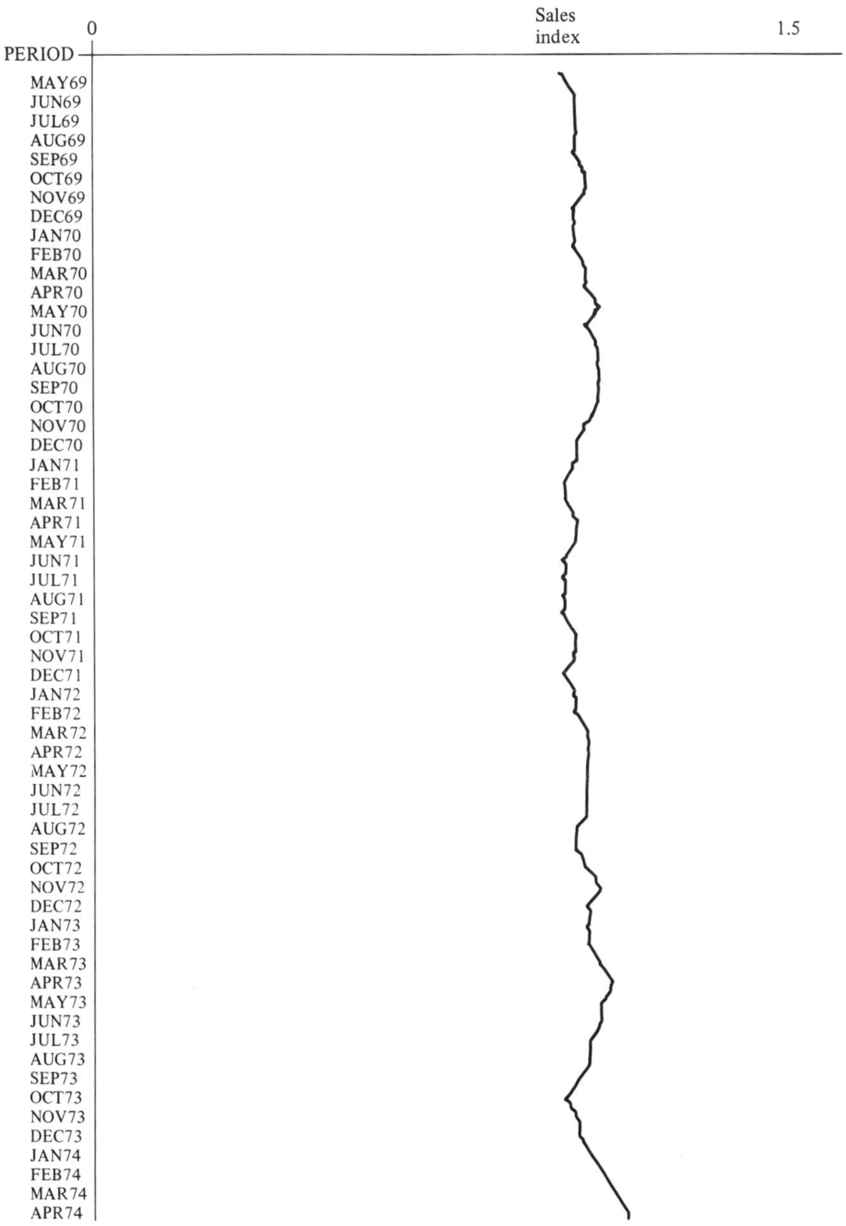

Figure 6. How, according to the curve, did advertising affect sales (model calculated)?

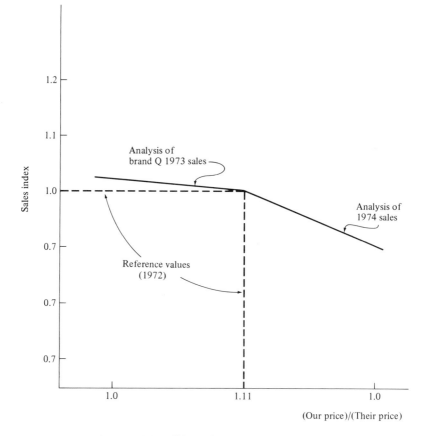

Figure 7. How did we determine price response?

The brand team detected a strong effect as the result of the buy-in period following a price change announcement. (See Figure 8.) The reason for the pattern was very similar to that for a trade performance promotion. An important finding from the team's analysis was that the relative magnitude of the buy-in effect peak and valley is very much affected by the trade's warehouse inventories. Those inventories are in turn affected by the number of months since the last promotion or price increase. The implications of this finding were that a price change could be used almost as a substitute for a promotion. The sales of brand Q were also affected by the basic uptrend in the product category sales. The increase in sales of the category averaged $2\frac{1}{2}$–3% per year. Figure 9 puts all of the model submodels together by multiplying all of the effect indices. The dotted lines are the predictions and the solid line represents the actual sales. The two periods in which the model was considerably off target were in the second half of 1971 and the second half of 1973, when the beginning and ending of

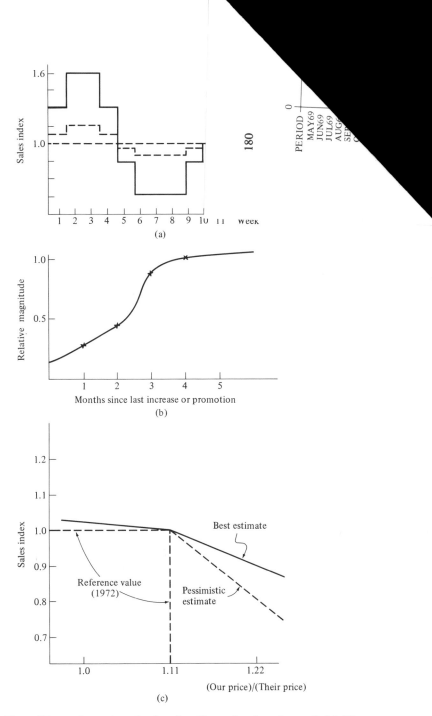

Figure 8. How did we determine the buy-in effect of price changes? (a) Time pattern of effect of buy-in; (b) relative magnitude of effect of buy-in; and (c) sales response to the price change.

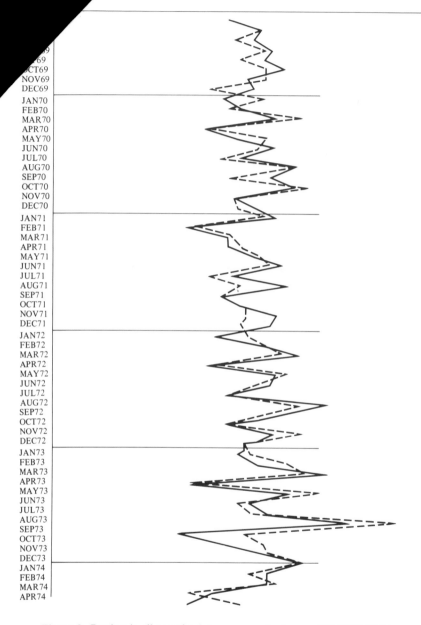

Figure 9. Putting it all together! (————, actual,- - -, BRANDAID.)

Table 6. Alternative BRANDAID Strategy Results

	1974		1975	
Strategy	Sales	Profits (×$1000)	Sales	Profits
Current plan	252	17.3	270	20.0
More newspaper coupons	253	17.2	276	19.7
More newspaper coupons; less advertising	252	18.0	262	20.0
More promotions; no newspaper coupons; no advertising	244	18.7	224	18.0
No marketing	243	19.3	222	19.9
No promotions; no coupons; more advertising	249	17.6	269	20.5
2¢ price increase	249	18.5	265	22.7
2¢ increase (pessimistic)	240	17.5	252	20.7

government price controls are hypothesized to have caused a good deal of the error. These phenomena were *not* specified in the model.

Once the model was parametrized by the team and was felt to track reasonably well, it was then used to develop implications of alternative strategies. Table 6 shows the sales and profit implications over the next two years of seven alternative marketing plans. What was apparent after all of the strategy runs was that it is possible to achieve very similar profits from strategies that result in tremendously different sales. The most attractive strategy was to maintain the current marketing plan, but increase the wholesale price. This would result in a modest sales decrease during the next year, but a nice profit increase, which could be used for further marketing activity or simply reported as profits. The price increase was indeed put into effect and the profit implications of the model were borne out by subsequent events. This price increase has become known within the company as the BRANDAID strategy. The yearly differences in profits from this strategy compared to the current strategy were in the middle seven-figure range.

Conclusions

What characteristics do these and other successful model implementations have in common? The most critical ingredient of success in these examples was an interface person who could relate the manager's needs to the model and decision support system and relate the model's outputs to the manager's needs. In order to make this interface person as effective as possible, all of these examples were done using interactive models that ran on time sharing. Also necessary was interactive access on time sharing to supporting data and statistical routines that were needed to parameterize the models. A combination of the interface person with the interactive computer system meant that managers could interact with the model and associated decision support system in hours and minutes rather than weeks. In all of these cases, this interaction helped the manager to understand exactly what the model was doing and essentially updated the manager's intuition about the world that the model was representing. In order to make sure that the manager was indeed in control of the model, all of the foregoing examples included both subjective and objective data sources. One of John Little's original decision-calculus requirements was for the model to be complete. In order for these models to be complete, subjective data were needed to consider phenomena that were not supported by empirical analysis.

All of the foregoing examples did not have optimization or statistical purity as a primary goal. The goal of all was helping managers to consider and evaluate more alternatives than they had prior to the use of the model. Many management science techniques for optimization or statistical estimation have been applied to marketing decision problems inappropriately, because they have sacrificed realism of the problem in order to structure their models so that they could be solved by mathematical programming techniques or complex statistical estimation routines.

Decision-calculus models are not necessarily mathematically or structurally different from other types of models discussed in other chapters. What is different is the method of implementation and the eclectic approach to model parametrization.

References

1. Fudge, W. K., and Lodish, L. M. "Evaluation of the Effectiveness of a Model Based Salesman's Planning System by Field Experimentation," *Interfaces* 8, No. 1, Part 2, 97–106 (1977).
2. Little, J. D. C. "Models and Managers: The Concept of a Decision Calculus," *Management Science* 16, No. 8, 466–485 (1970).
3. _____. "BRANDAID: A Marketing Mix Model, Part I: Structure," *Operations Research* 23, No. 4, 628–655 (1975).
4. Lodish, L. M. "CALLPLAN: An Interactive Salesman's Call Planning System," *Management Science* 18, No. 4, Part II, 25–40 (1971).
5. _____. "A Vaguely Right Approach to Sales Force Allocation Decisions," *Harvard Business Review* 52, No. 1, 119–124 (1974).
6. _____. "Sales Territory Alignment to Maximize Profit," *Journal of Marketing Research* 12, 30–36 (1975).
7. _____. "A Marketing Decision Support System for Retailers," Working Paper, Wharton School, Department of Marketing, University of Pennsylvania, 1979.

9

Evaluation of Stochastic Brand Choice Models*

Robert C. Blattberg

Marketing managers and researchers have long been dissatisfied with simply looking at market share changes and not being able to understand why and how they happened. To better understand these market share changes, management scientists began using stochastic models in conjunction with consumer diary panel data. This research, done in the middle fifties, led to a literature referred to as stochastic brand choice models. Since the late fifties, numerous articles and books have been written about stochastic brand choice models. However, what influence have these articles had on marketing managers, either directly through normative models or indirectly through descriptive models? The goal of this chapter is to evaluate the contribution stochastic brand choice models have made to marketing management and to consumer behavior research.

Several books have been written summarizing research on stochastic brand choice models, including that by Massy, Montgomery, and Morrison [32], along with review articles such as that of Montgomery and Ryans [34]. Since the purpose of this chapter is not simply to review past literature, it seems unnecessary to describe different types of stochastic brand choice models in detail. The reader can use Massy et al. [32] as a guide to the models and statistical procedures used. Also, many articles on stochastic brand choice models, without direct relevance to decision models, will not be discussed.

The term stochastic brand choice (SBC) model will refer to stochastic models in which the choice is a set of brands. Purchase incidence (PI)

*I would like to thank Hemant Jalan for his help in preparing this article.

models will refer to models that analyze the time between purchases for a brand or a product category. Although they appear to be different, these two types of models overlap in their use because one can analyze the choice of a brand on the basis of its incidence of purchase. Both types of models will be discussed here.

In trying to assess the effect of stochastic brand choice modeling on managerial decision making, certain caveats must be observed. First, a great deal of business research is unpublished, and therefore may be unknown to the research community. Second, research may not be directly applied to a specific problem, but still influence managers by offering general principles that aid in making decisions. In spite of these difficulties, an attempt will be made to evaluate the impact of stochastic brand choice models on managerial decision making.

The topics to be covered in this chapter are (1) the use of SBC and PI models to analyze marketing events (for example, a promotion) and predict future sales, (2) the use of PI models to forecast new product sales, (3) SBC models' contributions to consumer behavior theory, (4) SBC models as the basis of market response models, and (5) laws of behavior from stochastic models. The chapter will conclude with a summary and discussion of future research directions in stochastic modeling.

Stochastic Brand Choice Models to Analyze Marketing Events

One of the early applications of stochastic brand choice models was to project future brand sales after a marketing "event" (for example, a promotion) occurred (cf. Maffai [29], Herniter and Magee [17]). The early models usually used Markov chains to compute equilibrium sales, which were interpreted as the sales the brand would have obtained had no event occurred. The data base used for these analyses was consumer diary panels. In addition to predicting the sales of the marketing event, they also indicated how each brand was affected and what the long-run brand shares would do. Finally, the Markov SBC model could diagnose the source of the lost or gained business. This would allow the firm to understand competitive factors that were influencing the brand.

An example from Maffai [30, pp. 121–123] shows how the models were used. Suppose the transition matrix is

$$
\begin{array}{c}
\text{period } t+1 \\
\begin{array}{cc}
1 & 2
\end{array} \\
\text{period } t \quad
\begin{array}{c}
1 \\
2
\end{array}
\left(
\begin{array}{cc}
.5 & .5 \\
.25 & .75
\end{array}
\right)
\end{array}
$$

Brand 1 runs an advertisement and changes the transition matrix to

$$\text{period } t+1$$

$$\begin{array}{cc} & 1 \quad\ 2 \\ \text{period } t \quad \begin{matrix}1\\2\end{matrix} & \begin{pmatrix} .6 & .4 \\ .4 & .6 \end{pmatrix} \end{array}$$

The steady-state market share becomes 50% for each brand. The rate of convergence to this market share can also be computed.

The benefit of a stochastic brand choice model is that it offers diagnostic information about loss and gains from other brands. With only one brand, as was the case, it is less important. Buyers were also split into loyal and nonloyal as a first attempt to overcome the assumptions of homogeneity of buyers (cf. Harary and Lipstein [16]).

The key assumptions made in using stochastic brand choice models are that (1) the market is stationary and the marketing strategy for all firms will be the same in the future, which implies that competitors will not react to the firm's strategy change; (2) no new products are introduced; (3) the consumer's behavior is stationary; and (4) the population's behavior is homogeneous.[1] These assumptions, particularly (1) and (3), are very restrictive.

For marketing managers the Markov transition matrix served as a diagnostic tool, but was not very helpful in predicting future sales. A particular problem in using the model for prediction is that it does not consider nonbuyers of the category who might become buyers nor the differences in purchasing rate.

The use of the transition matrix as a measure of brand switching also came into disrepute. Frank [13] showed that what appears to be higher-order (nonzero-order) behavior may only be heterogeneity. Thus, brand-switching transition matrices appeared promising in principle but were shown to be not very useful in practice.

Although there are many problems with brand-switching matrices, diary panel companies use a similar system to analyze "sources of brand value." The "model" attempts to analyze the source of a brand's business. The sources are repeat buyers, other brands, and market expansion. The system analyzes individual switching behavior and then aggregates.

To see how this system works, consider two customers A and B. Suppose A's purchases are as shown in the accompanying table; then A's purchases

---

[1]Later this assumption was relaxed so that consumer's behavior was assumed to be heterogeneous.

can be characterized using the following matrix:

Brands	A's Purchases	
	Units in period 1	Units in period 2
1	4	2
2	2	3
3	2	3

		to			
	Brand	1	2	3	Total in period 1
from	1	2	1	1	4
	2	0	2	0	2
	3	0	0	2	2
	Total in period 2	2	3	3	

This matrix shows that consumer A's purchases in period 1 can be distributed to each of the three brands in period 2. The distribution begins by assigning to each brand the maximum repeat business. For brand 1, which went from 4 units in period 1 to 2 units in period 2, it is assumed that the 2 units are repeat business. The next question is how to distribute the other 2 units bought in period 1 to brands in period 2. This is done in proportion to their period-2 sales after eliminating the repeat-purchased units. Thus, brand 2 has 1 unit and brand 3 has 1 unit after repeat purchases are eliminated. The result is that each is allocated 1 unit from brand 1.

Suppose B's purchases are as shown in the accompanying table; then B's purchases can be characterized using the following matrix:

Brands	B's Purchases	
	Units in period 1	Units in period 2
1	4	5
2	1	1
3	1	0

		to			
	Brand	1	2	3	Total in period 1
from	1	4	0	0	4
	2	0	1	0	1
	3	1	0	0	1
	Total in period 2	5	1	0	

The total for the two consumers is then aggregated to produce the source-of-volume matrix, which for A and B is

$$
\begin{array}{cccccc}
 & & \multicolumn{3}{c}{\text{to}} & \\
 & & & & & \text{Total in} \\
 & \text{Brand} & 1 & 2 & 3 & \text{period 1} \\
 & 1 & \begin{pmatrix} 6 & 1 & 1 \\ & & \end{pmatrix} & & & 8 \\
\text{from} & 2 & \begin{pmatrix} 0 & 3 & 0 \end{pmatrix} & & & 3 \\
 & 3 & \begin{pmatrix} 1 & 0 & 2 \end{pmatrix} & & & 3 \\
 & \text{Total in} & & & & \\
 & \text{period 2} & 7 & 4 & 3 & \\
\end{array}
$$

For a more detailed discussion of the procedure, see "Description of NPD Volume-Oriented Brand Mix Shifting System" [9]. The problem with this approach is that it is difficult to interpret the results because of heterogeneity in purchase behavior. For example, suppose there were only two brands and two households. The purchasing behavior of households A and B is given below.

Brands	Household A		Household B	
	Period 1	Period 2	Period 1	Period 2
1	6	3	3	6
2	3	6	6	3

The brand-shifting matrix for the two households is

$$
\begin{array}{ccccc}
 & & \multicolumn{2}{c}{\text{to}} & \\
 & & & & \text{Total in} \\
 & \text{Brand} & 1 & 2 & \text{period 1} \\
\text{from} & 1 & \begin{pmatrix} 6 & 3 \\ 3 & 6 \end{pmatrix} & & 9 \\
 & 2 & & & 9 \\
 & \text{Total in} & & & \\
 & \text{period 2} & 9 & 9 & \\
\end{array}
$$

One would conclude from this matrix there is substantial loyalty, yet both households changed their preference from 0.67 to 0.33 for their favorite brand in period 1. This fact is lost in the analysis. Thus, heterogeneity in buying behavior may cause the interpretation of the brand-switching matrix to be spurious.

In conclusion, while brand-switching matrices sounded as though they had great promise for analysis of markets, heterogeneity in buying behavior meant that aggregate switching matrices did not capture all the relevant information. Aggregate switching matrices have been used much less in recent years because of the problems described above.

Brand Choice and Purchase Incidence Models

SBC models usually do not consider the time between purchase in addition to the probability of buying the brand. If one wants to predict the number of units bought of a brand in a given time period, it is necessary to model both interpurchase time and probability of buying. Such modeling is needed for commonly used statistics such as penetration and the number of "new triers" in a period.

Herniter [18] was one of the first model builders to create a joint purchase timing brand choice model. He assumed that time between purchases fit an Erlang distribution and that the brand choice distribution was Markovian. By assuming independence between brand choice and purchase timing, Herniter derived a closed-form solution for the number of purchases of brand j made during time t; other market statistics such as penetration could also be computed.

Zufryden [41], Bass, Jeuland, and Wright [3], and Bemmaor [4] have all extended Herniter's results using different models of purchase timing and brand choice models. By doing this, they have offered a procedure for analyzing the market statistics practitioners regularly produce.

Stochastic Models to Forecast Sales of New Products

Forecasting the sales of new products has been an area in which marketers have successfully used stochastic models. The first published research in this area was an article by Fourt and Woodlock [14]. Subsequently, models were developed by Massy [31], Parfitt and Collins [36], Ahl [1], and Eskin [12], as well as by diary panel companies, which produced a number of unpublished proprietary models. All of these models used consumer diary panel data, as is the case with SBC models.

These models disaggregated new product sales into trial and repeat buying. By disaggregating total sales for the brand into these two submodels, each of these subcomponents is forecasted separately. Before these models were developed, marketing researchers looked at the new product sales curve, such as that given in Figure 1, and tried to make forecasts by guessing the point (A, B, or C in Figure 1) at which sales would plateau. This obviously could not be done easily, and so long-run sales or market shares were usually poorly predicted. The models developed by Parfitt and Collins and by Ahl offered a new and far superior method of forecasting sales. By analyzing trial and repeat buying separately, sales were predicted much more accurately than by using the sales curves.

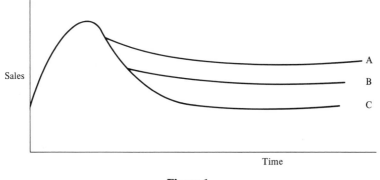

Figure 1

The use of these models for forecasting new product sales has been widely accepted by industry. These models have been used extensively by consumer diary panel companies to forecast new product sales in test markets. The major limitations of these models are that they fail to incorporate marketing variables such as advertising, price, promotion, and distribution into their forecasts, which in certain cases limits their usefulness. The models forecast success but do not offer diagnostic information about why a new product fails. In addition, it is difficult to plan a new product introduction from these models because changes in price, advertising, and distribution are not related to trial or repeat buying. This seems to be an important area for future research.

Stochastic Brand Choice Models: Understanding Consumer Behavior

Most of the stochastic brand choice modeling in the sixties and early seventies was designed to understand how consumers behaved. The objective was to determine whether consumers followed a Bernoulli, Markov, or linear learning model. It was felt that if marketing managers knew the answer to this question, they could design better marketing strategies because they could more accurately estimate the economic benefit of the strategy.

One of the earliest SBC models that tried to understand the purchasing behavior of consumers was developed by Kuehn [24], who tried to show that consumers followed a linear learning model. Frank [13] showed that the higher-order purchase behavior Kuehn found might be caused by heterogeneity across the population. Their work led to the development by many other researchers of more complex SBC models. For example, Morrison [35] developed the last-purchase-loyal Markov model and brand-loyal Markov model, Montgomery [33] the probability diffusion model, and Jones [22] the composite heterogeneous model, in which heterogeneity is across models as well as parameters.

Besides developing different model structures each paper usually tried to determine which model best fits the data. Statistical tests were used to evaluate which model best fit a series of purchase sequences obtained from consumer diary data. The statistic usually used was

$$\chi^2 = \frac{(O_i - E_i)^2}{E_i}, \tag{1}$$

where O_i is the observed sequence and E_i the expected sequence. The expected sequence was computed from each model.

Massy, Montgomery, and Morrison [32, p. 271] tested a number of models and found the following:

1. Both the linear learning and probability diffusion model provided reasonable fits to the data.
2. The last-purchase-loyal model developed by Morrison did not provide an adequate fit to the data. The brand-loyal Markov model did substantially better.
3. The more flexible models, the linear learning and probability diffusion models, outperformed the brand-loyal Markov model.

Unfortunately, other researchers have found different results. Part of the problem is the statistical tests used. Massy, Montgomery, and Morrison used p-values to select the best models. However, standard statistical tests such as the likelihood ratio might yield very different results. Also, they failed to use independent samples. Blattberg and Sen [5, 6] offer two alternative methods of discriminating between models and discuss the issue of nonindependent samples.

The answer as to which model consumers follow may be that not all consumers follow the same model. Jones [22] and Givon and Horsky [15] studied heterogeneity across models as well as parameters. Blattberg and Sen [7] showed that some consumers followed a Bernoulli process and others a Markov process, though the tests between the two models were not always direct.

Despite the amount of research available, it cannot be stated with any certainty which type of model consumers follow. Yet the answer to this question, if one does exist, is important in developing individual level models of the response of sales to advertising, promotion, and other marketing variables. The answer to this question should help determine the strategies marketing managers should follow.

The reasons that no answer exists to what appears to be a simple question are the following:

1. There is lack of stationarity in the product market because of changing strategies and new products being introduced into the market.

2. It is difficult to discriminate using statistical procedures and panel data between heterogeneity, nonstationarity, and higher-order stochastic processes.
3. No theory exists that explains what causes Markovian or linear learning behavior.

Based on these reasons, what methodology can be used to answer this question? Because the question cannot be answered strictly from data analysis, help must come from theoretical considerations. At present, almost no one is trying to develop theoretical reasons why certain behavior exists; instead most researchers are trying to develop new research techniques to analyze the data. It is unlikely that more powerful statistical tests can answer such questions because the quality of the data is not "rich enough." The data series must be short to ensure stationarity, which implies that it is difficult to discriminate between competing hypotheses. Therefore, some assistance in eliminating alternatives must come from theory.

Incorporating Marketing Variables into Stochastic Brand Choice Models

One of the objectives of Kuehn's [24] research was to build marketing response models with stochastic brand choice as the basis for individual buying behavior. Kuehn's model, in a simplified form, begins by assuming that individuals have a brand-switching matrix that assumes there is brand retention; that is, that the previous period's purchase influences the next period's purchase. Let r_i be the retention factor for the ith brand and M_i the influence of all marketing variables for the ith brand. Then, the brand-switching matrix is

$$
\begin{array}{cc}
 & \text{period } t+1 \\
 & \begin{array}{ccc} 1 & 2 & 3 \end{array}
\end{array}
$$

$$
\begin{array}{c}
\text{Brand} \\
\text{period } t \quad
\begin{array}{c} 1 \\ 2 \\ 3 \end{array}
\end{array}
\begin{pmatrix}
r_1+(1-r_1)M_{1,t+1} & (1-r_1)M_{2,t+1} & (1-r_1)M_{3,t+1} \\
(1-r_2)M_{1,t+1} & r_2+(1-r_2)M_{2,t+1} & (1-r_2)M_{3,t+1} \\
(1-r_3)M_{1,t+1} & (1-r_3)M_{2,t+1} & r_3+(1-r_3)M_{3,t+1}
\end{pmatrix}
$$

with

$$
r_i+(1-r_i)\sum_{j=1}^{3} M_j=1 \qquad \text{for all } i,
$$

which requires

$$
\sum M_j=1 \qquad \text{if} \quad M_i \geqslant 0.
$$

Next, let $S_{i,t}$ be the sales of the ith brand at time t and

$$I_t = \sum_i S_{i,t}.$$

It can be shown that if all individuals have the same brand-switching matrix, then

$$S_{i,t} = r_i S_{i,t-1} + M_{i,t}(1-\bar{r})I_t, \tag{2}$$

where

$$\bar{r} = \sum_i r_i \left(\frac{S_{i,t-1}}{I_{t-1}} \right).$$

The form of (2) looks similar to a distributed lag model with r_i being the lagged effect.

If $r_i > 0$, then there will be a carry-over effect to marketing variables. On the other hand, if $r_i = 0$ for all i, the brand-switching matrix would simply depend on the M_i's and a carry-over effect would exist only if the marketing variable (for example, advertising) led to a carry-over. Thus, when $r_i > 0$, variables such as dealing have future effects. This will, in turn, influence the profitability of a given marketing strategy.

Based on the foregoing discussion, it is obvious that the choice of the SBC model influences the marketing response model used and the strategy marketing managers should follow. The remainder of this section discusses how models of consumer behavior have been incorporated into the measurement of the effects of marketing variables.

Models of Advertising

One of the early applications of Markov models is the work of Telser [39, 40]. He tried to measure the effects of advertising on brand sales in the cigarette industry. As the basis of his advertising–sales model, he used a Markov transition matrix in which he assumed the transition probability depended on advertising. Telser did not consider such factors as heterogeneity in the population and some of the factors presently being incorporated into SBC models, but his research pioneered the use of SBC models as the basis for advertising–sales equations.

Despite its relevance, very few studies of advertising have incorporated consumer behavior theories directly into the model's structure as Telser's did. Given the early work of Telser, and its potentially promising directions, it is useful to try to understand why more research has not followed. First, the resulting models cannot be estimated using simple ordinary least squares models. Most researchers would rather use distributed lag models or multiplicative models to try to estimate the effects of advertising than to go to the complex structures and estimation tools required in Telser's model. Second, no one is certain about the appropriate stochastic brand choice process to assume (as has been discussed earlier).

An important issue that Telser's research raises is: Does assuming that the parameters of the model depend on marketing variables negate much of the SBC model research, which assumes stationarity? Very little research has been done to answer this question.

Another approach to the modeling of advertising in SBC models is that of Lipstein [27]. His model assumes that the elements of the brand-switching matrix depend on advertising (as does Telser). However, rather than directly relating advertising expenditures to the elements of the matrix, he assumes that a causative change matrix C is a function of advertising expenditures and attitudes, and that C influences the probability of buying brand i. Thus,

$$P_{ij} = g(a_{ij}) \quad \text{and} \quad a_{ij} = f(c_{ij}), \tag{3}$$

where

   P_{ij} is the probability of buying brand i given that brand j was the last brand bought,
   a_{ij} is the attitude change in brand i relative to brand j, and
   c_{ij} is the causative change element, which depends on the relative advertising expenditures and their effectiveness.

While Lipstein's model offers an interesting structure, the estimation questions are not discussed. With so many elements to estimate, it is not clear how useful his model is.

Another approach to the incorporation of advertising into stochastic models is that of Blattberg and Jeuland [8]. Rather than assuming an aggregate model for the advertising–sales relationship, they begin with micro assumptions about the individual's brand choice behavior. The underlying assumption is that behavior is zero order, but that the probability of buying depends on advertising. They then show that aggregating across time and individuals does not result in the types of models being estimated by most researchers in the advertising area. Carry-over effects of advertising were derived from memory decay and not Markovian behavior. Had a different micro model been assumed for specific purchase behavior, different sales equations would have resulted. Through aggregation and careful delineation of the process, the sales–advertising equations are consistent with micro assumptions about purchasing behavior.

Unfortunately, very few researchers in the area of advertising–sales modeling have tried to build a model consistent with assumptions about individual behavior that are then estimated. Obviously, this is an important area for modelers who worry about the types of micro models they are using to estimate the advertising–sales relationship. In summary, surprisingly little research has been done to incorporate advertising into SBC models.

Promotional Effects and SBC Models

Several models have been developed that incorporate, or at least can analyze, the effects of consumer promotions. Kuehn and Rohloff [25] used a linear learning model to see if there was recidivism in purchase behavior after a consumer promotion as well as to determine the effect of the deal on the probability of purchasing. They used the linear learning model to predict what the household would have done had the deal not occurred. In answering this question, they analyzed the next two purchases (the deal and subsequent purchase). This analysis can indicate the number of "new triers" and repeat purchasers. Analyzing past dealing behavior is important because if there is an increased probability of buying the brand after the deal (assumed in the linear learning model), then dealing will be more profitable.

Kuehn and Rohloff's model was followed by two further analyses. Lilien [26] also used the linear learning model to evaluate the effect of price on the probability of buying. His model is

$$P_{t+1} = (1-C)(\alpha + \beta X_t + \lambda P_t) + C\phi(\delta_{t+1}), \tag{4}$$

where

$$X_t = \begin{cases} 0 & \text{not buying brand,} \\ 1 & \text{buying brand,} \end{cases}$$

$$P_t = Pr(\tilde{X}_t = 1),$$

where

C is the price consciousness of the consumer,
ϕ_t the measure of price, and
$\delta(\phi_t)$ the value of the price response function with range $(0, 1)$.

The larger C is, the greater the price effect. This model implies positive feedback from a purchase event assuming that $\beta > 0$.

An article by Shoemaker and Shoaf [37] analyzed the effect of the next purchase after either a deal or nondeal purchase and showed that the probability of buying the brand was lower after buying that brand on deal than after making a nondeal purchase of that brand. Neither Kuehn and Rohloff nor Lilien incorporate this "negative" feedback into their model. Based upon Shoemaker and Shoaf's results, this appears to be an important omission.

Two models built used Markov transition probabilities to assess the effects of deals and price changes. Hinkle [20] studied the effects of deals in several categories, modeling the elements of the transition probabilities much the same as Telser did. Several strategic questions, including the timing of deals, were studied using this approach.

MacLachlan [28] also modeled the elements of the transition matrix and estimated the effects of deals and price. He then compared the variable transition matrix to a distributed lag model and concluded that the variable Markov model is as accurate as the distributed lag model and offers greater explanatory power.

The Shoemaker and Shoaf results show the important effect that marketing variables have on purchase probabilities and how consumer promotions have influenced these probabilities. Very few models consider these effects. Yet from the brand manager's perspective, the results influence the profitability of the marketing decision. Even with all the research done on SBC models, the effect of a deal on future purchases is unknown.

Models Incorporating Distribution

A final area is the matter of distribution or brand availability. Jeuland [21] considers the probability that a brand is available and incorporates this into a brand-switching matrix. The issue raised by this paper is the effect of availability on purchase probabilities. The retailer or distributor will stock the high-preference (share) brands, and therefore there is an interaction between preference and availability that influences the probability of purchase. Clearly, changes in availability greatly influence brand purchase probabilities.

Stochastic Models and Laws of Behavior

Overview

Several authors have posited that consumers behave according to well-defined models of behavior. The interesting theoretical issue resulting from this type of research is that it indicates that marketing variables may influence short-run behavior, but not necessarily long-run stationary behavior. The concept developed may help marketing managers evaluate their marketing strategies because it offers a very different perspective. The work that will be reviewed is that of Ehrenberg, Bass, and Herniter, as well as the Hendry system. The difference in their approaches is that Ehrenberg has studied purchase incidence and used a negative binomial model, whereas Bass, Herniter, and the Hendry system have assumed entropy as the basis for their approach. These issues and the implications for marketing decision models will be discussed.

Ehrenberg's NBD Model and Theory

Ehrenberg [11] developed a purchase incidence model to try to explain behavior. Based on this model one could calculate penetration statistics and the probability of trial for any given brand in the market for varying time periods. The model makes assumptions that are controversial: (1) a Poisson purchase rate for a given period of time, and (2) a heterogeneous population that follows a gamma distribution. These assumptions have been challenged as unreasonable.[2] Given these assumptions, however, one can derive a probability distribution, known as the negative binomial distribution (NBD) that allows one to calculate specific probabilities of events occurring.

To estimate the parameters of the NBD model, the number of purchases for a given period of time made by members of a consumer panel is required. For example, the percentage of households that make 0, 1, 2, etc. purchases for a fixed period (for example, a half year) is used. Based on the parameter estimates derived from the data just discussed, the model then computes the penetration and usage rate for any given time period, ranging from 1 to 52 weeks. Thus, the model can give the average number of purchases per buyer and the penetration rate for any length period, not merely the measurement period.

The NBD model makes two contributions: (1) it allows the firm to estimate long-run penetration based on quarterly or semiannual data; (2) it serves as a "null hypothesis" for marketing managers who feel that marketing expenditures will greatly change their brand's long-run sales. Ehrenberg [11, p. 17] states:

> The fundamental finding in the study of buyer behavior is that there are simple and highly generalizable patterns. This is by no means an obvious result....
>
> The theory applies to "stationary" situations, defined as there having been no change in the sales-level of the item being analyzed. This is the most usual situation for most brands in most markets.... This stationary theory can, however, also be used to interpret *non-stationary* situations.

To understand the contribution of Ehrenberg's NBD theory, an example is helpful. Table 1 gives the frequency of buying in a product category.

Table 1 shows that Brand A has a share of 46, Brand C a share of 6. The ratio is approximately 8:1. The penetration for Brand A is 62% of the market and for Brand C it is 17%, which is approximately a 4:1 ratio. The average number of units bought of Brand A is 10 and for Brand C it is 5, which is a 2:1 ratio. Therefore, the most significant cause of the difference between the high-share brand and the low-share brand is the ratio of penetrations rather than the number of units bought per trier. Ehrenberg views this as the critical factor in understanding share differences. This greatly differs from the view of those who believe that successful brand sales are primarily due to loyal buyers.

---

[2]The assumption of independence of purchases that the Poisson model makes is very unlikely to hold for short time periods. If a household bought very recently, it is unlikely to buy in the next time period.

Table 1. The Frequency of Buying a Brand and the Heaviness of Buying

Brand	Market share (%)	Population buying in year (%)	Number of purchases in year						Average per buyer
			1	2	3	4	5	6+	
A	46	62	18	9	8	7	6	52	10
B	12	32	32	18	11	6	5	29	5
C	6	17	38	16	13	7	3	23	5
D	5	14	45	20	9	3	0	23	4
E	6	12	36	12	6	5	6	36	7
Category		79	8	8	6	6	4	70	16

Source: A. Ehrenberg [11], *Repeat Buying*, Tables 3.2, 3.4.

Evaluation of the NBD Theory

While other authors refute the statistical assumption underlying the NBD theory, Ehrenberg's contribution is to show the importance of brand penetration in explaining behavior. To do this, Ehrenberg assumes that the market is stationary, but this is also a weakness of the model. As is the case with many other stochastic models, variables such as dealing, advertising, and product attributes are not related to changes in penetration and buying rates because the market is assumed to be stationary, and so is the brand strategy. No doubt increasing the amount of dealing increases the brand's penetration. Ehrenberg argues, however, that the source of a brand's volume is not the various marketing tactics, but rather the assumption that a brand's penetration and units are fairly constant over a long period of time. Therefore, he probably sees no reason to incorporate these other variables into the model.

Brand Duplication

Ehrenberg also argues that the joint purchasing of two brands, brand duplication, depends on the length of the time period, the brand's penetration, and a constant for the product category. For a fixed time period, except in the case in which certain segments or special attributes exist, the number of households buying both Brand A and Brand B is proportional to the brand's penetration. Duplication is defined as the number of households buying brand i and j in a given time period. Ehrenberg postulates that the duplication statistic $D_{ij} = kP_iP_j$, where P_i is the penetration of brand i and k is a product category constant. Ehrenberg is arguing that buyer behavior is highly predictable. This view of brand competition also appears in the work of Herniter and Bass and in the Hendry system and will be discussed later.

Summary of Ehrenberg's Theories

Ehrenberg has used a stochastic model, NBD, to explain buyer behavior. He has generated some simple rules of behavior that, he argues, explain far more of a brand's purchase behavior than do assumptions about loyalty, specially segmented brands, and marketing effects. His theory offers an excellent countervailing view to the brand manager who is enamored of the power of his marketing strategy. More research looking for regularities in data (or marketing generalizations), as Ehrenberg's has done, rather than for unique differences should be undertaken. Ehrenberg appears to have been able to utilize a stochastic model of brand behavior to find and test some of these regularities.

Entropy Model

Herniter [19] raised the following question: Can one fit brand-switching behavior assuming only that switching is a maximum? If the answer is yes, then purchasing behavior follows a simple law; that is, entropy is maximized. Further, it is possible to use market shares to predict brand and category-switching behavior.

For the brand manager, who devotes a great deal of energy to segmenting markets and trying to evaluate which brands are his major competitors, the theory developed by Herniter implies that brand shares contain all of the information necessary to predict brand switching.

Herniter's Model

Consider the case in which there are two brands in the market. A customer can follow one of three types of behavior: (1) purchase only brand 1, (2) purchase only brand 2, or (3) purchase brands 1 and 2. Let q_1 be the proportion of individuals buying only brand 1, q_2 the proportion buying only brand 2, and q_3 the proportion buying brands 1 and 2.

For the switching segment, segment 3, Herniter assumes that P_i is distributed across the population according to the distribution $f(P_i)$, and assumes that

$$S = -\left\{ \int_0^1 Pf(p)\ln[Pf(p)]\,dp + \int_0^1 (1-P)f(p)\ln[(1-P)f(p)]\,dp \right\}.$$

The problem becomes one of selecting $f(p)$ that yields the maximum entropy[3] (maximizes S) and fits the constraint that $\int_0^1 f(p)\,dp = 1$. Once $f(p)$ is found, one can then calculate q_1, q_2, and q_3 so that $\Sigma q_i = 1$ and brand switching is maximized.

---

[3] Entropy is defined as $S = -\Sigma_{i=1}^N P_i \ln P_i$, where P_i is the probability of buying brand i and N is the total number of brands.

Herniter also shows how to calculate the aggregate brand-switching matrix. For example, in a two-brand market, when market share for brand 1 is .1 and that for brand 2 is .9, the transition matrix is

$$
\text{period } t \quad \begin{array}{c} \\ 1 \\ 2 \end{array} \begin{array}{c} \text{period } t+1 \\ \begin{array}{cc} 1 & 2 \end{array} \\ \begin{pmatrix} .55 & .45 \\ .05 & .95 \end{pmatrix}. \end{array}
$$

Thus, a high-share brand has substantially greater loyalty, which is intuitively sensible.

Herniter's theory is independent of any information about the brand switching in the market. He uses only market share to derive the switching matrix. Thus, in any two-brand market in which brand 1 has a .1 share and brand 2 has a .9 share, the switching matrix given here holds.

The results given can be expanded to k brands in the market, though Herniter cannot easily derive the results as the number of brands increases beyond three because of the complexity of solving the entropy equation. To remedy this problem, Bass [2] tries to simplify the results so that only $k+1$ segments are needed rather than $2^k - 1$ segments. Bass assumes that all switching is part of a segment called the stochastic preference segment. Therefore, there are k segments who are loyal in the stochastic preference segment. Bass [2, pp. 5–11] derives two models that are much closer to stochastic brand choice models than Herniter's. Bass derives a measure he calls a category loyalty measure that helps fit the data.

Empirical Results

Both Herniter and Bass argue that their models fit actual switching data quite well. For the data sets Herniter studies, it is shown that χ^2 tests do not reject his model (Herniter [19, p. 373]). Bass [2, p. 18] states that "the reproduction of the actual switching behavior of the market is accurate enough to justify the conclusion that the evidence fails to falsify the theory."

Because the empirical methods in both articles are not described in much detail, it is difficult to evaluate them. The degrees of freedom in the estimation of the switching matrices appears to be small. Because $q_0, \ldots, q_k$ is being estimated based on a different set of assumptions than fitting the transition or joint probability matrix, it is difficult to estimate the exact number of degrees of freedom. However, it does raise the issue that with four brands and market shares given, there may not be very much chance to miss the true transition matrix. A null model is needed so that the entropy model can be compared to it. A possible null model is a Dirichlet prior and multinomial purchasing behavior. Research could then focus on the assumption of entropy and whether it is justified.

Evaluation of Research

Again, as with Ehrenberg, the research of Herniter and Bass has tried to show that there is a law governing purchasing behavior: Consumers switch brands at a maximum level given their segment membership. Their assumptions are similar to those of Ehrenberg, who assumes that duplication (for a fixed category and time period) is constant. They have not applied rigorous empirical tests to their models, as Ehrenberg and his coresearchers have done with the NBD theory. However, their research is much more recent (1973–1974), and so time is needed before further empirical testing of the entropy theory takes place.

Some aspects of the theory are contradicted with data. For example, in a panel of any reasonable length (for example, one year), very few households are totally loyal to a brand. Yet, for a three-brand market with shares of .3, .1, and .6, respectively, 40% of the households are assumed to be in the loyal group (Herniter [19, Table 3, p. 369]). If this is true, then why do Herniter and Bass do so well fitting data?

In summary, the research done raises an interesting question: Do market shares and the assumption of maximum entropy contain most of the information about brand switching? If the answer is yes, this is very useful for the brand manager who believes only certain brands are competitors. Herniter's work implies that product categories do not really partition; rather, shares and entropy explain brand switching.

The Hendry System

The Hendry system utilizes certain assumptions about choice behavior to (1) partition markets and (2) develop marketing strategies. It is an interesting application of stochastic brand choice models that is used to aid marketing management. The description of the Hendry system is based on the work of Kalwani and Morrison [23].[4]

According to Kalwani and Morrison's description, the model begins with a heterogeneous multinomial process that assumes zero-order purchase behavior and constant probability of purchasing over time. Next, heterogeneity in the population's probability of purchasing each brand is assumed. Which distribution is used for heterogeneity is not stated explicitly. It appears that the Dirichlet distribution is used [38, p. 129]. Given these assumptions, the Dirichlet and multinomial, the marginal distribution for a given brand's probability of being purchased is a beta binomial and brand switching is proportional to brand shares, that is, $P_{ij} = K_w P_i P_j$. The para-

---

[4]The difficulty in describing the Hendry system is that these articles do not delineate the models used. Therefore, it is necessary to use Kalwani and Morrison's description of their model.

meter K_w can be derived from the Dirichlet model.[5] If a multinomial distribution is used with Dirichlet heterogeneity, K_w is fixed across all brands.

The basis for this model is similar to that of Ehrenberg, who assumes that duplication is proportional to penetration. Under certain brand-switching assumptions, one can show that if Ehrenberg is correct and duplication is proportional within a product category, so then is K_w. Therefore, both Ehrenberg and the Hendry system are assuming that certain brand choice models fit consumer behavior. Based on these models, they then derive switching matrices and certain implications for managerial actions.

Managerial Implications of the Hendry System

A major use of the Hendry system is the dividing of brands in a market into either a form-specific or brand-specific structure. The example commonly used is margarine, which comes in two forms, sticks and tubs. Do consumers make their first choice on the basis of brand or on the basis of form? Figure 2 shows a form-specific market. Partitioning is done using K_w. It is assumed that K_w is a constant across brands within a partition. If the market is form specific, and one looks at the switching behavior across all brands, one finds out that K_w is not constant. It should be a constant within a specific form. Therefore, one partitions the market until K_w is constant for the brands within the partition.

The implications of the market structure for product introduction and advertising are important. If a product category is form specific, then a firm can introduce a new brand in a form in which they do not have an

Figure 2. Form specific market.

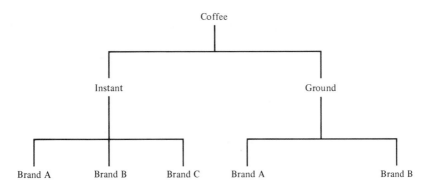

---

[5] If $f(P_1,\ldots,P_k)$ follows a Dirichlet distribution with parameters $V_1,\ldots,V_k$, and $V=\Sigma_{i=1}^k V_i$, then it can be shown that $K_w = V/(V+1)$.

entry and not cannibalize other brands sold by the firm. If, on the other hand, the market is brand specific, the firm should introduce into the market new brands rather than forms of existing brands.

The implications of the market structure are also important for advertising strategy. If a market is brand specific, one should try to advertise an overall brand concept to induce trial of a brand. On the other hand, if the market is form specific, one needs to advertise the brand within each form type.

The identification of the structure of the market is one of the important contributions of the Hendry system. Research is still needed to validate the structures. Further, the behavioral model underlying the Hendry partitioning is a two-stage choice model in which stage 1 is select form (or brand), and stage 2 is select brand (or form). Does their statistical procedure recover the appropriate structures if the choice processes are different?

In addition to the market structure, preference distributions are also studied. Based on the observed distribution for a market, attempts are made to set advertising budgets and to determine the categories in which to introduce new brands. The preference distribution can be interpreted as the joint distribution of the probability of buying k brands, that is, $f(P_1, \ldots, P_k)$ where P_i is the probability of buying brand i.

To set advertising budgets, one needs to know the shape of the preference distribution for a given brand. Advertising dollars have a dominant effect on consumers with a high preference for a brand, moderate influence on consumers with a moderate preference for a brand, a very limited effect on people with low brand preference [38, p. 24]. From empirical data, surveys, or panels, it becomes possible to analyze the percentage of people with high, medium, and low preference for a given brand.

Preference is defined as the percentage of the brand bought by each household.[6] Unfortunately, there are several problems with this theory. First, there is no evidence that buying a given brand is due to preference. Private labels often have loyal users but low preference. Second, there is no evidence that this theory of how advertising works is true. However, given this theory and data on preference, it is possible to derive the optimal advertising expenditure for a brand [38, p. 26].[7]

To identify which market to introduce a new product into, one again looks at the preference distribution. If a market has a high percentage of customers with strong preferences for different brands, then it is not a very good market into which to introduce a new brand. If on the other hand

---

[6]It should be noted that the probability of buying is not the same as preference, though it is not clear how preference differs from the probability of buying in the Hendry system.

[7]It may be that the Hendry system has more specific statements about how advertising is determined. Based on the article in the book *Speaking of Hendry*, the theory is very sketchy and it is difficult to understand exactly why it holds.

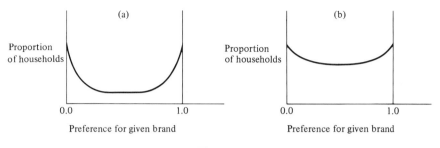

Figure 3

there are many customers with moderate preferences for the brands, a new brand is likely to do well.

If brands in a market have the preference distribution given in Figure 3a, then a new brand is unlikely to do well because customers have strong preferences. If brands have the preference distribution given in Figure 3b, then a new brand will do well because consumers do not have strong preferences for existing brands.

Evaluation of Hendry

Kalwani and Morrison state that the Hendry system has developed important marketing implications from stochastic brand choice models. Researchers need to study two questions:

1. Why should K_w be constant and why should K_w be the basis for partitioning markets?
2. What empirical evidence is there that the strategies developed by Hendry work?

Almost all of the empirical statements about the success of the Hendry system are the glowing testimonials from industry researchers, but no systematic evaluation of the system has appeared.

In spite of all of its limitations, the Hendry system raises many interesting questions. Obviously, more research is needed to evaluate the importance of these concepts. It is possible that the Hendry system has discovered laws of behavior. Academic researchers should attempt to validate the results, and if they are validated, determine why behavior follows these laws.

Future Research

Recently, there have been a number of interesting advances in SBC modeling mainly due to the success of the Hendry system. It offers academic researchers an interesting theory of behavior—that brand switching is maximized within the switching segments. The empirical fits to brand switching matrices are surprisingly good, given only market shares. Ehrenberg also posits similar relationships using brand duplication to study regularity of purchase behavior. Further empirical and theoretical research into these topics is needed so that these theories can be rigorously tested. If they are not falsified, then they offer brand managers of packaged goods products a useful perspective from which to evaluate their marketing efforts.

The other area in which more research is needed is the incorporation of marketing variables into SBC and PI models. Most of the research has tended to assume that marketing influences are constant and has then attempted to study brand choice behavior. Can researchers really make this assumption? Based on the empirical work of Shoemaker and Shoaf discussed earlier, it does not appear that these assumptions are valid. To be useful to managers, stochastic models need to incorporate major marketing factors influencing behavior.

Electronic point-of-purchase scanning is going to be a major source of consumer diary data in the future. Such problems as nonreporting and poor price data will be reduced. This revolution in data collection should give stochastic modelers the opportunity to have better information about the levels of each marketing variable. This, in turn, should help the modeler incorporate the effects of these variables into stochastic models.

Conclusion

This chapter has attempted to study the main directions of stochastic brand choice and purchase incidence models. Several interesting articles have recently appeared that have caused renewed interest in these models. The major problem from the manager's perspective has been that both SBC and PI models have failed to relate marketing tactics (advertising, dealing, etc.) to purchase behavior. In addition, questions about the order of purchasing behavior to determine whether there is purchase feedback have not been answered satisfactorily. It is hoped that future research can provide answers to some of these important questions.

References

1. Ahl, D. H. "New Product Forecasting Using Consumer Panels," *Journal of Marketing Research* 7, 160–167 (1970).
2. Bass, F. M. "The Theory of Stochastic Preference and Brand Switching," *Journal of Marketing Research* 11, 1–20 (1974).
3. Bass, F. M., Jeuland, A. P., and Wright, J. P. "A Multibrand Stochastic Model Compounding Heterogeneous Erlang Timing and Multinomial Choice Processes," *Operations Research* 28, 255–277 (1980).
4. Bemmaor, A. "Stochastic Models of Product Usage and Brand Choice: An Empirical Study," unpublished Ph.D. thesis, Purdue University, 1978.

5. Blattberg, R., and Sen, S. "An Evaluation of the Application of Minimum Chi-Square Procedures to Stochastic Models of Brand Choice," *Journal of Marketing Research* 10, 421–427 (1973).

6. Blattberg, R., and Sen, S. "A Bayesian Technique to Discriminate Between Stochastic Models of Brand Choice," *Management Science* 21, 682–696 (1975).

7. Blattberg, R., and Sen, S. "Market Segments and Stochastic Brand Choice Models," *Journal of Marketing Research* 13, 34–45 (1976).

8. Blattberg, R. C., and Jeuland, A. P. "A Micro-Modeling Approach to Determine the Advertising-Sales Relationship," Working Paper, University of Chicago, March 1979.

9. "Description of NPD Volume-Oriented Brand-Mix Shifting System," unpublished paper (Floral Park, New York: NPD Research).

10. Ehrenberg, A. S. C. "The Pattern of Consumer Purchases," *Applied Statistics* 8, 26–46 (1959).

11. Ehrenberg, A. S. C. *Repeat-Buying.* Amsterdam: North-Holland, 1972.

12. Eskin, G. J. "Dynamic Forecasts of New Product Demand Using a Depth of Repeat Model," *Journal of Marketing Research* 10, 115–127 (1973).

13. Frank, R. E., "Brand Choice as a Probability Process," *Journal of Business* 32, 43–56 (1962).

14. Fourt, L. A., and Woodlock, J. W. "Early Prediction of Market Success for New Grocery Products," *Journal of Marketing* 25, 31–38 (1960).

15. Givon, M., and Horsky, D. "Application of a Composite Stochastic Model of Brand Choice," *Journal of Marketing Research* 16, 258–267 (1979).

16. Harary, F., and Lipstein, B. "The Dynamics of Brand Loyalty: A Markovian Approach," *Operations Research* 10, 19–40 (1962).

17. Herniter, J. D., and Magee, J. F. "Customer Behavior as a Markov Process," *Operations Research* 9, 105–122 (1961).

18. Herniter, J. D. "A Probabilistic Market Model of Purchase Timing and Brand Selection," *Management Science* 18, 102–113 (1971).

19. Herniter, J. D. "An Entropy Model of Brand Purchase Behavior," *Journal of Marketing Research* 10, 361–375 (1973).

20. Hinkle, C. L. "Temporary Price Reductions as an Element of Marketing Strategy," unpublished Ph.D. thesis, Harvard Graduate School of Business Administration, 1964.

21. Jeuland, A. P. "The Interaction Effect of Preference and Availability on Brand-Switching and Market Share," *Management Science* 953–965 (1979).

22. Jones, J. M., "A Dual-Effect Model of Brand Choice," *Journal of Marketing Research* 7, 458–464 (1970).

23. Kalwani, M. V., and Morrison, D. G. "A Parsimonious Description of the Hendry System," *Management Science* 23, 467–477 (1977).

24. Kuehn, A. A. "An Analysis of the Dynamics of Consumer Behavior and Its Implications for Marketing Management, unpublished Ph.D. dissertation, Graduate School of Industrial Administration, Carnegie-Mellon University, 1968.

25. Kuehn, A. A., and Rohloff, A. C. "Consumer Response to Promotions," in P. Robinson (ed.), *Promotional Decisions Using Mathematical Models.* Boston: Allyn and Bacon, 1967.

26. Lilien, G. L. "A Modified Linear Learning Model of Buyer Behavior," *Management Science* 20, 1027–1036 (1974).

27. Lipstein, B. "A Mathematical Model of Consumer Behavior," *Journal of Marketing Research* 2, 259–265 (1965).
28. MacLachlan, D. "A Model of Intermediate Market Response," *Journal of Marketing Research* 9, 378–384 (1972).
29. Maffai, R. B. "Brand Preference and Simple Markov Processes," *Operations Research* 8, 210–218 (1960).
30. Maffai, R. B. "Advertising Effectiveness, Brand Switching, and Market Dynamics," *Journal of Industrial Economics* 9, 119–131 (1961).
31. Massy, W. F. "Forecasting Demand for a New Convenience Product," *Journal of Marketing Research* 6, 405–413 (1969).
32. Massy, W. F., Montgomery, D. B., and Morrison, D. G. *Stochastic Models of Buying Behavior.* Cambridge, Massachusetts: MIT Press, 1970.
33. Montgomery, D. B. "A Stochastic Response Model with Application to Brand Choice," *Management Science* 15, 323–337 (1969).
34. Montgomery, D. B., and Ryans, A. B. "Stochastic Models of Consumer Choice Behavior," in S. Ward and T. Robertson (eds.), *Consumer Behavior.* Englewood Cliffs, New Jersey: Prentice-Hall, 1973.
35. Morrison, D. G. "Testing Brand Switching Models," *Journal of Marketing Research* 3, 401–409 (1966).
36. Parfitt, J. H., and Collins, B. J. K. "Use of Consumer Panels for Brand Share Prediction," *Journal of Marketing Research* 5, 131–145 (1968).
37. Shoemaker, R. W., and Shoaf, F. R. "Repeat Rates of Deal Purchases," *Journal of Advertising Research* 17, 47–53 (1977).
38. *Speaking of Hendry*, The Hendry Corporation, 1976.
39. Telser, L. G. "Advertising and Cigarettes," *Journal of Political Economy* 60, 471–499 (1962).
40. Telser, L. G. "The Demand for Branded Goods as Estimated from Consumer Panel Data," *Review of Economics and Statistics* 44, 300–324 (1962).
41. Zufryden, F. S. "An Empirical Evaluation of a Composite Heterogeneous Model of Brand Choice and Purchase Timing," *Management Science* 24, 761–773 (1978).

10

Marketing Oriented Strategic Planning Models*

Yoram Wind

Marketing decision models have tended to focus on tactical marketing decisions concerning a limited number of marketing variables. Whereas some progress has been made in the development and utilization of more sophisticated and accurate models of this type, marketing modeling has had little impact on the strategic planning efforts of the firm. Planning in the more strategically oriented firms is often a separate corporate function, with few formal links to marketing. Marketing models, when utilized, tend to be employed by or for brand managers and rarely by the planners and top corporate management. Critical corporate decisions such as mergers and acquisitions tend to be made primarily on financial considerations with little attention to marketing inputs. Product portfolio models such as the Boston Consulting Group growth/share matrix ignore basic marketing considerations, such as the possible negative correlation between share and profit[1] and the different response elasticities to different marketing strategies of the various market segments.[2]

The marketing and planning literature accurately reflects this situation. The major strategic planning texts [e.g., 6, 36, 63] focus primarily on financial and organizational considerations. Their marketing discussion is generally limited, and at the level of an introductory marketing text with

*The author wishes to thank Professors Neil Beckwith, George Day, Vijay Mahajan, and Cynthia Fraser for their helpful comments.

[1]Whenever the profitability of a business is derived from a relatively small fraction of its customers (the 20/80 case) and the structure of its joint cost allows it, the company could improve its profitability by reducing its market share (dropping the less profitable customers).

[2]For a detailed discussion of the Boston Consulting Group product portfolio approach, see Abel and Hammond [1]. A critical evaluation of this approach and its comparison to other product portfolio models is given by Wind [73].

little attention to key marketing concepts and tools. Even the more technically oriented planning texts, such as the recent Naylor book on corporate planning models [47], and the articles appearing in *Planning Review*, the journal of the Society for Corporate Planning (as reflected, for example, in the recent collection by Allio and Pennington [4]), do not utilize the rich marketing concepts and tools which can be of enormous value in strategic planning. Naylor, for example, restricts his marketing discussion to some forecasting methods, a few examples of econometric demand models, and a policy simulation model.

The strategic planning literature neglect of marketing has not been one sided. The marketing literature has also ignored the needs of strategic planning. Most of the marketing modeling work has been at the tactical level. Furthermore, in a 1976 survey of 346 corporations, Naylor [47, p. 12] found that only 23% of the marketing respondents were very interested in the development of corporate modeling, compared with 30% of top management, 67% of planning, and 54% of finance. Similarly, one of every three marketing respondents indicated no interest in or indifference to corporate modeling, compared with only 9% of top management, 5% of planning, and 8% of the finance people. The few efforts at developing methods, concepts, and findings of relevance for strategic planning have been oversimplistic and often of questionable validity. Even the most grandiose marketing oriented strategic efforts—that of the PIMS (Profit Impact of Market Strategy) project [e.g., 15, 25, 58]—have been restricted by antiquated methodology (overreliance on cross tabulations and simplistic regression analyses).

The premise of this chapter is that marketing can and should be a dominant force in guiding corporate strategic planning efforts at both the corporate and strategic business units (SBU) levels. To realize such a potential, marketing needs to reallocate its research efforts; brighter scholars and practitioners should change their focus from the narrow tactical (and often trivial) modeling efforts to more complex modeling of marketing systems from a corporate management perspective. Such infusion of quantitative modeling efforts into the strategic marketing decision process would deemphasize the role of "war stories" and case discussion of strategies and offer management a rigorous and workable set of strategic models as input and guide to the critical strategic planning efforts of the firm.

In approaching this goal, we in marketing do not start from scratch. Developments in marketing modeling and measurement approaches provide a solid foundation for strategic modeling. The increasing concern and interest in strategic marketing issues as reflected in planning oriented marketing textbooks (such as that of Boyd and Massy [13] and of Hughes [33]), the growing interest in new product development systems [50], the recent focus on product portfolio analysis [20, 66], and the substantive findings of the PIMS project (see, for example Schoeffler [57] and other PIMS letters) offer some of the necessary substantive information and concepts required for strategic planning.

The objectives of this chapter are to synthesize our knowledge in these areas and, in particular, to focus on the following areas.

1. The key marketing concepts of relevance to strategic planning.
2. The three major types of strategic models.
   (a) models of systems of activities (such as marketing planning, new product development, and mergers and acquisitions);
   (b) models for resource allocation among products, markets, and distribution outlets; and
   (c) response models, which focus on response of specific segments to marketing programs and not just on a single marketing variable.
3. Some of the implementation problems and, in particular, the organizational implications of developing and utilizing marketing oriented strategic planning models.
4. Some of the needed conceptual and methodological developments.

Marketing Concepts for Strategic Planning

The design and implementation of strategic planning models require adherence to the concepts and techniques that govern all planning activities [2, 6] as well as some idiosyncratic marketing concepts and methods.

The general planning concepts include acceptable concepts such as management's need to focus on nonprogrammed areas and establish procedures for programmed areas [62]; the need to develop contingency plans; viewing planning as a continuous process, adaptable to changing conditions; avoiding suboptimization; obtaining top management and operating management involvement and commitment; engaging in both long-term and short-term planning; and the need to plan the planning process.

In addition to these and similar planning concepts, any strategic planning effort should include the following marketing concepts:

Following an Adaptive Experimentation Approach. In developing marketing strategy, it is important to consider an adaptive experimentation approach [3, 40]. To follow this approach it is necessary to design not a single strategy, but rather a *number* of marketing strategies based on an experimental design. The experimental results are used to update a sales response model, and marketing strategies are chosen to maximize the long-term objectives of the firm (for example, expected profit). To date, adaptive experimentation has been applied primarily to promotional spending and to a limited extent to other tactical decisions such as different message design, prices, and distribution outlets. The concept, however, is equally applicable to marketing strategies. Consider, for example, the benefit for management of knowing the market response function to alternative positioning strategies aimed at different market segments. Whereas adaptive experimentation is conceptually the *best* approach to assure the achievement of long-run optimal strategies, it can be costly and requires considerable implementation effort. Hence, in selecting the strategies to be experimented with, an explicit analysis of the cost versus value of information should be undertaken.

Application of the Market Segmentation Philosophy. Consistent with the market orientation, any product/service offering should be geared toward the satisfaction of the needs of specific target market segments; that is, products should not be developed and marketed for the "total market" but rather should be designed to satisfy the needs of specific and identifiable segments.

Consistent with this philosophy is one of the major findings of the PIMS project (Schoeffler, undated), that a business's absolute and relative share of its served market—the specific segment of the total potential market (defined in terms of products, customers, or areas) in which the business actually competes—has a positive impact on its profits and net cash flow.

Application of the Marketing Concept of all Stakeholders. The survival and growth of any firm depends not only on its customers, but increasingly on a large number of stakeholders. These include government agencies, suppliers, competitors, consumer and other environmental groups, security analysts, and others with a stake in the future of the corporation. Design of corporate strategies requires understanding of the current and likely needs, attitudes, and behavior of these groups. A marketing approach to the understanding of these groups and the design of strategies to reach them are therefore essential components of modern strategic planning.

Search for and Implementation of a Strategy with a Differential Advantage. Corporate strategy should be designed to benefit from the firm's special competitive advantages and to focus on those strategy components that offer the firm a unique differential advantage as reflected, for example, in a unique product positioning.

The importance of a unique positioning (as one of the expressions of a strategy with a differential advantage) is clearly evident in the following findings from the PIMS project: "Quality, defined as the customers' evaluation of the business's product/service package as compared to that of competitors, has a generally favorable impact on all measures of financial performance" [57].

Encouraging Creativity. The generation of innovative product and marketing strategies requires strong emphasis on creativity and original thinking. Given the strong pressures for continuation of current strategies or the introduction of "me too" strategies, it is especially important to encourage the generation of new creative strategies.

Use of Appropriate Marketing Research Techniques. Most planning decisions require inputs on likely consumer needs, problems, and reactions to new product and marketing concepts, as well as information on likely changes in environmental conditions and competitive activities. In collecting, analyzing, and disseminating such information, appropriate research techniques should be used. Familiarity with multivariate statistical techniques is essential, and research programs that incorporate a number of research techniques are of special value.

Developing a "User-Oriented" Marketing Information System. Planning requires continuous inputs of market, competitive, and environmental conditions, as well as information on the performance of the firm's products and services. The volume of such inputs requires the design of a user-oriented information system, that is, a system that provides only relevant information in a form that is easy to comprehend and utilize.

System Models

System models, unlike typical marketing models (such as media selection, salesmen allocation to territories, or estimated sales and share of a new product), are not intended to offer a solution in terms of selection of a specific course of action from among a number of alternatives. Rather, they are designed to offer a framework for organizing a series of activities involving data collection, analysis, and dissemination; allocation and optimization modeling; and implementation procedures. System models range from the most comprehensive strategic planning models to relatively specific systems for design and development of new products, identification and selection of merger and acquisition candidates, and the identification of products that should be modified or deleted. These models provide the framework for organizing the activities and strategic decisions required to achieve the corporate long-term objectives, given alternative environmental scenarios and internal resources.

The value of such frameworks has long been recognized; they constitute the core of the formal strategic planning orientation. More recently, there have also been a number of studies that established explicitly the value of strategic planning. Consider the following examples.

A content analysis of successful and unsuccessful (in terms of return on equity and sales) firms in the food processing industry found that the less successful firms complained more about the environment and talked less about possible changes in it and less about their product/market portfolio and the direction in which they are going [12].

A study of Belgian firms found that firms with consistent product policy tended to outperform (in terms of average return on equity over six years) those having weak product policy [32].

Planning firms[3] in each of three industries—machinery, chemicals and drugs, and electronics—outperformed over a ten-year period (in terms of annual growth of sales, earnings per share, net income, and mean annual operating margin) nonplanning firms [35].

Based on acceptance of the value of strategic planning, the premise of this chapter is that strategic planning should be designed with a marketing orientation. In addition to the key modeling concepts for strategic planning discussed earlier, which should guide the design of corporate strategies,[4] a corporate strategic plan should incorporate a specific marketing program. This program should include a target portfolio of products/markets and distribution outlets, a specific positioning for the various products (by market segments), detailed product/service offerings at appropriate prices, and an associated advertising and promotion campaign.

Such a program should be integrated with the planning of the other business functions. Product decisions, for example, require inputs from finance, accounting, research and development (R&D), manufacturing, personnel, and top management. At the same time, product decisions affect all of these functions; hence, product/marketing planning requires strong and continuous coordination of the product/marketing planning function with the plans of the other business functions. Of special importance in this respect is the design of a new product development system as an operational link between marketing, R&D, production, finance, and personnel. The program should avoid the dominance of one function (whether marketing or R&D) and strive for a balanced and coordinated

---

[3]Karger and Malick [35] used a very restrictive definition of planning as (a) the presence of a written plan for the overall organization, for each division, and for each plant within each division with (b) the plan having at least a five-year horizon accompanied by a more detailed one- or two-year plan, (c) the written plan distributed to the involved executives, and (d) the CEO using the plan in marketing decisions.

[4]For a discussion of the integration of these concepts in other system models for (a) new product development, (b) product modification and deletion, and (c) mergers and acquisitions, see Wind [69, 71]. A more detailed discussion of the mergers and acquisitions model is also given by Wind [70].

operation that takes into account the relevant perspectives and expertise of the various functions and integrates them into a cohesive operational system that is tied into the corporate resource allocation system and budgetary procedure. The profit and resource requirements should be clearly stated and included as an integral part of any plan transmitted for corporate approval. In addition, product plans should include an explicit allocation of resources among products and markets over time.

The resulting system (*process and specific outputs*) should "fit" the unique characteristics of the strategic business unit and the firm. This required compatibility with the user organization has been defined by Schultz and Slevin [59] as "organizational validity," which together with the technical validity of the model (the model capability of providing some solution, often an optimal one, to the stated problem) increases the probability of having a successful model and outcomes. No planning system should be transferred directly from one company to another. The fact that a given system has proved successful in company X does not imply that it will be appropriate for company Y. Planning systems should be designed to fit the idiosyncratic characteristics of the given company— its management style, objectives, resources, and competitive advantages.

An Illustrative Marketing Planning Model

Figure 1 presents an illustrative marketing planning model[5] that has been applied in a number of cases and is based on seven interrelated phases:

1. determination of corporate mission, objectives, resources, and constraints;
2. monitoring of the current and anticipated (domestic and multinational) environment;
3. situation analysis;
4. market/product portfolio analysis and decisions;
5. generation of alternative marketing programs;
6. evaluation of alternative programs and selection of the "best" ones; and
7. organization for marketing action, implementation, and control.

The first three phases and the market/product portfolio analysis constitute the marketing activities that provide the necessary inputs to all the marketing activities of the firm. The decision part of the fourth phase and the content of the fifth and sixth stages are the set of unique product-marketing decisions. The process followed in phases 5–7, on the other hand, are common to all planning models. Some of the major features of the first six stages are briefly outlined next, whereas the seventh stage is discussed in the last section of this chapter.

---

[5]The model is fully developed by Wind [73]. It is also presented by Wind [71].

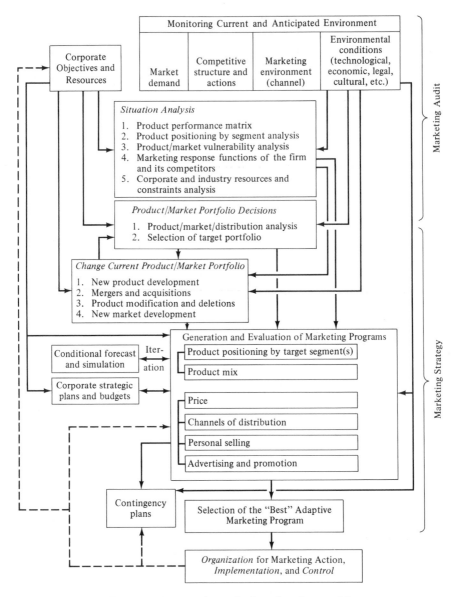

Figure 1. A strategic marketing planning model.

Setting Objectives. The determination of the corporate and marketing objectives requires two major steps: identification of the relevant objectives and determination of the relative importance of each.

The identification of corporate and strategic business unit objectives is a relatively easy task that can be performed in the context of a management brainstorming session. This can further be aided by the identification (using unstructured research approaches) of the criteria used by relevant publics (such as security analysts) and various management levels to evaluate corporate performance. The objectives should be consistent with the stated corporate mission, which in turn should not be viewed as a given constraint but rather should be subject to critical examination. The mission definition is critical for the determination of the acceptable boundaries for the firm's product/market portfolio and should be subjected, not unlike the objectives, to periodic examination.

Having identified a set of relevant corporate objectives and derived from them the appropriate marketing related objectives (criteria), the key question is, how important is each? To establish the relative importance of the various objectives, the relevant group(s) of managers can be asked to evaluate them directly or to respond to a conjoint analysis task [28]. In both of these cases the task should be done in a group setting allowing for an explicit discussion of any disagreement and leading to consensus or, in extreme conflicts, to the forcing of a specific point of view. The complexity of the process of establishing the relative importance of the various objectives is quite evident if one considers questions such as the following:

Who should be involved in the process?

If both "top down" and "bottom up" approaches are being used, what is the best iterative procedure, and how can conflicting objectives be reconciled?

In case of unresolvable conflicts, whose position should be accepted?

What should be the long versus short-term trade-off among objectives?

How often should objectives be reevaluated and how responsive should they be to changes in environmental conditions and performance measures?

The explicated criteria provide guidelines for the evaluation of all marketing decisions (ranging from the corporate product/market portfolio to specific brand decisions). The objectives are influenced not only by management preference structure but also by the corporate resources and corporate environment.

Monitoring the Environment. The monitoring of the relevant environment and projection of its trends are major inputs to all the marketing and corporate planning activities of the firm. In particular, four sets of environmental forces should be monitored:

1. market demand;
2. competitive structure and actions;
3. marketing (for example, channel) environment (including the power relation in the channel); and
4. technological, economic, social, cultural, and legal environment.

It is this last set of environmental conditions that are the most complex and difficult to monitor. Yet all planning activities require detailed input on the current and projected state of these environmental forces, their interrelationship (cross impact), direction and magnitude of change, and likely effect on the firm's operations.

Given the extremely large number of environmental factors and their complex interrelationship, effective planning calls for the identification of a relatively few environmental scenarios. These scenarios should be spelled out and include at least the extreme scenarios of disaster and most optimistic conditions and the continuation of the status quo. Having identified the key (manageable number of) scenarios, strategic corporate (and marketing) planners should take explicitly into account the likely occurrence of each scenario and assure that the accepted plan could be achieved under (adopted to) any scenario. In addition, the explication of the various scenarios provides the framework for the development of a series of contingency plans and the identification of the events that should trigger these activities. Whereas the scenarios are the culmination of environmental analysis, the collection, analysis, and projection of each environmental force can offer additional valuable inputs to the generation of marketing strategies for the base and contingency plans of the firm and the relevant SBUs.

Situation Analysis. Situation analysis is an essential part of any marketing planning procedure. It offers answers to questions "Where are we?" and "Where are we going, assuming no changes in our marketing strategies, competitive actions, or environmental conditions?" To provide answers to these questions a fivefold procedure is suggested, based on an analysis of the firm's current position and historical and projected trend.

1. *Product (business) performance.* A product performance matrix [74] can be utilized to assess the current and anticipated changes in the products' (and business's) sales, profits, and market share positions by market segment. Data on these or other performance measures consistent with management objectives are essential for both the continued *control* of product performance and input to the generation and evaluation of new strategies. In addition, to the extent that it is desirable to compare the product/business performance to some norms, PIMS data on PAR ROI reports [26] can be used to provide the following:

   An estimate of the normally expected rate of return for the business given its

   market attractiveness,
   competitive position,
   differentiation from competitors,

capital/production structure,
discretionary budget expenditures,
a comparison of the trend in actual ROI relative to PAR ROI, and
an indication of the sensitivity of the PAR rate of return of this
business to changes in each data input.

2. *Product positioning by market segment.* This analysis [67] can provide insights into the way various consumer segments, and other relevant publics, perceive and evaluate the firm's products vis-à-vis its competitors on the relevant determinant attributes. Understanding the current positioning (by segment) of the firm's products and the changes in it over time (in response to the competitive marketing activities) offers critical insight into the competitive position of the firm as perceived by relevant market segments. It can also identify product weaknesses, assess changes in competitive activities, and identify gaps in the current product offerings.

3. *Product vulnerability.* This analysis [68] attempts to supplement market share data by identifying the users' degree of positive attitudes toward the product. Users with negative attitudes are viewed as vulnerable to competitors, whereas nonusers with positive attitudes are potentially convertible to clients. The size of the vulnerable segments of the firm versus that of its competitors is an important indication of the strength of the firm's market franchise and its trend.

4. *The market response functions to the firm's marketing efforts.* Understanding the market response elasticities to advertising and other promotional and marketing activities is an essential input to the firm's decision how to allocate its marketing resources. In addition, if the current marketing activities are not effective, it can offer an incentive for the development of new marketing tools. Such analysis requires a well-organized information system and the implementation of straightforward econometric models. The assessment of the market response function can be further aided if management follows an explicit adaptive experimental program involving large changes in the type and range of marketing variables employed.

5. *Corporate and industry resources, constraints, strengths, and weaknesses.* Some of these factors have been included in the GE, McKinsey, and Shell portfolio analyses. Yet, to the extent that management uses a portfolio model that does not include all these variables, an explicit analysis of the following variables should be included as part of the firm's situation analysis.

   Corporate and industry technology and production facilities. Current technological strengths and weaknesses, trends in technological developments, the technological competitive advantages of the firm, and the production (facilities, personnel, and material) resources of the firm and its competitors.

Corporate and industry investments and financial resources. The cost of
entry to and exit from the industry, the importance of capital
investment and its sources, the rate, size, and type of assets, and
especially the current and potential liquid financial resources available to the firm and its competitors.

Corporate and industry management style and competitive profile.
Management style, capabilities, and competitive actions offer clues
to the likely internal receptivity to various courses of action. A
similar analysis of the firm's major competitors offers insights into
their likely competitive behavior, including likely response to competitive actions and the nature of such activities. The identification
and forecast of competitive activities is a critical yet mostly ignored
input to the strategic decisions of most businesses.

Corporate and industry marketing strengths and weaknesses. The size
and type of marketing resources and activities of the firm and its
competitors, for example, the nature and strength of the firm's
distribution system, corporate image, and advertising and sales
promotion clout.

The analysis of these factors is geared not only toward an understanding
of the firm's *current* strengths and weaknesses, but primarily toward the
identification of *future* strengths and weaknesses. In this context, these
analyses are closely tied to the environmental analyses since it is extremely
important, for example, to identify *future* competitors (who might employ
drastically new technology that today is *not* considered competitive).
Consider, for example, the watch industry prior to digital watches, or the
x-ray industry prior to computer tomography.

Product/Market Portfolio Analysis and Decisions. After the situation
analysis, the next step in the corporate marketing planning focuses on the
firm's portfolio of products/markets and distribution outlets. This phase
involves:

1. an analysis of the current product/market/distribution portfolio; and
2. the selection of the *desired* portfolio of products/markets/distribution
   outlets.

The analysis of the current product/market/distribution portfolio of the
firm follows one of two major approaches: factor listing or the framework
proposed by one of the product portfolio models. *Factor listing* takes into
consideration those factors used in making decisions on the width and
depth of the product mix and the associated marketing program required
to reach effectively the desired market segment(s). These factors include
corporate objectives, resources, current marketing strengths and weaknesses, current and potential demand estimates (reflecting customer inter-
ests, problems, and purchase plans), competitive offerings (type and range

of products offered by competitors and their market position), and other environmental factors.

The *product portfolio* models offer a more structured set of dimensions on which the current product portfolio of the firm can be analyzed. These dimensions include market share (as a measure of the business's strength), growth (as a measure of the business's attraction), and other specific dimensions, such as profitability, expected return, and risk. Most models tend to focus on two dimensions, company (product) capabilities and market attractiveness. Yet the specific dimensions vary from one portfolio model to another and include both models with a normative set of dimensions, such as the Boston Consulting Group's growth/share dimensions [20] or the risk/return dimensions of the financial portfolio model [66], and models such as the product line matrix approach [74] which allow management to identify dimensions they consider relevant. Figure 2 lists in schematic form and Table 1 summarizes some of the key characteristics of the major portfolio models. (For further discussion of these models, see Wind and Mahajan [78].)

Following a classification of the existing (and occasionally, potential new) products of the firm on the specific dimensions, the major managerial task is to decide on the desired target portfolio. A target portfolio should not be limited, however, to products and should ideally include target market segments and distribution outlets. Such a portfolio reflects management's objectives, desired direction of growth, and the interactions among products, markets, and distribution outlets. The specification of a target portfolio should be accompanied by specific guidelines for allocation of resources among the components of the portfolio.

Having decided on the desired target portfolio, to the extent that it differs from the current portfolio, the next step is an explicit evaluation of the most appropriate ways of reaching the target portfolio. These courses of action can include (a) the addition of new products, either through internal development or mergers/acquisitions; (b) the modification or (c) the deletion of existing products; and (d) changes in the allocation of resources to the various products (and markets). Decisions whether to invest/grow or to harvest/divest have significant implications for each element of marketing strategy as well as for the overall effort placed behind each product. In addition, since desired portfolios should focus on products, markets, and distribution outlets, the determination of desired changes in the current portfolio should encompass an examination of the internal and external (mergers and acquisitions) methods that can be employed to change (develop, add, or delete) markets served by the firm and distribution outlets employed to reach these markets.

Development and Evaluation of a Marketing Program. Having established corporate objectives, assessed the current and anticipated environment,

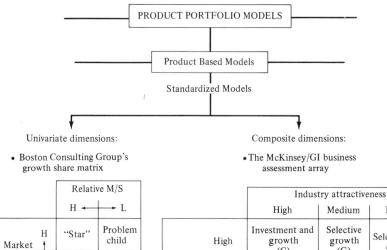

PRODUCT PORTFOLIO MODELS

Product Based Models

Standardized Models

Univariate dimensions:

- Boston Consulting Group's growth share matrix

		Relative M/S	
		H ← → L	
	H	"Star"	Problem child
Market Growth			
	L	Cash cow	Dog

Composite dimensions:

- The McKinsey/GI business assessment array

		Industry attractiveness		
		High	Medium	Low
Business Strengths	High	Investment and growth (C)	Selective growth (G)	Selectivity (Y)
	Medium	Selective growth (G)	Selectivity (Y)	Harvest (R)
	Low	Selectivity (Y)	Harvest (R)	Harvest (R)

- A. D. Little business profile matrix

		Stage of industry maturity			
		Embryonic	Growth	Mature	Aging
Competitive position	Dominant				
	Strong				
	Favorable				
	Tentative				
	Weak				

- Shell International directional policy matrix

		Prospects for sector profitability		
		Unattractive	Average	Attractive
Company's competitive capabilities	Weak	Disinvest	Phased withdrawal / Custodial	Double or quit
	Average	Phased withdrawal	Growth	Try harder
	Strong	Cash generation	Growth / Leader	Leader

Figure 2. Portfolio models.

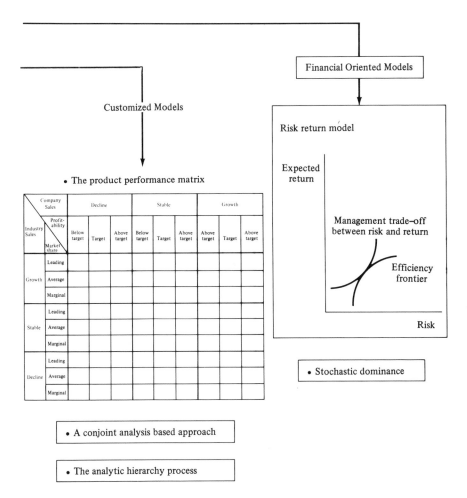

Figure 2 (*continued*)

completed the situation analyses, and made the basic decisions concerning the desired product/market/distribution portfolio, management is now ready to design its marketing program.

The program itself is based on two parts: (1) the product decisions, involving the determination of desired positioning by segment as well as the specific product mix to be offered; and (2) the interrelated marketing decisions of price, distribution, personal selling, advertising, and promotion. Since management can easily generate a very large number of possible product/marketing programs, it is essential first to assure the generation and evaluation of a *manageable* number of strategies that cover the entire range of possible strategies and are not limited to minor variations around the current strategies. There is no rule as to how many

Table 1. Key Characteristics of the Nine Portfolio Models

Model	Degree of adaptability	Specific dimensions
1. BCG growth/share matrix	None. A rigid framework	1. Relative market share (cash generation) 2. Market growth (cash use)
2. McKinley/G.E. business assessment array	Limited through the selection of variables used to determine the two composite dimensions	1. Industry attractiveness 2. Business strengths
3. A.D. Little business profile matrix	Same as McKinsey/G.E.	1. Competitive market position 2. Industry maturity
4. Shell International directional policy matrix	Same as McKinsey/G.E.	1. Profitability of market segment 2. Competitive position in the segment

strategies should be generated and evaluated. Given the typical time and money constraints, management patience, and the different resource requirements of the strategy generation and evaluation activities, one solution would be to generate as many diverse and creative strategies as possible, then group them into types of strategies and evaluate in depth only *types* of strategies. Alternatively, a two-step evaluation procedure can be developed, one for initial screening of the larger number of strategies and a followup detailed evaluation of the surviving strategies. Next, the evaluation of the strategies requires a quantification of the expected outcome of each program. This suggests the need to develop conditional forecasts of sales, profit, and market share (or other performance measures) for each product/marketing program. The program should be further related to the corporate strategic plans and budgets to assure their compatibility with the corporate objectives and resources. Furthermore, since the product/marketing plans are designed for the future, they should take explicitly into account alternative futures. Hence, a series of contingency plans should be designed for each reasonable future scenario.

Allocation rules	Comments
1. Allocation of resources among the four categories (move "cash" to "problem child," etc. 2. Consideration for product deletion (e.g., "dogs") 3. No explicit portfolio recommendation except with respect to the balance of cash flows	Widely used but conceptually questionable given the forcing of two dimensions, the unique operational definition, and lack of rules for determining a portfolio of "dogs," "stars," etc. No consideration of risk, no weighting of dimensions
In its simplistic use, it offers a slightly greater precision than BCG (nine cells vs four and better definition of dimensions). In its more sophisticated uses (as by G.E.), the classification of products on these two dimensions is used only as input to an explicit resource allocation model.	Forcing of two dimensions which might not be the appropriate ones. The empirical determination of the correlates of the two dimensions is superior to the BCG approach, yet, given the tailoring of factors to each industry, comparability across the industries is difficult. No consideration of risk
Same as McKinsey/G.E.	Same as McKinsey/G.E.
Same as McKinsey/G.E.	Same as McKinsey/G.E.

(*continued*)

The selection of a specific plan should be in accord with (1) the achievement of the corporate mission and the corporate and SBU's objectives, such as sales, profit, and market share levels; (2) corporate resources and differential advantages; (3) the most likely scenarios concerning the future; and (4) the "adaptive experimentation" philosophy.

Upon completion of the selection procedure, an evaluative mechanism should be designed to provide continuous feedback on the performance of the marketing program and supply the input for continuous adjustment and changes aimed at achieving the firm's long-term objectives.

Thus the program development and evaluation procedure requires three distinct sets of skills: (1) the creative skill to generate a large, diverse, and innovative set of alternative programs utilizing some of the information generated in earlier stages of planning process; (2) a managerial evaluative skill involving the ability to evaluate the various courses of action, select a course of action, and determine the size, allocation, and sources of required resources; and (3) an implementation skill to carry out effectively the selected course of action.

Table 1 (*continued*)

Model	Degree of adaptability	Specific dimensions
5. Product performance matrix	Considerable. The specific dimensions are selected by management	1. Industry sales 2. Product sales 3. Market share 4. Profitability all by market segment
6. Conjoint analysis based approach	Fully adaptable to management needs	No general dimensions. The dimensions determined by management judgment
7. Analytic hierarchy process	Fully adaptable to management needs	As with conjoint analysis, determined by management judgment
8. Risk/return model	None. A theory derived model	1. Expected return (mean) 2. Risk (variance)
9. Stochastic dominance	Same as risk/return model	The entire distribution of return

Allocation Models

Whereas system models specify the framework for organizing a set of activities required for designing and implementing the given strategic plans, many of the corporate strategic decisions involve a resource allocation decision, specifically, the determination how to allocate corporate resources among current product, current and new products, current markets, current and new markets, etc. Product portfolio models should offer guidelines for these resource allocation decisions. Yet, as seen in our brief discussion of the various portfolio models, most of them do not offer rigorous specific guidelines for resource allocations, and at best can only

Allocation rules	Comments
Same as BCG but based on projects results in response to alternative marketing strategies	Limited applications (major user: International Harvester), yet it offers the conceptual advantage of management-determined performance dimension and allocation of resources based on projected rather than historical performance. No weighting of dimensions.
Based on computer simulation which incorporates management utility functions (for the dimensions of the portfolio), and product performance data (supplemented to the extent needed by management perceptions of current and new products and businesses)	Limited applications. Very demanding of management time
Optimal allocation among all items of the portfolio (e.g., products, market segments) determined algorithmically	Limited applications. Conceptually and mathematically very appealing. Allows management to evaluate strategic assumptions and allocate resources across products, market segments, and distribution networks optimally under different scenarios of market and competitive conditions. Weighting of dimensions explicitly considered
Determination of optimal portfolio	Conceptually the most defensible, yet, difficult to operationalize for the product portfolio decision. Limited real-world applications
Same as risk/return	Same as risk/return

suggest the need for further examination of specific actions such as further investment to build share, or divestment. In contrast to the product portfolio models, allocation models such as mathematical programming, system dynamics, game theory, and computer simulations, although designed to give specific guidelines to resource allocation, have a number of serious limitations, since they tend to focus on

1. "optimization" of a single objective (in contrast to the frequent situation of multiple objectives, such as profitability, market share, and sales growth);
2. existing alternative courses of action (and not future courses of action

under alternative competitive conditions and environmental scenarios);[6]
3. a single decision maker (ignoring the fact that most corporate decisions involve a number of intracompany participants with diverse and often conflicting views and preferences);
4. tangible dimensions (ignoring the intangible but critically relevant dimensions that encompass the "political" setting of the organization); and
5. researcher-designed models (whether accurately reflecting the respondent's "true model" or not) without allowance for model modification to reflect the respondent's experience or other personal characteristics.

Given these limitations, many managers have been willing to live with the restrictive nature of the conventional resource allocation models when applied to relatively narrow tactical decisions, using judgments and organizational political considerations for the key strategic decisions of the firm. Given the importance of correct resource allocation at the strategic level, it is desirable to formulate a different resource allocation model that is not subject to the above limitations. The analytical hierarchy process (AHP) is one such process and is briefly discussed next.

The Analytical Hierarchy Process

The analytical hierarchy modeling and measurement process [52, 53] is a recent addition to the various approaches used to determine the relative importance of a set of activities or criteria. The novel aspect and major distinction of this approach is that it structures any complex, multiperson, multicriterion, and multiperiod problem hierarchically. Using a method for scaling the weights of the elements in each level of the hierarchy with respect to an element (for example, criterion) of the next higher level, a matrix of pairwise comparisons of the activities can be constructed where the entries indicate the strength with which one element dominates another with respect to a given criterion.

This scaling formulation is translated into a largest eigenvalue problem that results in a normalized and unique vector of weights for each level of the hierarchy (always with respect to the criterion in the next level), which in turn (by a principle of hierarchical composition) by means of a series of multiplications results in a single composite vector of weights for the entire hierarchy. This vector measures the relative priority of all entities at the lowest level that enables the accomplishment of the highest objective of the heirarchy. These relative priority weights can provide the guidelines for

---

[6]Some simulations do overcome this limitation; see, for example, Schultz and Dodson [60].

the allocation of resources among the entities at the lower levels of the hierarchy. When a hierarchy is designed to reflect likely environment scenarios, corporate objectives, and alternative product, market, and distribution options, the analytic hierarchy process (AHP) could provide a framework and methodology for the determination of the firm's target product/market/distribution portfolio, and resource allocation among the components of the portfolio.[7]

The basic premise of the analytic hierarchy process is that measurement evolves out of comparisons, particularly pairwise comparisons. Let us suppose that we have n objects $A_1, \ldots, A_n$ whose vector of corresponding weights $w = (w_1, \ldots, w_n)$ is known. Let us form the matrix of pairwise comparisons of weights

$$
A = \begin{array}{c} A_1 \\ \vdots \\ A_n \end{array}
\begin{array}{ccc} A_1 & \cdots & A_n \end{array}
\left(\begin{array}{ccc} w_1/w_1 & \cdots & w_1/w_n \\ \vdots & & \vdots \\ w_n/w_1 & \cdots & w_n/w_n \end{array} \right).
$$

We note that we can recover the scale of weights $w_1, \ldots, w_n$ by multiplying A on the right by w, obtaining nw, and then solving the eigenvalue problem $Aw = nw$, which has a nontrivial solution since n is the largest eigenvalue of A. (The matrix A has unit rank; hence, all but one of its eigenvalues $\lambda_1, \ldots, \lambda_n$ are zero. Since

$$
\sum_{i=1}^{n} \lambda_n = \text{trace}(A) = n,
$$

n is the maximum eigenvalue.)

In general, we do now know the ratios w_i/w_j, but we may have estimates of them from data and experiments or even from experienced judges. We would elicit a judgment and automatically enter its reciprocal in the transpose position. In that case we have perturbations of A, which lead to perturbations in the eigenvalues of A. We can show that now we must solve the problem $Aw = \lambda_{\max} w$ to obtain an estimate of the weights w. Saaty [52] proved that $\lambda_{\max} \geq n$ always and that $(\lambda_{\max} - n)/(n - 1)$ serves as

---

[7]Note that the application of the AHP is only to the selection of a target portfolio and the allocation of resources among is components. It is not concerned, at this stage, with the identification of the current portfolio of the firm (the portfolio analysis part, which is at the core of the existing approaches to product portfolio such as the Boston Consulting Group's model).

a consistency index, which gives the departure from consistency in estimating the ratios w_i/w_j, with consistency (which is stronger than transitivity) holding if and only if $\lambda_{max} = n$. Consistency is defined by the relation between the entries of A: $a_{ij}a_{jk} = a_{ik}$, which means that if we have n entries that form a spanning tree, the remainder of the matrix can then be generated from them. In the AHP approach to measurement, inconsistency is admissible provided one can specify its effect on the final results.

To provide numerical judgments in making pairwise comparisons, Saaty [53] developed a reliable and workable scale.[8] The scale assumes that the elements involved in any comparison are of the same order of magnitude; that is, their relative weights do not differ by more than 9. If they do, they are separated into different clusters. The nine-point scale used in typical analytical hierarchy studes is presented in Table 2.

With the scale, a pairwise comparison reciprocal matrix is used to compare the relative contribution of the elements in each level of the

Table 2

Intensity of importance	Definition	Explanation
1	Equal importance	Two activities contribute equally to the specific objective.
3	Weak importance of one over another	Experience and judgment slightly favor one activity over another.
5	Essential or strong importance	Experience and judgment strongly favor one activity over another.
7	Demonstrated importance	An activity is strongly favored and its dominance is demonstrated in practice.
9	Absolute importance	The evidence favoring one activity over another is of the highest possible order of affirmation.
2, 4, 6, 8	Intermediate values between the two adjacent judgments	When compromise is needed
Reciprocals of above nonzero	If activity i has one of the above nonzero numbers assigned to it when compared with activity j, then j has the reciprocal value when compared with i.	

---

[8] For a discussion of the specific scale used and its justification, see Saaty [53].

hierarchy to an element in the adjacent upper level. The principal eigenvector of this matrix is derived and weighted by the priority of the property with respect to which the comparison is made. That weight is obtained by comparing the properties among themselves as to their contribution to the criteria of a still higher level. The weighted eigenvectors can now be added componentwise to obtain an overall weight or priority of the contribution of each element to the entire hierarchy.

This process of principal eigenvector extraction and hierarchical weighting and composition leads to a summary unidimensional scale of the priorities of the elements in any level of the hierarchy. The resulting priorities represent the intensity of the respondent's judgmental perception of the relative importance of the elements represented in the hierarchy considering the importance of and trade-offs among the criteria.

The major attractive features of the AHP as the conceptual and measurement approach for the determination of the firm target portfolio and allocation of resources within it are

- a flexible formulation of the hierarchy reflecting management value systems.

- a flexible hierarchy that can incorporate *any* objectives (of varying units of measurement) and *any* courses of action (current and innovative as well as competing and complementary activities) under *any* set of environmental scenarios;

- a measurement procedure based on the relevant managers' perceived relationship among the various forces, actors, actions, and personal and organizational objectives;

- a built-in extension to incorporate the judgments of any number of decision makers and to resolve conflicting views among them [23]; and

- a flexible *process* allowing for iteration in both the structure of the problem (for example, alternative hierarchies) and judgments.

To understand the application of the AHP to the resource allocation problem, consider the following simplified illustration, which is based on an actual application of the AHP in a large insurance company to the selection of a desired target portfolio of products/markets and distribution outlets, and allocation of resources among the portfolio's components.[9]

A hierarchy was developed jointly with the company president and is presented in a disguised form in Figure 3. This hierarchy was based on three major levels.

---

[9]This application is borrowed from Wind and Gross [76], and is based on a project conducted jointly with Thomas L. Saaty.

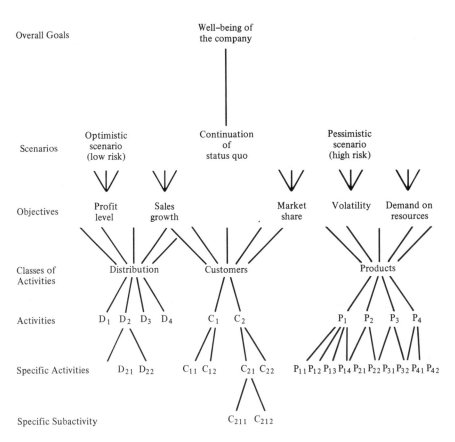

Figure 3. A disguised analytical hierarchy for the selection of the target product/market/distribution portfolio for Colonial Penn Insurance Company.

1. The *environmental scenarios*, expressed as three summary scenarios reflecting
   an optimistic environment (low-risk and potentially high-return environmental conditions),
   continuation of the status quo, and
   a pessimistic scenario (high-risk and potentially low-return environmental conditions).

2. *Corporate objectives*—the criteria for the evaluation of the various courses of action. Five objectives were identified:
   profit level,
   sales growth,
   market share,
   volatility, and
   demand on resources.

3. The *courses of actions—activities*. These include the three sets of products, markets, and distribution outlets but went into considerably greater specificity of potential activities, including various new distribution outlets not currently used by the firm, new market segments, and specific new product activities.

Given the sensitive nature of information on the firm's plans for allocation of its resources among alternative courses of action, the actual options are disguised and referred to by letters and numbers that do not correspond in any order to the items listed above.

Having selected the hierarchical structure outline in Figure 3, the president evaluated all pairwise comparisons using the nine-point scale discussed earlier. These evaluations take the form of reciprocal matrices of the components of each level against the items in the level above. Consider, for example, the evaluation of the three major sets of activities against the objectives. This involved five pairwise matrices of the importance of products, custom, and distribution with respect to each of the five objectives. One of these five pairwise matrices is illustrated in Table 3.

In this case, the president judged distribution to be of strong importance (5) over product in leading to the achievement of the firm's target profit level, but somewhat less important when compared to customers (4). In evaluating customers versus products, the president judged customers to be less important than products (3). Given the three judgments, the reciprocals were added and the president continued with the pairwise comparison tasks. These tasks included the evaluation of

scenarios against the overall objective of the firm,

objectives against each scenario,

the class of activities (and subactivities) against each of the objectives, and

the cross-impact evaluation of the likely occurrence and impact of each component given each of the other components at the same level of the hierarchy.

These data provided the input to the eigenvalue analysis [52], and a resulting partial hierarchy is presented in Figure 4.

Table 3

Profit level	Products	Customers	Distribution
Products	1	$\frac{1}{3}$	$\frac{1}{5}$
Customers	3	1	$\frac{1}{4}$
Distribution	5	4	1

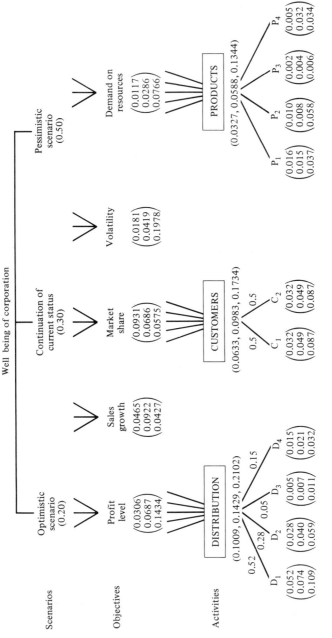

Figure 4. An analytic hierarchy of the products/customers/distribution portfolio of an insurance firm.

An examination of this figure suggests explicit rules for allocating the firm's resources in development of products, markets, and distribution vehicles under three alternative scenarios. In the disguised example presented in Figure 4, the president has a strong preference for the development of distribution outlets. In fact, the allocation of the developmental resources of the firm under this example should be 0.44 to the development of new distribution outlets, 0.34 to the development of new markets, and 0.22 to the developments of new products. This allocation rule is based on allocating resources in proportion to the priorities. Other resource allocation rules, such as the ratio of priorities (benefits) to costs, can also be used. The output as presented in Figure 4 provides a significant amount of information, such as

The perceived likelihood of occurrence of the three scenarios:
    optimistic,   0.2,
    status quo,   0.3,
    pessimistic,   0.5.
The relative importance of the five objectives.
    profit level,   0.24,
    sales growth,   0.18,
    market share,   0.21,
    volatility,   0.25,
    demand on resources,   0.11.
The relative importance of the various objectives varies considerably by the anticipated scenario:
    Sales growth is twice as important under continuation of the status quo than the other two scenarios (0.92 versus 0.045 and 0.042).
    Market share is most important under an optimistic scenario (0.93 versus 0.68 and 0.057).
    Profit level, volatility, and demand on resources are most important under pessimistic scenarios.

A sensitivity analysis was conducted using alternative hierarchical formulations, as well as different assumptions concerning the likely occurrence of the various scenarios. These analyses resulted in a *range of priorities*. This range, which suggested an allocation of resources significantly different from the firm's current resource allocation pattern, has led the president to reevaluate his firm's activities and to assign task forces to those aspects of the portfolio (as suggested by the detailed priorities of Figure 4) that have not received the attention and resources they deserve.

These task forces used the AHP to clarify their one preference structure and evaluate a larger number of alternative courses of action. The judgments of the task force were reached in a number of group sessions, which provided the vehicle for open discussion among the members on assumptions, information, and preferences leading to the identification and resolution of a number of conflicts.

Although other procedures, such as conjoint analysis, can be and have been used to assess the relative importance of management's objectives [29], conjoint analysis, to date, has not been used on problems such as the resource allocation problem of the firm. For this class of problem, the AHP is more appropriate given the type of output it generates and its track record in allocating the transportation resources of the Sudan [52], electricity to industry in case of shortage [56], and research funds of the electric power research institute [55].

Both AHP and conjoint analysis can be used in a number of evaluative areas, and two such comparative studies are currently being conducted by the author with respect to the determination of the relative importance of objectives and consumer and management evaluation of new products.

Multivariable and Segment Response Models

The analytical hierarchy process has been found, in the few cases in which it has been applied, to be a useful way of establishing management's preference for allocation of resources among new and existing products, markets, and distribution outlets. This approach can be supplemented for existing products and markets with the more conventional market response models. Market response models are at the core of most management science marketing models. These response models, however, tend to be designed in most cases for a single product, focus on a single marketing variable (for example, level of advertising or price), and assess the total market response to it. From a strategic point of view, response models should be extended to have a more *realistic* coverage.

The Desired Coverage of Strategic Response Models

Strategically relevant response models should cover for each product in the firm's product portfolio the following features.

All Relevant Marketing Variables. Response functions should be generated in response to all relevant marketing variables (defined in terms of *specific* type of activities, level, and scheduling of effort) and their interactions. This requires one of two research procedures. The first is econometric modeling of the response to the firm marketing variables and the competitive actions. The major obstacle to the implementation of this approach is data availability, which encompasses the relatively simple situation in which data exist or can be generated, and the problem is the collection and organization of the data, as well as the more serious case in which a certain type of data cannot be obtained or certain variables are never present independent of some other variables (as in the case of a food company that, in order to protect its market share, never had a price change without an accompanying increase in advertising or promotional activities, hence restricting the ability to assess the price sensitivity to its products). The second procedure is an adaptive experimental approach using experimental designs such as Latin square or Greco-Latin square designs to measure the market response to a number of marketing variables.

Some of the more sophisticated market response models do include a number of marketing mix variables and to a limited extent, their interaction and carry-over effects. Yet most of the current econometric response modeling efforts, including most of the new product forecasting models such as DEMON [17] NEWS [9], Tracker [11], Sprinter [65], and the N. W. Ayer model [19], as well as the marketing decision models such as BRANDAID [41, 42], do not include all marketing mix variables and the response by market segments.

Response of Various Market Segments. Given the heterogeneity of all markets, effective control of marketing performance and design of a new marketing strategy require the development of market response data by relevant market segments. The segment response data should encompass, to the extent necessary, response by geographical location, distribution outlets, and any other relevant market groupings.

Projected Response Under Alternative Environmental and Competitive Scenarios. Strategic perspective requires the development of *projected* response functions (including the assessment of market potential). Historical response functions are by themselves of limited interest and their value is in providing one of the bases for projecting the likely response functions. Simple extrapolation of past response, although often very accurate for short-term projections (next-year sales can often be predicted quite accurately by a time series projection), is typically of limited value for long-term projections. This weakness of time series projections is due to the likelihood of changes in the environment, the competitive activities, the consumer needs, problems, expectations, lifestyles, etc. Hence, a critical feature of strategically relevant response functions is the development of response functions conditional on various environmental (including competitive) scenarios.

This requirement also has implications for the analysis of historical response data, which should incorporate, to the extent possible, an analysis of the effect of the various environmental forces (including competitive activities) on the response function.

Multiple Response Functions. The frequent reliance on a single sales response function is not sufficient as input to the strategic decisions of the firm. Response functions should incorporate all the performance measures used by the firm to evaluate the performance of their products and assess their product portfolio. Hence, if a firm uses the Boston Consulting Group portfolio approach, it should include at least two response functions—market share and product class sales. Given the conceptual advantages of letting management determine the portfolio dimensions (as suggested by the product performance matrix approach), one can envision a situation such as in the case of International Harvester, in which four response functions—product and industry sales, share, and profitability—should be developed.

Of these response functions the most complex is the profit function,[10] since it requires not only a revenue projection (under alternative scenarios) but also cost projections. Cost projections are often based on historical data and subjective adjustments. The unstable inflationary pressures and increased turbulences in the supply of resources (the energy shortage and dramatic price increases, raw material shortages, etc.) involve a heavy dependence on international political/economic considerations in determining both availability and price of critical resources. More attention should, therefore, be given to cost projections and many of the marketing research tools can and should be utilized to project the availability and cost of necessary materials and operation.

Explicit Examination of Multiproduct Interdependence. Market response functions, not unlike most marketing modeling, focus on individual product performance, ignoring to a large extent multiple product interdependencies. An explicit examination of this interdependency is essential for an accurate portfolio analysis and also serves as a basis for product line decisions. Of special interest in this context is cannibalization analysis and its use as an offensive or defensive strategy.

Multiple Brand Models. To the extent that data are available, developing market response functions for the firm *and* its major competitors and examining their interrelationships can provide greater insights into the market behavior.

Methodology of Response Modeling

The discussion so far has focused on the required content of strategically relevant market response models. Methodologically one can use a number of modeling approaches. The most common ones are econometric, stochastic, simulation, and a hybrid of these.

---

[10] Insights into profitability and its determinants can be gained from analysis of the PIMS data base. In addition to analysis of the profitability of the specific business versus other relevant business, the PIMS project has generated a number of general findings (their "Laws of the Marketplace") that explain 80% of the observed variance in operating results (across different businesses). These nine regularities (Schoeffler, undated) are summarized in Figure 5.

Econometric response models are the most frequently used approaches. Despite their conceptual attractiveness—"their implied world view," according to Parsons and Schultz [49]—and their ability to handle marketing decision variables (in linear and nonlinear forms and with carry-over and feedback effects) and appropriate testing procedures, most of the econometric response models are single-equation models with nonvarying parameter structures. Single equation models are quite naive since they assume a unidirectional flow of influence. Hence, the major development to watch for (which is of particular importance in the design of strategically oriented response models) is that of multiple-equation models. Lambin [39], Beckwith [10], and Clarke [18], for example, used multiple-equation models to estimate simultaneously market share relationships. Similarly, one should watch for the development of time-varying parameter structure, which allows for changes in the coefficients of the marketing variables and environmental forces. Such changes might be quite critical in long-term response models, which are more appropriate as inputs to the strategic decisions of the firm. A number of procedures for dealing with time-varying parameters have been proposed and implemented and are discussed by Parsons and Schultz [49].

Stochastic response models [e.g., 44], which do not incorporate marketing decision variables, are of limited value. There have been a few attempts to overcome this shortcoming [e.g., 43], but most practical applications of stochastic models have not used them as response functions.

Simulations have been used to model sales response processes for the last 20 years. The early work of Balderston and Hoggatt [7] was further expanded in the late sixties [e.g., 5, 31]. More recently simulations have been widely used to forecast the likely performance of new products in studies based on conjoint analysis [29, 77].

Hybrid approaches integrate the three approaches—econometric, stochastic and simulation—to the modeling of response functions into a research system. Such a hybrid system is most appropriate as input to strategic marketing decisions and has to be modeled for each situation separately to capitalize on the available data, precise modeling requirements, management-unique information needs, and management style.

Encouraging Developments

Recent years have witnessed a number of encouraging developments:

1. The use of log linear models to allocate resources among the various components of the marketing mix. Carroll, Green, and DeSarbo [16] have illustrated that if data are available on the various marketing variables and product/business performance, the regression coefficients of the log model measure accurately the market response to these variables and hence offer the optimal allocation rule among the

various marketing variables. When applied to pharmaceutical products the model was further improved when assessed separately for each medical specialty, allowing for allocation of resources among the market mix variables *and* market segments. A more general solution to the problem has been obtained by Bultez and Schultz [14].

2. The developments of flexible segmentation [69] and componential segmentation [26, 27], which emphasize the need to consider the market segmentation decision jointly with the positioning decision; that is, the selection of the "best" target segment for a given product positioning (and product features) or alternatively the selection of the best positioning (and product features) for reaching a segment selected a priori.

3. The use of optimization procedures to select the best product features and target market segments either in the context of Green's POSSE model [51] or in the more conventional context of market segmentation analysis [27].

4. The developments of methodology appropriate for hybrid research methods. Random coefficient regression [8, 64] is one such development, whereas market simulators such as SIMPLAN [78] incorporate sales and share forecasting models with econometric policy simulation models.

5. The increased use of marketing experimentation in the marketplace and in particular in simulated test markets.

6. Recent extensions of the concept of positioning from a narrow focus on product positioning to a broader scope of "corporate positioning." This extension [72] has been prompted by the increased importance of stakeholders other than consumers (such as government, media, and consumer advocates). In this context one of the primary responsibilities of top management is the selection of a desired corporate position for its various stakeholders and the employment of marketing strategies (at the corporate level) to implement and achieve the desired corporate positioning. Such an overall corporate positioning should also provide the guidelines for individual product positioning, since incongruent positioning might lead to dysfunctional results.

7. The increased attention to the development of strategically oriented marketing information systems that incorporate various data bases with appropriate modeling efforts.

8. The development of comprehensive models that integrate analysis of historical data with subjective management judgment, field experimentation, tracking, and adaptive controls. BRANDAID [41, 42] is an excellent example for such modeling effort for the brand manager level of decisions. Missing, however, are similar modeling efforts for the strategic decisions of the firm.

9. Increased methodological sophistication resulting in the development of more realistic econometric market response models, which can

1. Investment intensity generally produces a negative impact on percentage measures of profitability or net cash flow.

2. The higher the value added per employee, the higher the profitability.

3. The business's share of its served market (both absolute and relative to its three largest competitors) has a positive impact on profits and net cash flow.

4. Growth is generally favorable to dollar measures of profit, indifferent to percentage measures of profit, and negative to all measures of net cash flow.

5. Customer's evaluation of the product/service as compared to that of competitors has a generally favorable impact on all measures of financial performance.

6. New product introduction, R&D, and marketing efforts generally produce a positive effect on performance if that business has strong market position.

7. For business in mature and stable markets, vertical integration (that is, make rather than buy) generally impacts favorably on performance.

8. The rate of cost increases has complex impacts on profit and cash flow depending on how the business is positioned to pass along the increase to its customers and/or to absorb the high costs internally.

9. *Changes* of any of the above factors have frequently opposite effects to that of the factor itself.

Figure 5. Illustrative substantive strategic findings (based on PIMS data). *Source*: Schloeffler [57, pp. 3–4].

include, for example, nonlinear effects, carry-over effects, interactions, and time-varying parameter structures.

10. The development of generalizable substantive findings on the nature of market response measures and their determinants. Most notable of these efforts are the findings of the PIMS program. Figure 5 summarizes some of these key findings. The potential of the PIMS data in this respect is enormous and is most likely to add markedly to our understanding of the strategic determinants of corporate performance.

Implementation Issues

The design of marketing oriented strategic planning models is relatively straightforward. It is based on our current understanding of marketing concepts and methods, the nature of strategic planning, and the idiosyncratic characteristics of the firm and its management. The difficulties arise not so much in the design of these models but in their implementation. It is essential, therefore, to plan an implementation program. Such a program can be viewed as a special case of the general procedures a firm should follow in the implementation of any modeling efforts. (For a discussion of the general problems of the procedures for implementation of decision models, see Schultz and Henry [61]). The implementation of strategic marketing models does not raise new types of implementation factors. It does, however, add some complexities to three key aspects of the implementation program.

1. The design of a comprehensive marketing research program and associated marketing (and other relevant) information system that would

provide on an ongoing basis the needed information to the various strategic decisions.

Such an information system should provide the ongoing environmental monitoring function discussed in Figure 1 as well as the information for the situation analysis and marketing performance evaluations and the portfolio of the firm and its key competitors. The information system should include not only the collection of data but its evaluation (with respect to its reliability, accuracy, and pertinence), analysis, storage, and dissemination. For a discussion of marketing information systems for strategic planning, see Montgomery and Weinberg [46].

Such an information system, which is comprehensive in scope, requires inputs from various organizational units (for example, cost data and production schedules), is continuous in nature, likely to be expensive, difficult to implement, and politically sensitive. Yet having such continuous information is a critical component of any strategic planning system and should be integrated with the firm's control function.

2. The development and implementation of an organizational design and climate that would facilitate the implementation of marketing oriented strategic plans. Despite the growing interest in organization design and the increasing number of studies on this topic [24, 37], little is known about the organizational characteristics that are most conducive to the implementation of strategic planning models.

Organizational arrangements are often a major obstacle for the implementation of marketing oriented strategic planning. Consider, for example, the case in which an organization has both a V.P. for planning and a V.P. of marketing. If conflicts between the two arise, it is quite likely that the long-range strategic plan will not be marketing oriented. Similarly, if in a decentralized organization the divisions have strong planning units with no corporate planning department, it is likely that there will be no corporate level planning and that most efforts will be conducted by individual divisions, with little coordination among them.

An organizational design conducive to marketing oriented strategic planning should be planned with specific tasks, structure (and in particular incentive system), technology, and personnel consistent with the corporate idiosyncratic characteristics and the specific planning requirements. Since no single organizational design can fit all firms, no specific organizational solutions are presented, but two suggestions are offered for consideration: (a) there should be a combined corporate marketing/planning function;[11]

---

[11]If such an organizational arrangement is selected, the innovative V.P. position, which was suggested elsewhere [75] as one of the organizational solutions to the need to stimulate creative product/market development, can report to the senior V.P. in charge of planning and marketing.

(b) marketing research should report to corporate planning, since corporate planning is more likely than marketing (if the functions are separated) to allocate the research efforts to the areas of greatest potential for the firm's future.

Organizing a strategic planning system that is marketing oriented, encompasses all levels of operations, is acceptable by management, is consistent with the planning concepts discussed earlier, and is well integrated in the overall operations of the firm is not an easy task. It requires explicit design efforts and cannot be assumed to "happen" with the reorganization into the now popular strategic business unit structure.

3. Related to the organizational design issue is the critical question how to attract management attention to the strategic issues facing the firm. Despite lip service to the need for long-range strategic planning, the top executives in many firms are overly occupied with tactical day-to-day decisions, ignoring or paying too little attention to the strategic issues facing the firm. A possible solution to this problem is the design of a high-level organizational position (V.P. or even executive V.P.) for strategic planning. A complementary solution is to allocate a certain percentage of top management time (for example, a day a month, or ideally a day a week) for strategic planning.

Directions for Future Developments

Marketing oriented strategic planning models and concepts present a point of view concerning the role of an explicit research-based modeling approach in strategic corporate planning. Whether one adopts the specific models suggested here or other models is immaterial, as long as an effort is made to formalize the strategic planning process, design it following a marketing orientation, and fit it to the idiosyncratic characteristics of the firm.

The premise of this chapter is that a formal marketing approach to strategic corporate planning increases the likelihood of making the "right" decisions (that is, decisions that are at least consistent with management's objectives). The implementation of these or similar models however, requires answers to a number of key questions. Specifying these questions could help summarize some of the key dimensions of these models and suggest directions for future research.

No attempt is made to develop an exhaustive research agenda. Rather, the selected research areas are those viewed as relevant to practical management question *and* a conceptual or methodological challenge. These research areas are organized along the major components of the strategic marketing planning model (Figure 1) and include the following.[12]

---

[12] These needed developments were first identified in the context of product planning and discussed by Wind [10].

Determining the Relevant Objectives

How to Determine Corporate Objectives and Criteria. The identification of relevant objectives and criteria at all levels of management (for example, corporate, the strategic business unit, the product line, and individual product level) is essential for the determination of the boundaries for the product/market decisions of the firm and of the dimensions of the product/market portfolio, as well as of the criteria for evaluating alternative strategies. Yet there are a number of unanswered questions concerning how to identify the relevant product/market boundaries, what levels of abstraction to employ, how to identify and resolve conflicting objectives among the relevant management team, how to change objectives in response to changes in environmental conditions, etc. These and similar questions suggest the need to study the perceptions and preferences of corporate management. In fact, most of the research approaches used in consumer studies can be employed in the study of corporate executives.

How Explicit Should Management Objectives and Criteria Be? A number of approaches such as conjoint analysis and the AHP have been used successfully to explicate the relative importance of various criteria. Given the political/negotiative environment of many firms, there might be situations where not knowing the explicit criteria is preferable. What are these conditions, and how would lack of explicit criteria affect the "quality" of management decisions?

Marketing Audit

A relatively neglected concept is that of the marketing audit. The audit is a comprehensive periodic assessment of the firm's market environment, objectives, strategies, organization, and systems for the purpose of assessing the effectiveness and efficiency of the firm's marketing strategies, practices, and procedures [38]. This audit incorporates most of the components of the first four phases of the marketing planning model (Figure 1). The design and implementation of the marketing audit requires, however, the resolution of a number of key conceptual and methodological issues, including the following:

How to Design and Implement a Monitoring System and Forecasting Model(s) of Changes in Environmental Conditions and Firm Performance. Many current marketing information systems offer disjointed environmental information. Little effort is given to the development of a systematic scanning system of the relevant environment (consumption, competitive, technological, legal, economic, and so forth). Similarly, little attention has been given to the ongoing monitoring of the firm's performance (for example, situation analysis). Furthermore, most of the monitoring systems do not include *projections* of trends or cross-impact analyses. User oriented

MIS should therefore be designed that incorporate advances in information dissemination technology (for example, on-line information systems) and forecasting methods (especially environmental forecasting techniques). In addition, greater attention should be given to (a) the development of new data collection analysis and dissemination methods and (b) the explicit implementation and modification of existing *methods*, adjusting them to the needs imposed by continuous monitoring of *changes* in relevant environmental forces and in the firm's performance.

How to Adopt the Various Static Research Approaches and Analytical Models to the Dynamic Nature of the Market. Given that marketing decisions should be based on likely *future* behavior of consumers and other relevant stakeholders, it is necessary to develop *dynamic models* that offer managment forecasts conditional on alternative marketing strategies under alternative environmental conditions.

How Often Should Marketing Studies Be Conducted? Given the rapidly changing environment, marketing studies for the generation and evaluation of alternatives should be scheduled to ensure accurate capturing of changes in consumers' attitudes and behavior and market and environmental conditions.

Design of Marketing Strategy

Following the inputs from the marketing audit, the major managerial task is the generation and evaluation of marketing strategies. This area, despite the widespread attention it has received in the marketing management literature, still requires the resolution of a number of conceptual and methodological issues, including the following.

How to Encourage the Generation of Truly Innovative and Creative Strategy Alternatives. The generation of new product ideas has received a considerable amount of attention in the marketing and R&D literature. Yet little attention has been given to the systematic generation of creative marketing and corporate strategies.

How to Design and Implement Resource Allocation Models Among Products, Markets, and Marketing Programs. The analytical hierarchy process was found to be a useful procedure for allocating resources within the product/market/distribution portfolio of one firm. Can it be applied to other firms, and what are the organization and research implications of such an approach? How consistent are the results obtained by AHP with those of other allocation models?

How to Integrate Marketing Decisions (and Orientation), with Other Business Functions—Finance, R & D, Production, Personnel, Procurement, Legal and Top Management. What are the implications of the need for such integration for organizational design and the research and modeling activities of the firm? Successful development and implementation of strategic planning models calls for close links between marketing and the other business functions. Ways to achieve such links should be explained and the strategic planning models developed, utilizing inputs from all relevant functions and aimed at satisfying the diverse needs of multiple organizational users.

How to Schedule (Allocate Resources Over Time) the Various Corporate and Marketing Strategies of the Firm. Scheduling is often viewed as a tactical decision. Yet strategic planning requires careful scheduling of resource allocation and activities over time.

What Procedures Can Be Developed for the Translation of Research Findings (Such as Consumer Perception of and Preference for Various Product Attributes) into Physical (and Imagery) Product Attributes and Marketing Strategies? Multidimensional psychophysics and conjoint analysis studies (with actual product prototypes) have been used successfully in a few cases. Yet greater attention should be given to the translation problem: how best to execute the planning corporate strategies.

Design of a Strategic Planning System

One of the most complex and difficult aspects of strategic planning is the design and implementation of a strategic planning process. The design of an effective system that utilizes the relevant marketing concepts and tools still requires the resolution of a number of key conceptual and methodological issues including the following.

How to Assess Operationally the "Cost Versus Value" of the Various Concepts Such as Adaptive Experimentation and Contingency Plans and Research and Management Science Tools (Such as Environmental Monitoring Programs and Forecasting Models) and How to Reconcile Possible Conflicts Between the Desired Approaches and Political Realities in the Firms. The cost versus value of information concept, although widely accepted, has rarely been applied to the strategic planning process and its research and modeling component. Given the frequent pressure to sacrifice strategic (long-term) objectives for tactical (short-term) ones, the explicit evaluation of the cost versus the value of each research and modeling project is of great practical importance. In addition, the *process* that has to be developed in order to assess the value and cost of various projects offers a vehicle for better communication among the relevant decision makers and explicit examination of their assumptions and preferences.

How to Determine the Best Mix of Research Approaches to the Generation and Evaluation of Alternatives. Given the diversity of research approaches, it is necessary to determine which mix of approaches is most appropriate under which conditions, and to integrate them in a user oriented marketing information system.

Given that most planning efforts have been undertaken by large consumer and industrial firms, a critical question is, *What changes, if any, are required in the explicit approaches to (and concepts and techniques employed in) strategic product planning of* service-oriented firms (versus firms who manufacture products); intermediate marketing organizations (versus manufacturers); nonprofit firms (versus profit oriented firms); small (versus large) firms; and firms involved with multinational (versus domestic) markets?

Organizing for Strategic Planning

A key ingredient for the effective implementation of strategic planning models is an appropriate organizational design. The strategic planning, marketing, and organizational behavior literature offers few clear-cut guidelines for the development of such organizational designs. Hence, a major area for future research is the design of effective organizations for strategic corporate planning and implementation as well as the testing of the effectiveness of alternative organizational designs. These designs should incorporate the functions of strategic planning, marketing, marketing research, and management information systems; their interrelationships; and their coordination with top management operations.

Concluding Remarks

In recent years we have witnessed two unrelated developments: (a) tremendous interest in strategic planning and (b) increased utilization of tactical marketing models. New product forecasting models based on concept testing, simulated test markets, or actual test market data are, for example, widely used. In the context of specific marketing decisions, marketing practitioners should not be concerned with whether analytical approaches work, but rather with which of the many analytical approaches is better suited for their firm and the specific product/market situation involved. The challenge, however, is in developing and implementing new analytical approaches for the strategic planning decisions.

The basic premise of this chapter has been that both the marketing and strategic planning literature would benefit if marketing scholars and practitioners were to focus more on the development of SBUs and corporate strategic marketing models. As illustrated in this chapter, the design and implementation of strategic marketing models can benefit from a number of concepts and methods. Even though there are still a number of unanswered basic research questions, enough is known to allow for the development and implementation of real-world marketing oriented strategic planning models. Such models require top management recognition that marketing, and in particular marketing research and modeling activities, can offer viable inputs and guidelines for the strategic decisions of the firm. If marketing is to have its deserved impact on corporate decisions, the development of such recognition is essential. It is particularly critical in the more complex management areas, such as international marketing operations and the diversification activities of the firm.

The international marketing area is especially intriguing since it entails a second layer of decisions beyond those that are usually required in domestic marketing operations, that is, the country selection/mode of entry decision. These decisions have traditionally been made on a haphazard basis, such as management's familiarity with the given country, or the initiative of an importer or broker. Yet the high risk and tremendous potential of international operations call for a *systematic*, portfolio driven approach to the country selection and mode of entry decision. The need for more rigorous and advanced modeling and research activities characterizes *all* of the strategic planning activities of the firm that involve decisions that, in the long run, can make the big difference between growth or decline.

The necessary conceptual and methodological developments in this area and the challenge of implementing such procedures when developed make the marketing oriented strategic planning model an exciting and challenging area for research. Progress in this area requires, however, close collaboration between the academic researcher and the industry practitioners who provide the real-world laboratory for developing, testing, and implementing new analytical approaches so necessary for making marketing oriented corporate strategic planning models a reality.

References

1. Abel, D. F., and Hammond, J. S. *Strategic Market Planning.* Englewood Cliffs, New Jersey: Prentice-Hall, 1979.
2. Ackoff, R. L. *A Concept of Corporate Planning.* New York: Wiley (Interscience), 1970.
3. _____ and Emshoff, James R. "Advertising Research at Anheuser-Bush, Inc., 1963–68" and "1968–74." *Sloan Management Review* 16 (Winter), 1–15 (1975), (Spring), 1–15 (1975).

4. Allio, R. J., and Pennington, M. W., eds. *Corporate Planning: Techniques and Applications*. New York: AMACON, 1979.

5. Amstuz, A. *Computer Simulation of Competitive Market Response*. Cambridge, Massachusetts: MIT Press, 1967.

6. Ansoff, H. I. *Corporate Strategy*. New York: McGraw-Hill, 1965; "The State of Practice in Planning Systems," *Sloan Management Review* 18 (Winter), 1–24 (1980).

7. Balderston, F. E., and Hoggatt, A. C. *Simulation of Market Processes*. Berkeley California Institute of Business and Economic Research, University of California, 1962.

8. Bass, F. M., and Wittink, D. R. "Pooling Issues and Methods in Regression Analysis with Examples in Marketing Research," *Journal of Marketing Research* 12 (November), 414–425 (1975).

9. BBD&O. "The Theoretical Basis of NEWS," Management Science Department, unpublished newsletter, 1971.

10. Beckwith, N. W. "Multivariate Analysis of Sales Responses of Competing Brands to Advertising," *Journal of Marketing Research* 9 (May), 168–176 (1972).

11. Blattberg, R., and Golanty, J. "Tracker: An Early Test Market Forecasting and Diagnostic Model for New Product Planning," *Journal of Marketing Research* 15 (May), 192–202 (1978).

12. Bowman, E. H. "Strategy and the Weather," *Sloan Management Review* 17 (Winter), 49–62 (1976).

13. Boyd, H. W., Jr., and Massy, W. F. *Marketing Management*. New York: Harcourt Brace Jovanovich, 1972.

14. Bultez, A. V., and Schultz, R. L. "Decision Rules for Advertising Budgeting and Media Allocation," Institute Paper No. 694, Krannert Graduate School of Management, Purdue University, May 1979.

15. Buzzell, R. D., Gale, B. T., and Sultan, R. G. M. "Market Share—A Key to Profitability," *Harvard Business Review*, 53 (January–February), 97–108 (1975).

16. Carroll, J. Douglas, Green, Paul E., and DeSarbo, Wayne S. "Optimizing the Allocation of a Fixed Resource: A Simple Model and Its Experimental Test," *Journal of Marketing* 48, 51–57 (1979).

17. Charnes, A., Devoe, J. K., and Learner, D. B. "DEMON: Decision Mapping via Optimum GO/NO Networks—A Model for Marketing New Products," *Management Science* 12 (July), 865–887 (1966).

18. Clarke, D. G. "Sales-Advertising Cross Elasticities and Advertising Competition," *Journal of Marketing Research* 10 (August), 250–261 (1973).

19. Claycamp, H., and Liddy, L. E. "Prediction of New Product Performance: An Analytical Approach," *Journal of Marketing Research* 6 (November), 414–420 (1969).

20. Day, George S. "Diagnosing the Product Portfolio," *Journal of Marketing* 41 (April), 29–38 (1977).

21. FitzRoy, Peter T., and Wind, Yoram. "On the Multi-Dimensionality of Market Share," Wharton School Working Paper, July 1978.

22. Fogg, C. Davis. "The New Business Planning Process," *Industrial Marketing Management* 4, 273–285 (1975).

23. Frawley, S. G., and Saaty, Thomas L. "Political Behavioral and Analytical Hierarchies: Implications for Group Decision Making," University of Pennsylvania Working Paper, November 1978.
24. Galbraith, J. *Organizational Design*. Reading, Massachusetts: Addison-Wesley, 1975.
25. Gale, B. T. "Planning for Profit," in R. J. Allio and M. W. Pennington (eds.), *Corporate Planning: Techniques and Applications*. New York: AMACOM, 1979, pp. 160–171.
26. _____, Heany, D. F., and Swire, D. J. *The PAR ROI Report: Explanation and Commentary on Report*. Cambridge, Massachusetts: The Strategic Business Institute, 1977.
27. Green, Paul E., and DeSarbo, Wayne S. "Componential Segmentation in the Analysis of Consumer Trade-Off," *Journal of Marketing* 43 (Fall), 83–91 (1979).
28. _____ and Wind, Yoram. "New Ways to Measure Consumers' Judgment," *Harvard Business Review* 53 (July–August), 107–117 (1975).
29. _____ and _____. *Multiattribute Decisions in Marketing: A Measurement Approach*. Hinsdale, Illinois: The Dryden Press, 1973.
30. Hamelman, Paul W., and Mazze, Edward M. "Improving Product Abandonment Decisions," *Journal of Marketing* 36 (April), 20–26 (1972).
31. Herniter, J. D., and Cook, V. "A Multidimensional Stochastic Model of Consumer Purchase Behavior," University of Chicago Working Paper, Center for Multitudinal Studies in Business and Economics, June 1970.
32. Heyvaert, H. "Strategic Managment and Performance," quoted in D. Montgomery and C. Weinberg, "Strategic Intelligence Systems," in A. Shocker (ed.), *Analytic Approaches to Product and Marketing Planning*, pp. 147–176. Cambridge, Massachusetts: Marketing Science Institute, 1979.
33. Hughes, G. David. 1978. *Marketing Management: A Planning Approach*. Reading, Massachusetts: Addison-Wesley, 1978.
34. Johnson, Samuel C., and Jones, Conrad. "How to Organize for New Products," *Harvard Business Review* 35 (May–June), 49–62 (1957).
35. Karger, D. W., and Malick, Z. A. "Long Range Planning and Organizational Performance," *Long Range Planning* 8 (December), 60–65 (1975).
36. Katz, R. L. *Management of the Total Enterprise*. Englewood Cliffs, New Jersey: Prentice-Hall, 1970.
37. Khandwalla, P. N. *The Design of Organizations*. New York: Harcourt Brace Jovanovich, 1977.
38. Kotler, P., Gregor, W., and Rogers, W. "The Marketing Audit Comes of Age," *Sloan Management Review* 18 (Winter), 25–43 (1977).
39. Lambin, J. J. "Optimal Allocation of Competitive Marketing Efforts: An Empirical Study," *Journal of Business* 43 (October), 468–484 (1970).
40. Little, John D. C. "A Model of Adaptive Control of Promotional Spending," *Operations Research* 14 (November) 1075–1097 (1966).
41. _____. "BRANDAID: A Marketing Mix Model, Part 1: Structure," *Operations Research* 23 (July–August), 628–655 (1975).
42. _____. "BRANDAID: A Marketing Mix Model, Part 2: Implementation, Calibration and Case Study," *Operations Research* 23 (July–August), 656–673 (1975).

43. MacLachlan, D. L. "A Model of Intermediate Market Response," *Journal of Marketing Research* 9 (November), 378–384 (1972).
44. Massy, W. F., Montgomery D. B., and Morrison, D. G. *Stochastic Models of Buyer Behavior*. Cambridge, Massachusetts: MIT Press, 1970.
45. McCann, J. M. "Study of Market Segment Response to the Marketing Decision Variables," *Journal of Marketing Research* 11 (November), 399–412 (1974).
46. Montgomery, D. B., and Weinberg, C. B. "Strategic Intelligence Systems," *Journal of Marketing* 43 (Fall), 41–53 (1979).
47. Naylor, T. H., ed. *Corporate Planning Models*. Reading Massachusetts: Addison-Wesley, 1979.
48. _____, Mayo, R. B., and Schauland, H. "SIMPLAN: A Planning and Modeling System," in T. H. Naylor (ed.), *Corporate Planning Models*. Reading, Massachusetts: Addison-Wesley, 1979, pp. 361–384.
49. Parsons, L. J., and Schultz, R. L. *Marketing Models and Econometric Research*. New York: North-Holland, 1976.
50. Pessemier, E. A. *Product Management: Strategy and Organization.* New York: Wiley, 1977.
51. Rogers National Research. "Product Optimization and Selected Segment Evaluation." Toledo, Ohio, 1979 (a brochure).
52. Saaty, Thomas L. "A Scaling Method for Priorities in Hierarchical Structures," *Journal of Mathematical Psychology* 15 (June), 234–281 (1977).
53. _____. *The Analytic Hierarchy Process*. New York: McGraw-Hill, 1980.
54. _____ and Bennett, J. P. "A Theory of Analytical Hierarchies Applied to Political Candidacy," Behavioral Science 22 (July), 237–245 (1977).
55. _____ and _____. "Theoretical Aspects of Negotiating with Terrorism," in Robert Kupperman and Darrel M. Trent (eds.), *Terrorism: Threat, Reality, Response*. Stanford, California: Stanford Hoover Institution, 1979, pp. 244–284.
56. _____ and Mariano, Reynaldo S. "Rationing Energy to Industries; Priorities and Input–Output Dependence," Energy Systems and Policy 8 (Winter), 85–111 (1979).
57. Schloeffler, S. "Nine Basic Findings on Business Strategy," PIMSletter on Business Strategy No. 1 (undated).
58. _____, Buzzell, R. D., and Heany, D. F. "Impact on Strategic Planning on Product Performance," *Harvard Business Review* 52 (March–April), 137–145 (1974).
59. Schultz, R. L., and Slevin, D. P. "A Program of Research on Implementation," in R. L. Schultz and D. P. Slevin (eds.), *Implementing Operations Research/Management Science*. New York: American Elsevier, 1975, pp. 31–48.
60. _____ and Dodson, J. A., Jr. "An Empirical Simulation Approach to Competition," in J. Sheth (ed.), *Research in Marketing* 1, 269–301 (1978).
61. _____ and Henry, M. D. This volume, Chapter 12.
62. Simon, Herbert A. *The New Science of Management Decision*. New York: Harper, 1960.
63. Steiner, G. A. *Top Management Planning*. London: Macmillan, 1969.
64. Swamy, P. A. V. B. *Statistical Inference in Random Coefficient Regression*

Models. New York: Springer-Verlag, 1971.
65. Urban, G. L. "Sprinter Mod III: A Model for the Analysis of New Frequently Purchased Consumer Products," *Operations Research* 18 (September), 805–854 (1970).
66. Wind, Yoram. "Product Portfolio Analysis: A New Approach to the Product Mix Decision," in Ronald C. Curhan (ed.), *Combined Proceedings.* Chicago: American Marketing Association, August 1975, pp. 460–464.
67. _____. "The Perception of the Firm's Competitive Position," in F. Nicosia and Y. Wind (eds.), *Behavioral Models for Market Analysis: Foundations for Marketing Action.* Hinsdale, Illinois: Dryden, 1977, pp. 163–181.
68. _____. "Brand Loyalty and Vulnerability," in A. Woodside, J. Sheth, and P. Bennett (eds.), *Consumer and Industrial Buying Behavior.* New York: Elsevier, 1977, pp. 313–319.
69. _____. "Issues and Advances in Segmentation Research," *Journal of Marketing Research* 15 (August), 317–337 (1978).
70. _____. "A Research Program for a Marketing Guided Approach to Mergers and Acquisitions," in Neil Beckwith, Michael Houston, Robert Mittelstaldt, Kent B. Monroe, and Scott Warzl (eds.), *1979 Educators' Conference Proceedings.* Chicago: American Marketing Association, 1979, pp. 24–28.
71. _____. "Product-Marketing Planning Models: Concepts, Techniques, and Needed Development," in A. Shocker (ed.), *Analytic Approaches to Product and Marketing Planning.* Cambridge, Massachusetts: Marketing Science Institute, 1979, pp. 39–66.
72. _____. "Going to Marketing: New Twists for Some Old Tricks," *Wharton Magazine* 4 (Spring), 34–39 (1980).
73. _____. *Product Policy: Concepts, Methods, and Approaches.* Reading, Massachusetts: Addison-Wesley, 1980.
74. _____ and Claycamp, Henry J. "Planning Product Line Strategy: A Matrix," *Journal of Marketing* 40 (January), 2–9 (1976).
75. _____ and Goldhar, Joel. "Organizing the Marketing–R & D Interface for Innovation"; a summary is presented in Y. Wind, *Product Policy.* Reading, Massachusetts: Addison-Wesley, 1980, Chapter 16.
76. _____ and Gross, Daniel. "An Analytic Hierarchy Approach to the Allocation of Resources Within a Target Product/Market/Distribution Portfolio," paper prepared for the ORSA/TIMS Workshop on Market Measurement and Analysis, Stanford University, 26–28 March 1979.
77. _____, Jolley, S., and O'Connor, A. "Concept Testing as Input to Strategic Marketing Simulation," in E. Mazze (ed.), *Proceedings of the 58th International AMA Conference,* 120–124 (April, 1975).
78. _____ and Mahajan, Vijay. *Portfolio Analysis and Strategy.* Reading, Massachusetts: Addison-Wesley (in press).

11

Marketing Models in Public and Nonprofit Organizations

Charles B. Weinberg

After a decade of writing and lecturing by marketing academics, a substantial number of administrators in public and nonprofit organizations (PNPs) appear willing to adopt and utilize a marketing framework as part of their management system. Indeed, Lovelock and Weinberg's recent review article "Public and Nonprofit Marketing Comes of Age [11]" demonstrates just that fact. This new maturity, however, poses a problem—just what do marketing models have to offer PNPs? Although there are many similarities between the marketing management problems in business and PNPs, there are also substantial and significant differences, and nowadays few would naively ask, as did one author in the 1950s, "Why can't you sell brotherhood like you sell soap?"

Three differences between businesses and PNPs seem particularly salient for the marketing modeler. First, the objective function is not (even theoretically) profit maximization. This obviously complicates any optimum-seeking algorithm. Second, few PNPs meet all their costs from user fees alone, which means that they must design marketing programs that appeal and provide benefits to both users and funding sources, be they donors, taxpayers, or government agencies. For example, many public school districts have belatedly found out that providing superior educational services to students is not sufficient in itself to influence voters to approve tax levies and bond referenda. The third difference is that PNPs predominantly deal in intangibles; while many businesses also provide services, the bulk of the theoretical and practical work in analytical marketing has been concerned with the marketing of goods. Some particular problems that arise when dealing with services are (1) that limited inventorying of services can take place (an unused theater seat on a Monday night is empty forever and cannot be used, for example, on the following Saturday night), and (2) that substantially more of the total cost often varies with the capacity of the system rather than with the number of users. This suggests a need for coordination among service operations and marketing management and, presumably, management science approaches to support this coordination. Yet, to date, with some exceptions such as Edelstein and Melnyk's model [4] for Hertz Rent-A-Car, relatively little management science work has been done in this area.

Of course, in some areas, virtually identical marketing model approaches may be employed for both PNPs and businesses. For example, media scheduling algorithms that either evaluate media plans or develop schedules to meet reach and frequency targets are probably equally valuable in both settings. Even here, however, some differences exist because many PNPs have access to free media space. Moreover, PNPs using free media space have little control over the placement of their advertisements and, in some cases, whether they will be run at all. So perhaps a media scheduling model that includes these uncertainties is required here. As is discussed in this chapter, similar analytic approaches to demand estimation appear to be applicable in both PNPs and businesses.

This chapter is primarily concerned with discussing the role of marketing models in PNPs. Consequently it focuses on models that operate at the organization or market (or market segment) level and not on the individual or micro level. Although individual level models can provide valuable insights and, at least theoretically, be aggregated, it is at this aggregate level that marketing managers generally make decisions. The chapter is divided into four major sections. First, the structure of marketing models and the ways in which they can help marketing managers are briefly reviewed. Second, we show that the difference in objective functions between a nonprofit organization and a business and also the potential of attracting donations and subsidies lead to different marketing mix decisions. We also specify a framework for the marketing mix problem in nonprofit organizations. Third, the published literature on marketing models for PNPs is reviewed. This review is divided into two parts—(i) analytic approaches to demand estimation, for which a number of cases can be reported, and (ii) decision models, an area in which there is only limited work. Fourth, and finally, the history of development and implementation of marketing models in one nonprofit organization is reviewed in depth.

Structure of Marketing Models

A model is a representation or abstraction of a real-world system. Being an abstraction, it is a less than perfect reflection of the real world, but it is much easier to manipulate and work with than its real-world counterpart.

The model builder continually has to counterbalance model completeness (and thus validity) with simplicity (and thus usability).

There are two broad classes of models: descriptive models and decision models.[1] Descriptive models are developed either to predict or to help provide understanding of a process. When a descriptive model is used to evaluate several decision alternatives, it becomes a decision model.

A descriptive model involves constructs and relationships between constructs. First, there are input constructs. These may be under the control of the decision maker, such as price level, or they may be uncontrollable, such as the advertising expenditures of competitors. In any case, they are inputs to the model. Second, there are output constructs, such as number of users or revenues, which are the model outputs of interest to the manager. Finally, models can include intervening constructs, such as consumer attitudes or number of inquiries.

The model structure involves the determination of the relationship between constructs at three levels of specificity. First, there is the identification of the link between constructs: for example, the advertising expenditure generates positive consumer attitudes, which in turn precipitate a revenue stream over time. Second, there is the nature of the functional form of this relationship—whether it is, for example, linear or nonlinear, immediate or lagged, additive or multiplicative. Finally, there is the ultimate need to estimate the parameters of the functional relationship.

The relationship between the constructs should reflect causal flow if understanding of the process is one of the model's goals. If the goal is "simply" prediction, understanding the causal links is desirable but not necessary. It may not matter, for example, for prediction purposes, if advertising increases usage directly or if advertising creates a positive attitude that in turn increases usage; it is sufficient to know that changes in advertising expenditure result in changes in usage.

When descriptive models are used to evaluate two or more decision alternatives—alternative values of controllable input constructs—they become decision models. Search procedures are then needed to determine the various decision alternatives to consider. These procedures can be informal searches based on the judgment of the decision maker or formal mechanistic search procedures built into the model itself. Some writers prefer to reserve the term "decision model" for systems in which the mechanistic search process is built into the model. Others are willing to allow the term to be used when the overall modeling system provides a convenient means for management to make evaluations of alternatives.

---

[1] A fuller discussion of the issues raised in this section may be found in the work of Aaker and Weinberg [1] and Montgomery and Weinberg [14].

Building a descriptive model involves determination of relevant and valid constructs and development of the relationships between these constructs. Constructs and their relationships can be determined by judgmental evidence or arguments, by data-based methods, or by a combination of both, such as Weinberg and Shachmut's ARTS PLAN [18].

Judgmental approaches can be drawn from marketing theory, economics, psychology, or other disciplines, or from the experience of the decision maker. An economist might argue, for example, that price will affect sales, and marketing theory might suggest that distribution is a relevant construct. Perhaps the most powerful source of model building information, however, is the decision maker. Often he or she has assimilated an enormous amount of relevant information about constructs, about their causal relationships, and even about such specifics as parameter estimates. One of the misconceptions about models is that they must be based primarily or exclusively on large amounts of hard data. Grayson [8], for example, claimed that one of the reasons why management science was not used at the Price Commission of the early 1970s was the inaccessibility of data. Yet many successful models rely extensively on "soft" information that reflects the decision maker's knowledge.

Advantages of Models to Marketing Managers

A wide range of benefits from using models, particularly computer-based ones, can be realized by the manager. A computer-based marketing model may

1. help to better utilize a manager's judgment and available data,
2. limit a manager's tendency to overact,
3. provide quick and convenient evaluation of alternatives,
4. search for better solutions,
5. allow emergence of "unmentionable" solutions,
6. improve prediction,
7. help with the formal statement of (a) input assumptions and (b) the logic of analysis,
8. provide vocabulary with which to discuss problems,
9. organize data, and
10. provide a guide to research (a) through sensitivity analysis and (b) by exposing gaps in knowledge.

The purpose of descriptive models is to predict, or provide greater understanding of, the system being modeled. Thus, a descriptive model can be used as a forecasting tool or to help determine which constructs are relevant to the decision maker and the nature of the causal relationships between them. A decision model is expected to aid the decision maker directly by providing relatively objective evaluations of decision alternatives in an efficient manner. The capacity of the computer to incorporate complex structures and to perform calculations quickly is of enormous practical help to the decision maker.

Models also have a set of less obvious benefits. They act as information summarizers. A single interpretable output construct, for example, can serve to summarize a mass of objective and subjective input data. The various constructs and relationships can serve to organize information and to provide a common vocabulary for discussing complex issues. By providing a formal statement of input assumptions and logic of analysis, models can provide a basis for clearer understanding and a means for exposing hidden assumptions and logical flaws. Decision models can sometimes generate solutions that would otherwise not be thought of or would be "politically unmentionable" in an organization. Models can also guide research by identifying areas in which information is needed and to which the model output is sensitive.

Models can be an aid to decision makers, but some cautions must be stated explicitly. Successful models usually need to be custom designed for the organization and the particular management problem. Although a management scientist is expected to be a master of a set of techniques and may begin with modular components, successful implementation depends on the appropriateness of the model built. A second caution is that the manager and management scientist must work together if the model is to be implemented effectively. Third, as the organization changes, the nature of the models needed and their role and use as a decision aid can be altered.

Comparison of Objective Functions

A critical difference between nonprofit organizations and businesses is that many nonprofits incur substantial deficits and thus require either government grants or private benefactions. Some nonprofits, such as performing arts groups and hospitals, charge a price for their services so that users bear some of the costs of the provided services. Other organizations, such as libraries and religious groups, often make no direct charge for their services.

The marketing task of the nonprofit is more complex than that of a business, which generally prospers if it can satisfy consumer needs better than the competition. The nonprofit organization must not only provide goods and/or services (generically referred to as "products") that meet user needs, but it also must satisfy the donors from whom it attracts resources. For some nonprofits, this often means that the products offered to users must appeal to the donors' intuitive appraisals of client needs and may limit the range of services provided. An example of this is the limitations that some donors place on the counseling and educational services that family planning agencies can offer to their clientele.

In many cases, an organization's success in serving clients will lead to success in raising funds from benefactors. For example, a manager of one performing arts series explained that he turned to an aggressive marketing policy to build an audience for several reasons, one being that it is easier to raise money for a performing arts series that is sold out at half price than for one that is half empty at full price.

Specification of the objective function for making marketing mix decisions is, of course, crucial. In the business sector, the objective function for determining the optimal marketing mix is usually based on profit maximization. Although the definition of profit in an actual organizational setting is never as straightforward as theoretical treatments would suggest, and few would suggest that a firm will make *every* decision based on profit maximization, most will agree that profit is a goal of nearly every business enterprise—probably the predominant one. Few business executives deliberately pursue policies that they think will in the long run yield profits far below what otherwise could be earned. Among the alternatives to profit maximization are satisficing behavior, sales maximization, market share maximization, cost minimization, long-run survival, personal goals of managers, and growth.

By definition, nonprofit organizations are not profit maximizers. In order to achieve insights into the nature of the marketing mix decision for nonprofits and to be able to compare their decisions to those of businesses, we need to specify an objective function that captures the distinctiveness of the nonprofit sector and is broad enough to cover a range of nonprofit organizations as well. Consequently, in this chapter we assume that the objective function for a nonprofit organization, when making marketing mix decisions, is *maximization of the amount of its products or services that are consumed or utilized*, subject to the amount of *revenues and donations* being at least equal to the cost of providing the service.[2] If revenues and donations are fixed, and consequently independent of any marketing efforts by the organization, then the objective leads to a resource allocation problem. The more general case is the one in which both revenues and donations are conditional on the marketing mix.

---

[2] Conceptually we might attempt to use multicriteria optimization approaches to setting the marketing mix. Although these approaches offer considerable promise, successful, insightful applications of multicriteria optimization to the marketing problems of nonprofit organizations have not yet been made, to the knowledge of this author. The development that follows is based on Weinberg [17].

Framework and Model Specification

In order to specify the marketing mix model mathematically, the following notation is needed:

p is the price per unit of consumption,

x is the marketing expenditures to users,

y is the marketing expenditures to donors,

$q = f(p, x)$ is the quantity of services used by clients,

$s = g(q, y)$ is the subsidies raised, and

$c = h(q)$ is the cost of producing q units.

The functions f, g, and h are assumed to have all necessary derivatives. The symbols x and y represent variables, but the model can be extended to include x and y as vectors. The model formulated here does not explicitly account for multiperiod effects, such as the carryover of advertising. However, similar comparative conclusions to those developed below about optimal marketing mix decisions for profit maximizing and nonprofit organizations will hold in the multiperiod and the single-period cases.

It should be noted that the subsidies or donations function, $s = g(q, y)$, is dependent on the quantity q. This is included to capture two effects. First, donors may perceive organizations that have larger user bases as being more worthy of support. Foundations often require that organizations indicate the level of community support they have as part of the grant application. An organization that provides food and shelter for the needy, for example, might expect that the more needy people it serves, the likelier it is to attract donations. The second reason for including q is that it affects the size of the target market for many organizations. For example, the results of a fund raising campaign for a university should be dependent on the number of graduates of the school. Or, as a second example, a performing or visual arts institution may find its audience to be a primary target for fund raising efforts.

The marketing mix problem for the nonprofit organization can be stated as follows:

$$\text{max} \quad q = f(p, x) \tag{1}$$
$$\text{subject to} \quad pf(p, x) - h(q) - x + g(q, y) - y = 0. \tag{2}$$

The nonnegativity constraints on p, x, and y will not be stated and will be assumed to be met throughout. The optimal solution to this problem will be denoted p^*, x^*, and y^*.

If the nonprofit organization cannot raise donations, then (2) can be modified so that the term $g(q, y) - y$ is omitted. If the nonprofit organization has a fixed subsidy, independent of q and y, then the term $g(q, y) - y$ can be replaced by the amount of that subsidy.

A profit maximizing business's objective can be stated as

$$\max \quad \Pi = qp - h(q) - x. \tag{3}$$

Weinberg [17] examines extensively the comparative solutions of (1) and (2) and of (3). For present purposes, however, it is sufficient to confine our discussion to the case in which the response functions $f(p, x)$ and $g(q, y)$ are represented by power functions and costs by a linear function. These functional forms are frequently used in empirical work and the main comparative results will hold if other functional forms are used.[3] Thus, we have the following demand, subsidy, and cost functions:

$$f(p, x) = \alpha_0 p^{-\alpha_1} x^{\alpha_2} \quad (\alpha_0, \alpha_1, \alpha_2 > 0), \tag{4}$$

$$g(q, y) = \beta_0 q^{\beta_1} y^{\beta_2} \quad (\beta_0, \beta_1, \beta_2 > 0), \tag{5}$$

and

$$h(q) = c_f + c_v q \quad (c_f, c_v \geqslant 0), \tag{6}$$

where c_f and c_v are fixed and variable cost, respectively.

Although the optimal solution to this marketing mix problem can be stated in general form, in order to provide a more compact representation it is convenient to assume that $\alpha_1 + \alpha_2 = 2$ and $2\beta_1 + \beta_2 = 1$. For this case, the optimal price strategies (p^*) for the profit maximizing firm and for usage maximizing organizations that can and cannot obtain contributions are given in Table 1.

The optimal marketing effort to users x^* can be stated in terms of p^* in all three cases to be the following:

$$x^* = \left(\frac{\alpha_0 \alpha_2}{\alpha_1} \right)^{1/(1-\alpha_1)} (p^*)^{-1}. \tag{7}$$

Further, for nonprofit organizations that can obtain donations, the optimal marketing expenditures directed to the contributer market are given by

$$y^* = \left[\frac{\alpha_1}{\alpha_2} \left(\frac{\alpha_0 \alpha_2}{\alpha_1} \right)^{1/(1-\alpha_1)} (\beta_0 \beta_2)^{1/\beta_1} \right]^{1/2} (p^*)^{-1}. \tag{8}$$

If there are fixed costs ($c_f > 0$), then both the profit and nonprofit organizations would not operate if those costs could not be met from revenues and contributions.

---

[3] The reader is cautioned that some of the assumptions of the power function model may be untenable in some situations. For example, a value of zero for x results in no demand and a value of zero for y implies no donations. Also, the model assumes constant elasticity. These functional forms are chosen for illustration; a more comprehensive discussion is beyond the scope of this chapter.

Table 1. Optimal Price Strategies[a]

Profit maximizing firm

$$p^* = \frac{c_v \alpha_1}{\alpha_1 - 1}$$

Nonprofit firm without donations

A. Fixed cost $= c_f$

$$p^* = \frac{(k_2 - k_1) - \sqrt{(k_2 - k_1)^2 - 4 c_f c_v k_2}}{2 c_f}$$

B. No fixed costs ($c_f = 0$)

$$p^* = \frac{c_v \alpha_1}{2(\alpha_1 - 1)}$$

Nonprofit firm with donations

A. Fixed cost $= c_f$

$$p^* = \frac{(k_2 - k_1 + k_3) - \sqrt{(k_2 - k_1 + k_3)^2 - 4 c_f c_v k_2}}{2 c_f}$$

B. No fixed costs ($c_f = 0$)

$$p^* = \frac{c_v k_2}{k_2 - k_1 + k_3}$$

---

[a] Assume $\alpha_1 + \alpha_2 = 2$, $2\beta_1 + \beta_2 = 1$. Notation:

$$k_1 = \left(\frac{\alpha_0 \alpha_2}{\alpha_1} \right)^{1/(1 - \alpha_2)}; \quad k_2 = \frac{\alpha_1}{\alpha_2} k_1; \quad k_3 = \frac{2\beta_1}{\beta_2} (\beta_0 \beta_2)^{1/2\beta_1} k_2^{1/2}.$$

Illustrative Example

In order to illustrate the implications of the marketing mix decision rules, a numerical example is developed in this section. The parameter values chosen are hypothetical, although they would appear to be representative of at least some nonprofit organizations. The numerical examples are summarized in Table 2.

In particular, demand for service is given by

$$q = \alpha_0 p^{-\alpha_1} x^{\alpha_2}$$
$$= 1000 p^{-1.6} x^{0.4} \tag{9}$$

and contribution responsiveness is described by

$$s = \beta_1 q^{\beta_1} y^{\beta_2}$$
$$= 50 q^{0.4} y^{0.2}. \tag{10}$$

The coefficients of price ($\alpha_1 = 1.6$) and marketing effort ($\alpha_2 = 0.4$) represent a moderate degree of sensitivity of demand to the price and marketing variables. Similarly, contributions are moderately sensitive to total usage of

Table 2. Numerical Example of Optimal Decisions[a]

	p^*	x^*	y^*	Gross user revenue	Profit from users
Profit maximizing					
No fixed costs	$2.67	$3720	—	$14,882	$5581
$c_f = \$5000$	$2.67	$3720	—	$14,882	$581
Usage maximizing, no donations					
No fixed costs	$1.33	$7441	—	$29,764	0
$c_f = \$5000$	$2.02	$4921	—	$19,682	0
Usage maximizing, donations					
No fixed costs					
$\beta_0 = 10$	$1.25	$7915	$378	$31,659	−$1512
$\beta_0 = 50$	$0.90	$10,984	$3922	$43,934	−$15,687
$c_f = \$5000$					
$\beta_0 = 10$	$1.72	$5763	$275	$23,051	−$1101
$\beta_0 = 50$	$1.02	$9705	$3466	$38,823	−$13,862

[a] Constants for the numerical example: $\alpha_0 = 1000$, $\alpha_1 = 1.6$, $\alpha_2 = 0.4$; $\beta = 0.4$, $\beta_2 = 0.2$; $c_v = \$1.00$.

the service ($\beta_1 = 0.4$), but somewhat less sensitive to effort devoted to the benefaction market ($\beta_2 = 0.2$). In other words, a 50% increase in usage would increase donations by 20% ($1.5^{0.4} = 1.2$); increasing marketing effort by 50% would increase donations by 10% ($1.5^{0.2} = 1.1$). The α_0 and β_0 are scale values; Table 2 gives an alternative value of β_0 (10) that provides 80% fewer contribution dollars at any value of q and y.

In order to show the effect of fixed costs on the optimal solution, Table 2 shows the optimal values of the decision variables for the cases of zero fixed cost and for $c_f = 5000$. Variable cost c_v is $1.

As can be seen in Figure 1, the usage maximizing organization not only charges a lower price than the profit maximizing firm, but also spends more money on marketing ($10,984 versus $3720). For the nonprofit organization, the loss from users is exactly equal to the amount by which donations (for example, $19,509) exceed the marketing expenditures to the donor market (for example, $3922). Both the price and the marketing expenditures for the nonprofit organization that cannot raise donations are intermediate between the other two organizations. By definition, the nonprofits show no deficit. When the potential of the benefaction market is reduced ($\beta_0 = 0.10$), the optimal price is increased from $.90 (below variable cost) to $1.25 in the case of no fixed costs.

The effect of fixed costs on the level of service offered differs for the profit and nonprofit firms. For the profit maximizer, assuming that fixed costs are covered by revenues so that the firm remains in business, there is no effect on the optimal values of p^* and x^*. The nonprofit firm, however,

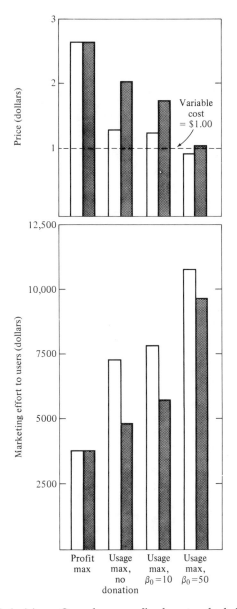

Figure 1. Optimal decisions. Open bars: no fixed costs; shaded bars: fixed costs are $5000.

because it cannot incur a deficit, must increase p^* (from \$0.90 to \$1.02) and decrease x^* (from \$10,984 to \$9705) as compared to the case of no fixed costs. Nevertheless, output is still higher than for the profit maximizing firm.

In summary, the numerical examples illustrate the degree to which a nonprofit organization should optimally charge lower prices and spend more on marketing than a profit maximizing firm facing identical demand and cost functions.

Review of Marketing Models

A limited number of marketing models have been explicitly developed either for the products or for the markets that are frequently dealt with by PNPs or for PNPs themselves. This section briefly reviews this work. There are two major divisions of these models, paralleling the distinction made earlier between descriptive and decision models. That is, some models focus primarily on estimation of the responsiveness of contributions and demand for goods and services to marketing variables, while others are embedded in a system that attempts to help a manager determine his or her marketing plan. The latter models, of course, usually include a descriptive model as part of their overall structure.

Demand Estimation and Descriptive Models

Demand estimation in businesses and PNPs is essentially similar, although one has to recognize that PNPs deal primarily with services. Thus there is considerable opportunity for the transfer of work between businesses and PNPs. Quite often, a researcher's decision to use a PNP setting is made for his or her convenience and testifies to the similarity of the business and nonbusiness sectors for the purposes of demand estimation. Indeed, to the extent that the analytical work being carried out is solely for descriptive purposes, the nature of the sponsoring organization is essentially immaterial from the standpoint of the analyst. The positive aspects of this interchangeability can be illustrated by the work of Farley and others on the marketing of contraceptives. For example, Farley and Leavitt [7] deal with the impact of alternative distribution strategies on contraceptive sales in Jamaica; Farley and Harvey [6] deal with the effectiveness of different copy strategies on direct mail sales of contraceptives in the United States. The first paper assesses various private sector solutions to a public sector problem; the second paper uses data supplied by a nonprofit organization.

There have been several other studies of the effect of marketing mix variables on demand in PNPs. Epps [5], for example, analyzes the United States Army's 1971 paid advertising campaign and concludes that it had a positive effect on short-term recruitment. Another example is Blattberg and Stivers's finding [2] that transit promotion in Pittsburgh significantly increases ridership in the off-peak but not the peak hours. There have been several statistical studies, primarily carried out by economists, on the relationship between price and demand for mass transit. These studies focus primarily on absolute price levels and not on other aspects of pricing policy. A more marketing oriented perspective on pricing is provided in McDonald's [13] study of the impact of charging for directory assistance service (that is, 411 in the United States).[4] This article is discussed in more detail later in the section on decision models.

In the performing arts, Weinberg and Shachmut [18] examine the relationship of attendance at performing arts events at Stanford University to performance type, seasonality, and other factors. The development of this model is discussed extensively in the last section of this article. The model has recently been extended and utilized at UCLA by Cooper [3]. In other work in the performing arts, Hanssens [10] carries out an econometric analysis of the effectiveness of advertisements in various media (for example, newspapers, magazines, and radio and TV) on ticket sales and revenues.

Finally, there has been almost no published analytical work on the relationship between marketing mix variables and donations or contributions. Weinberg [17] has reported a small scale study of gift giving to a university. This study finds the annual contributions are significantly related to expenditures on fund raising and to whether the university declared the year to be a "special campaign year."

In summary, there have been a substantial number of econometric analyses of the relationship of demand to marketing effort in the private sector. Although these studies provide a resource base and can provide guidance in determining demand sensitivity in PNPs, there is a need for substantial empirical work in this area. This is especially true because most PNPs offer services rather than goods and require contributions, donations, and/or subsidies, while most of the private sector studies are concerned only with the demand for goods.

Models of Consumer Preference for Multiattribute Alternatives. Since the early 1970s there has been considerable interest in the use of conjoint analysis to estimate the utilities that individuals place on the different

---

[4]Although the Bell System is a private company, it should be noted that telephone service is a key public utility that is heavily regulated by government agencies in the United States and has been nationalized in most other industrialized countries. Hence, the inclusion of directory assistance is entirely appropriate.

levels of the multiple attributes of goods, services, and other objects.[5] The nature of the technique can best be indicated by an illustration. Wind and Spitz, in their study of hospital choice by prospective patients [19], suggest that hospital management would like to know the attributes (such as proximity, quality of facilities, and price) that are important to patients and how influential different levels of each attribute are in forming preferences. For example, would a prospective patient for elective surgery prefer to stay in a nearby nonteaching community hospital that has average facilities or in a very modern teaching hospital located in a downtown area? Conjoint measurement proceeds not by asking the respondent directly for his or her utility for each level of each attribute, but by estimating these utilities based on the respondent's rank ordering of stimuli. The stimuli can be pairs of attributes that the respondent has to trade off against each other or a set of multiattribute alternatives that the respondent is asked to rank order. Using any of a variety of computer algorithms (and some assumptions), the ordinal data are then converted into a metric utility function for each individual.

Once developed, these individual utility functions can be used in a variety of ways. They can be used essentially as a descriptive model in order to estimate the demand for various alternatives. When used in this way, the individual utility functions are often aggregated into segments. Another approach, which moves farther along the continuum from descriptive to decision models, is to use individual utility functions as the basis for a computer-based simulation routine. Market share for different alternatives can then be calculated for this simulated market; the alternatives themselves can be generated either by the user or by a computer algorithm. An example of the simulation approach is a Department of Defense study [12] of enlistment in the United States Armed Forces. Finally, some models, such as Parker and Srinivasan's [15] study of rural primary health care facilities, include an algorithm for determining the optimal product configuration for a given market structure.

Decision Models and Decision Support Systems

There are very few marketing mix models for PNPs that appear to be designed to aid managers to make marketing decisions, other than by just providing an estimate of demand as a function of marketing mix variables. Although demand estimation is valuable, few managers can be expected to use regression results (or the output of other estimation techniques)

---

[5]Although these are individual level techniques, as discussed below there has been some work on aggregation of these utilities. An extensive review of conjoint analysis has been made by Green and Srinivasan [9].

directly. Rather, a decision support system that is responsive to the manager's needs usually has to be constructed. Such a decision support system enhances the likelihood that a manager will receive the full range of model benefits listed above. In this section, two implemented modeling systems are reviewed.

Urban [16] proposes a model for managing a family planning system that is developed, tested, and implemented with the Atlanta Family Planning System. The basic approach used is to build a deterministic, macro-process flow model. The process model traces movement of the target-group population through postpartum and nonpostpartum program states such as the following: request for an appointment, pregnancy, and choice of sterilization. The rates of flows between states are influenced by both marketing and nonmarketing variables such as outreach recruitment, postpartum checkups, referral, advertising response, and contraceptive method effectiveness. Both data-based and subjective estimation procedures are used in the model. The model provides a variety of output benefit measures—total active patients, couple-years of protection, and births prevented—that would seem to be of particular value to a manager who has to deal with multiple objectives and constraints. Finally, it should be noted that the model is implemented as an on-line, conversational program that facilitates management involvement and usage of the system.

McDonald's work on pricing policies for directory assistance (information) service [15] is oriented toward helping management to make a policy decision. The underlying problem is how to cope with a steady increase (7% a year) in the number of directory assistance calls and a usage pattern in which (i) 60% of the requested numbers are in the caller's own directory and (ii) 10% of the customers account for more than half of the calls. The modeling process involves several steps. An econometric model is developed to estimate the impact that charging would have on the volume of customer demand for the information service. This model can be modified by subjective estimation; sensitivity analyses are also performed. Additional models are constructed of the impact of charging on several other measures of concern, such as revenue, operator work time, and costs. The charging plan itself is actually multidimensional and the demand and impact models reflect this. Some of the dimensions that need to be considered are selectivity (whether a charge is imposed only for directory assistance calls within the subscriber's area), break point (how many, if any, free or lower-cost directory assistance calls should be allowed), and price per call below and above the break point. In addition, market research surveys of consumer reaction to the plan have been carried out. The set of studies was important in persuading senior management to propose charging and the studies "have been quite effective in convincing local regulatory bodies that charging for directory assistance service is equitable, efficient, and in the public interest" [15, p. 18].

Summary

Although there have been a number of successful marketing models developed in public sector settings, many problems remain unstudied, at least in the published literature. Work in the area of decision models is particularly sparse. In the final section of this paper, the evolutionary development and utilization of one decision model is discussed in detail.

Development and Utilization of a Decision Model

In this section, we describe the development and utilization of an interactive marketing planning system, ARTS PLAN [18], which has been used for three seasons by the management of the "Lively Arts at Stanford" as an aid in product line planning and in making marketing mix decisions. The model consists of three major components: (1) a forecasting system to predict attendance at an event, (2) an interactive planning model by which the manager can test the impact of different choices of performing arts events on total attendance for the year, and (3) a routine for assessing the impact of extensive promotion on different events.

In developing a procedure to forecast number of tickets sold, data were available for 93 performances over a 3-year period ending in spring 1976. A dummy-variable multiple linear regression with an R^2 of 0.79 was estimated, based on the type of performing arts event (for example, dance, jazz, chamber music), the quarter in which it was presented (fall, winter, spring), and other factors (see Table 3). Most important, and surprising,

Table 3. Regression Results for Predicting Attendance

Variable[a]	Coefficient	F[b]
Spring	−127	5.5
Dance (A)	231	12.3
Dance (B)	804	74.1
Guitar	481	27.0
Jazz	732	79.6
Young concert artists	−400	33.0
Group A	178	4.1
Year 2	−113	6.0
Constant	647	

$F = 43.7$; adjusted $R^2 = 0.79$; $n = 90$.

[a] All variables are categorical (0, 1) variables describing the performance type, season of the year, or year held. One chamber music group (group A) appeared more than five times and is represented by a separate dummy variable. The broad category dance was subdivided into two classes, class B representing three particularly well-known groups.

[b] $F_{0.05(1,90)} = 4.0$, $F_{0.01(1,90)} = 6.9$. All coefficients are significant at the 0.05 level or above.

was the finding that, in general, the name of the individual performer was not needed.[6] This meant that a forecasting system could be built for performers who had not previously been on campus and that seasonal effects could be segregated from others.

The ARTS PLAN system is user oriented, as is illustrated in Table 4. The number of options considered in the example problem is relatively

Table 4. Excerpts from a Sample Run[a]

Arts Planning Model.
Do you wish to investigate an entire season, or a single quarter (S=Season; Q=Quarter)? Q
Which quarter do you wish to investigate
    (Fall=1, Winter=2, Spring=3)? 3
Will data come from keyboard (K) or file (F)? K
Number of performances planned for quarter (Max=17)? 4
The following table presents the base-case attendance percentages which will be used in generating the first-round attendance projection.

Estimated Attendance Percentages (Historical)*

	Fall	Winter	Spring
(1) Chamber Music	87	87	70
(2) Dance	52	52	44
(3) Guitar	104	104	92
(4) Jazz	81	81	74
(5) YCA	71	71	34
(6) Other (700)	90	90	72
(7) Other (1700)	38	38	31

*In addition the following supplementary effects have been observed:
    (G) Gala Quartet   25
    (P) Popular Dance Group   47
At this step you are asked to provide specific information on the program you are planning.

Performance Number 1
Enter Performance Name (Maximum 12 characters)? *Beth*
Enter Performance Type (use code number:)
    1=Chamber Music   3=Guitar   5=Young Concert Artists (YCA)
    2=Dance   4=Jazz   6=Other (700)
    7=Other (1700)
? 2
Enter Capacity of Hall? 1700
    Popular Dance Group   (Y=Yes, N=No)? Y

(*continued*)

---

[6] It should be noted that this statement does not imply that any group of the specified type would do equally well. Rather, it suggests that for the range of groups that LAS books, the name of the individual group is not statistically significant in this regression. In general, LAS books groups which are relatively well known and highly talented. However, there are literally hundreds of groups that fall into this category, so the statistical results are important.

Table 4 (*continued*)

(Remainder of initial input deleted.)				
Attendance Predictions for Spring Quarter				
Performance number	Performance name	Percentage attendance	Capacity of hall	Attendance
1	Beth	P 91	1700	1547
2	Sari	74	1700	1258
3	Amy	34	350	119
4	Michelle	45	1300	585
Totals	*	69	5050	3509

Do you want to save Table on a file (Y or N)? *N*
Do you wish to make any changes? (Y = Yes, N = No)? *Y*
Enter number of performance you wish to change? 2
Current status of performance number 2

Name	Sari
Type	(4) Jazz
% Attend	74
Capacity	1700
Attendance	1258

Indicate by code number the parameter you wish to change
Enter one only: 1 = Performance Name 3 = Percentage Attendance
               2 = Performance Type 4 = Capacity of Hall
? 3

Old percentage attendance: 74
New percentage attendance expected? 85
Any other changes to this performance (Y = Yes, N = No)? *N*

Attendance Predictions for Spring Quarter				
Performance number	Performance name	Percentage attendance	Capacity of hall	Attendance
1	Beth	P 91	1700	1547
2	Sari	RV 85	1700	1445
3	Amy	34	350	119
4	Michelle	45	1300	585
Totals		73	5050	3696

Do you wish to make any modifications to the planned season (Y = Yes, N = No)? *Y*
Input type of change desired (one only).
    1 = Add a new performance
    2 = Delete an old performance
    3 = Replace an existing performance with another
    4 = Make changes to an existing performance
? 2
Which performance do you wish to delete?
    (Enter performance number)? 2

Do you wish to examine promotional impact (Y = Yes, N = No)? *Y*
At this stage you are asked to estimate the impact of devoting considerable
promotional effort to a particular performance.

(*continued*)

Performance name	Projected % attendance	Estimated % attendance with promotion
Beth	P 91	? 95
Amy	34	? 34
Michelle	45	? 75

The following table lists performance by order of increase in attendance due to promotion:

Performance number	Performance name	Projected attendance	Increase from promo	Attendance with promotion
3	Michelle	585	390	975
1	Beth	P 1547	68	1615
2	Amy	119	0	119

Which performance, if any, do you want to promote. Indicate by performance number. If none, enter zero...? 3
Performance number or zero if no more...? 0
Attendance with Promotions chosen is now estimated

Attendance Predictions for Spring Quarter				
Performance number	Performance name	Percentage attendance	Capacity of hall	Attendance
1	Beth	P 91	1700	1547
2	Amy	34	350	119
3	Michelle	* 75	1300	975
Totals		79	3350	2641

[a] User answers are underscored. For a more complete description of this model, see Weinberg and Shachmut [18].

small, because of space limitations, but in an actual application can be considerably increased. Table 4 is largely self-explanatory and only limited supplementary comments will be made here.

After identifying the time period to be examined and setting the number of performances, the program prints out the historical record. The program then requests the user to identify each performance by name and type, given the capacity of the hall it is to be held in, and indicate any special effects that may exist. An option is provided to override the base case projections because of additional information that the manager has available. The manager can also examine the impact of adding, deleting, or replacing a performance with another. When all the adjustments are completed, a planning base forecast for the quarter is established.

The manager has the opportunity in the next phase of the program to investigate the impact of allocating promotional effort to one or more performances. First, the manager is asked what would be the impact of promotion on percentage of capacity sold for each performance. The performances are then ranked in order of increase in attendance. This ranking reflects the promotion responsiveness of a performance, capacity of the hall, and attendance without promotion.

The user then selects the performances to be promoted in light of the foregoing results and any other information available. An attendance projection by performance and for the quarter, including the effect of promotion, and a variety of summary statistics are then output. The user has the option to revise estimates or make schedule changes before terminating the session.

Implementation Experience

The ARTS PLAN system has been used as an aid in the management of an ongoing season and in the planning of a future season. Before the start of the 1976–1977 season, attendance forecasts were made for the 26-performance schedule. Selected performances in the winter and spring were scheduled for intensive promotion.

The forecast was first reviewed at the end of the fall quarter. At this time, the only large deviation found was the unexpected sellout of a performance that had received rave notices when it played the week before at a nearby university. The review also indicated that some winter and spring performances would achieve their attendance goals even without normal promotion, but that the performances selected for intensive promotion truly needed that effort. The model was fundamental in focusing management attention on these issues. Toward the end of the winter season, sales to date and predicted attendance for the spring quarter were compared by the manager. At this time, it was found that one event, which was budgeted for normal promotion, had unexpectedly low sales. The manager was then able to take appropriate corrective action.

At the end of the 1976–1977 season, the actual and predicted attendances were compared. An R^2 of 0.80 between actual and predicted was obtained. Further, the total attendance prediction of 20,875 was virtually identical to the actual attendance of 20,882.

The system was also used to help plan a forthcoming season's schedule. Three 2–3-hour computer terminal sessions were employed in this process. Prior to each session, the manager prepared a schedule and a set of changes to that schedule. The manager evaluated the alternatives and generated new ones in response to the forecasted results. It appears that the questions the manager was asking were these: (1) Does a schedule meet attendance goals with or without promotion, (2) is the effort required to manage a season within the resources of the organization (for example, not too many different performers), and (3) does the schedule meet the artistic goals of the manager? The quantitative forecasts, however, did not replace the manager's qualitative goals. For example, while evaluating one schedule, it appeared that booking a well-known but mediocre group would help the manager solve a seasonal attendance problem. The manager, however, said, "What am I trying to do?" and rejected that group. The system has become an aid to the manager's planning, but does not dominate it.

Year 2 of Implementation. By this time, there had been three directors of the arts program since model development had begun. Interestingly, the regression coefficients had become one means of preserving organizational history. Several times, differences of opinion about the drawing power of events were resolved by referring to previous runs of the ARTS PLAN model.

At the end of the 1977–1978 season, an analysis was again made of the accuracy of the ARTS PLAN system's forecasts. As in the previous year, the total forecast was highly accurate, with an actual attendance of 19,372 and a predicted of 19,135; however, the correlation R^2 between actual and predicted dropped to 0.27. This result is due to a number of factors that provide insights on how managers may use models.

As discussed above, the manager used the forecast as a control device, so that if several weeks before the actual event sales-to-date (plus an estimate of expected sales prior to the performance) were much below forecast sales, aggressive promotion could be undertaken to boost sales. If sales were above or near the forecast, normal promotion could be reduced. Thus, to a certain extent, it appears that management worked toward the forecast. This, of course, would tend to increase the correlation between predicted and actual.

A reason for the lower correlation, one that has interesting policy implications, is the apparent reaction to the high significant coefficient for spring. That is, with all other factors held constant, the expected number of seats to be sold for an event scheduled in the spring would be 127 below that expected if the event were scheduled in the fall or winter. Once the impact of this factor was recognized, management's reaction to this coefficient may have been to devote more effort both to planning and to managing the marketing of tickets for the spring season. An analysis of the difference between actual and estimated ticket sales supports this contention. Thirteen events were presented during the spring seasons of 1977 and 1978. Of the 13 events, 10 had actual attendance greater than forecast, 2 forecasts were essentially "on target" with forecast and actual attendance within 25 seats of each other, and 1 event had forecast greater than actual. When the spring coefficient was removed from the forecast, that is, 127 was added to the forecast, the pattern of residuals was much more balanced:

Actual greater than adjusted forecast	6 events
On target (within 25)	3 events
Actual less than adjusted forecast	4 events

Personal conversations with the management suggest that more attention is now paid to the spring season than in the past.

There were several other reasons for the decline in forecast accuracy. The variety of events scheduled was lessened, so that there were no jazz performances, only one guitar concert in 1977–1978, and approximately half the events were chamber music concerts. In addition, the new management had different policies, procedures, and emphases than the previous management. For example, the new management was more restrictive in providing additional temporary seating when the fixed capacity was sold out.

In summary, the decline in R^2 is, to a large extent, a consequence of the use of the model and changes in management policy. In fact, management's use of the model as a planning device in choosing performers to book has declined. One possible reason for this is that management has learned how, from usage of the interactive computer system, to anticipate what the model forecast will be and can utilize that information without formally using the model itself.

However, the underlying regression model and the interactive system continue to provide the basis for analytical work. The current management is particularly interested in the sales of series (subscription) tickets, an approach that had been only modestly used in the past. This interest has raised questions about the effects of price and price discounts on sales and to what extent the sales of subscriptions "cannibalize" single-ticket sales. Fairly simple models of these effects have been built and installed as a supplement to the ARTS PLAN system. The ARTS PLAN forecasts are used as the base case, assuming traditional pricing and subscription policies. The manager provides subjective estimates of price elasticities and cross-elasticities between subscription and single-ticket sales; the model is then used to examine what would happen if a variety of different price and discount policies were tried. (The more promising strategies were also tested against alternative elasticity estimates.) The model became a key part of the manager's decision process for the subscription program. One impact of use of the model is particularly instructive. Originally, it had been planned to offer different discount percentages for different series. However, once a near-final strategy emerged, it was shown by testing that there was only small effect on total seats sold and revenue of this variation of subscription, discount, and consequently it was decided to consolidate all discounts at one level. This then became one of the major copy themes of the subscription campaign, that is, "Save 30%."

Models such as ARTS PLAN can serve multiple purposes. They can aid managers in making both strategic and tactical decisions. Over time, an implemented model may become obsolete, may be used in different ways, and may serve as the building block for the evolutionary development of analytic approaches to marketing management problems.

Conclusion

Public and nonprofit organizations that have adopted marketing as a significant management function have considerable need for analytic approaches and marketing models. The marketing problems of PNPs and business have much in common, but there are significant differences as well. The model builder should be aware of both. He or she should seek to capitalize on the similarities and recognize and respond to the differences. While some limited progress has been made, much remains to be done.

References

1. Aaker, D. A., and Weinberg, C. B. "Interactive Marketing Models," *Journal of Marketing* 39 (October), 16–23 (1975).
2. Blattberg, R. C., and Stivers, S. R. "A Statistical Evaluation of Transit Promotion," *Journal of Marketing Research* 7 (August), 293–299 (1970).
3. Cooper, L. G. *Forecasting Ticket Sales and Revenue for a Performing Arts Concert Series*. Los Angeles: Study Center for Cultural Policy and Management in the Arts, 1978.
4. Edelstein, M., and Melnyk, M. "The Pool Control System," *Interfaces* 8, (November), 21–36 (1977).
5. Epps, T. W. "An Econometric Analysis of the Effectiveness of the U.S. Army's 1971 Paid Advertising Campaign," *Applied Economics* (December) 261–269 (1973).
6. Farley, J. U., and Harvey, P. D. "Marketing Contraceptives by Mail," *Journal of Advertising Research* 12 (October), 15–18 (1972).
7. Farely, J. U., and Leavitt, H. T. "Private Sector Logistics in Population Control: A Case Study in Jamaica," *Demography* 5, 449–459 (1968).
8. Grayson, C. T., Jr. "Management Science and Business Practice," *Harvard Business Review* 51 (July–August), 41–48 (1973).
9. Green, P. E., and Srinivasan, V. "Conjoint Analysis in Consumer Research: Issues and Outlook," *Journal of Consumer Research* 5 (September), 103–121 (1978).
10. Hanssens, D. M. "Evaluating Media Effectiveness in the Marketing of Arts Organizations," in *Proceedings, 1978 UCLA Conference of Professional Arts Managers*. Los Angeles: Study Center for Cultural Policy and Management in the Arts, 1978.
11. Lovelock, C. H., and Weinberg, C. B. "Public and Nonprofit Marketing Comes of Age," in G. Zaltman and T. Bonoma (eds.), *Review of Marketing 1978*. Chicago: American Marketing Association, 1978, pp. 413–452.
12. Martin, A. J., Carr, R. P., Jr., Liveris, R., and Howen, R. "Marketing Research Applications in Recruiting: Meeting Manpower Requirements in the All-Volunteer Armed Forces," in S. Jain (ed.), *1978 Educators' Proceedings*. Chicago: American Marketing Association, 1978, p. 363. (See also the United States Department of Defense report "Conjoint Analysis of Values of Reserve Component Attributes," OMB #22S-77006.)

13. McDonald, J. "The Use of Management Science in Making a Corporate Policy Decision—Charging for Directory Assistance," *Interfaces* 7 (November, Part II), 5–18 (1976).
14. Montgomery, D. B., and Weinberg, C. B. "Modeling Marketing Phenomena: A Managerial Perspective," *Journal of Contemporary Business* 2 (Autumn), 17–43 (1973).
15. Parker, B. R., and Srinivasan, V. "A Consumer Preference Approach to the Planning of Rural Primary Health-Care Facilities," *Operations Research* 24, 991–1025 (1976).
16. Urban, G. L. "A Model for Managing a Family Planning System," *Operations Research* 22 (March–April), 205–233 (1974).
17. Weinberg, C. B. "Marketing Mix Decision Rules for Nonprofit Organizations," in J. Sheth (ed.), *Research in Marketing*, Vol. 3, Greenwich, Connecticut: JAI Press, 1979.
18. Weinberg, C. B., and Shachmut, K. M. "ARTS PLAN: A Model Based System For Use in Planning a Performing Arts Series," *Management Science* 24 (February), 654–664 (1978).
19. Wind, Y., and Spitz, L. K. "Analytical Approach to Marketing Decisions in Health-Care Organizations," *Operations Research* 24, 973–990 (1976).

12

Implementing Decision Models

Randall L. Schultz and Michael D. Henry

If marketing decision models are a technology designed to improve marketing decisions, then the value of such models must clearly be defined in terms of their impact on organizational effectiveness. This insight about the role of models in organizations, and their evaluation, stems from a series of studies on the implementation of operations research and management science.[1] In this chapter, major findings of empirical research on implementation are reviewed and then shown to be relevant to the management of organizational innovation. It turns out that although many questions remain to be answered, certain key variables seem to be the principal determinants of implementation success. By monitoring and controlling these variables, the likelihood of a marketing decision model's meeting its objectives (and hence the organization's objectives) can be significantly increased. Before examining the research or its implications, however, it will be useful to clarify the meaning of "implementation" and of "successful implementation."

Implementation Success

One of the more interesting classes of marketing decision models, and the one to which this discussion primarily relates, is a model designed for multiple users such as sales managers, brand managers, and buyers. Of course, some marketing decision models are built as an aid to single managers or, what is the same, a single management group or decision area, such as a model designed to set optimal advertising budgets. But even

---

[1] The basic argument is developed elsewhere [26, pp. 25–47; 29; 30; 33].

in the latter situation, the issues relating to implementation are substantially similar to the more general case of multiple users.

We have, then, the following scenario. A manager (or management group) recognizes a problem, such as the need to improve the quality of sales managers' sales forecasts. Based on this problem perception, some search process for a solution is initiated. At this point, operations research or management science may be engaged; that is, an analyst is brought into the picture to solve the forecasting problem by developing a (decision) model. It does not matter to the analysis of the process whether the analyst is an in-house staff person or an outside consultant. The opportunities and problems for project success or failure remain much the same.

Initial problems, for example, may be caused by the relationship between the manager and the researcher. They may not understand one another, may communicate in different languages, may not have mutual respect, and so on. It is not surprising that "client–researcher relationship" appears in implementation research as a factor determining both the shape and the outcome of the model development process. As model development proceeds, many other factors mediate the process.

Depending to some extent on the institutionalization of OR/MS in the organization, top management may provide a high level of support for generalized OR activities or for this particular MS project. Or such support may be low or nonexistent. Additional factors such as urgency for results (of the sales forecast improvements) and goal congruence (between the manager and the researcher) may also affect the nature of model development.

It is not possible to be exhaustive of these kinds of variables here, only suggestive, but at some juncture a model may be produced that seems to fit the needs of the manager (without making a type III error, solving the wrong problem). The model will have certain characteristics—say, empirical, interactive and, perhaps, costly—all of which also play a role in the manager's decision to accept the model and suggest that it be used by the sales managers.

Note this last point. In a two-stage implementation process such as this, the first direct outcome is management acceptance and the second is user adoption. Even with management acceptance and both management and top management support, the ultimate users, the sales managers, may not adopt the new sales forecasting model. Such factors as personal stake in the model, user decision (cognitive) style, and other personal/situational variables may overweigh the organizational "mandate."

If the model is used, other questions arise, such as trial use versus repeat use, impact of use on user performance (recall that this was the purpose of the model), and overall user and manager satisfaction with the model. In this entire process, feedbacks occur as between user adoption and user knowledge and, in the long run, presumably, between user performance and user decision style and between user performance and top management support.

The upshot of this example is that the model development and implementation process is not simple, but not unresearchable either. What does seem to be critically important is what is meant by implementation success, for that is the object of the whole enterprise.

Implementation and Successful Implementation

Implementation refers to the actual use of OR/MS output (projects, models, or solutions) by managers that *influences* their decision processes. Influence is thus the key to understanding the notion of implementation, for if management science, designed to influence decision making, does not in fact influence the decision process, then a model (or management science) can hardly be thought of as being implemented. It is possible, of course, that organizational decision-making processes could be influenced without the *particular* OR/MS output being actually used, although in this case the benefits of operations research are more correctly attributable to organizational intervention or consulting in general.

Marketing decision models seek to improve decision making, but that does not mean that all of them do just that. Improved decision making implies changed decision making, but not all changes in decision processes are improvements, a point worth noting since it suggests that not all decision models *should* be implemented. In fact, implementation can be thought of as *changed* decision making and successful implementation as *improved* decision making. Thus, any OR/MS intervention in decision making that changes decision making (or decisions) is "implemented." If decision making is improved, then implementation is "successful."

Model Success and Implementation Success

A successful model is one that adequately represents the phenomena being modeled and is used for the purpose for which it was designed. So model success is a more narrow concept than implementation success, since the former is defined in terms of the model's goals and the latter in terms of the organization's goals. A marketing decision model designed to optimize advertising expenditures, for example, is successful only to the extent that it is used for this purpose and accomplishes its goal. But since models need not be "used" to have a change in decision making, a kind of fringe benefit of the attempt to adopt the model may accrue to the organization. It is even possible that, in an indirect way, the advertising decision process is improved. So successful OR work may or may not imply the success of a model.

A behavioral perspective of implementation would include the development and the use of a decision model that results in a positive change in *organizational effectiveness.* In the scenario above, this would mean that the sales forecasting model was successfully developed and was adopted by sales managers (model success), and that it in fact improved the process of sales forecasting (implementation success). In this scheme, user and manager satisfaction are appropriately tied to user performance and hence to organizational effectiveness.

Management science activity involves (1) intervention, (2) implementation, and (3) improvement. *Intervention* occurs when OR/MS activity takes place (a model is built, a project is done, consulting takes place, etc.). *Implementation* occurs when decision making is changed (that is, the decision process is influenced in some way as a result of the intervention). *Improvement* obtains when there is a positive change in decision making or organizational effectiveness.

Research Approaches

Research on the implementation of operations research/management science can be classified into five different although not entirely exclusive categories: philosophical papers, cases, factor studies, model building, and change process research.[2] In Figure 1 most of the key work in these areas is arranged into a framework based on the Schultz–Slevin paradigms of model building and the extensions of Hildebrandt and of Manley. Although an attempt has been made here to select the most representative work, no attempt has been made to be exhaustive; indeed, a recent bibliography by Schultz, Slevin, and Henry [35] lists nearly 400 references to implementation research.

Model Building Paradigms

Different model building or implementation strategies have been proposed to deal with some of the problems of implementation. One approach is to distinguish between traditional, evolutionary, and behavioral model building [32]. Traditional model building, which characterized most management science activity until recently, implies that the model is created independently from the user and the organization. The manager and the researcher have very little interaction and hence very little mutual understanding of problems, processes, goals, and so on.

In order to remedy some of this lack of understanding, evolutionary model building would involve the user in successively more complex versions of a decision model, providing the researcher with a measure of

---

[2]Although most of this work has not been done by marketing researchers, two notable exceptions are the interesting study by Larréché and Montgomery [12] and the excellent volume by Naert and Leeflang [24].

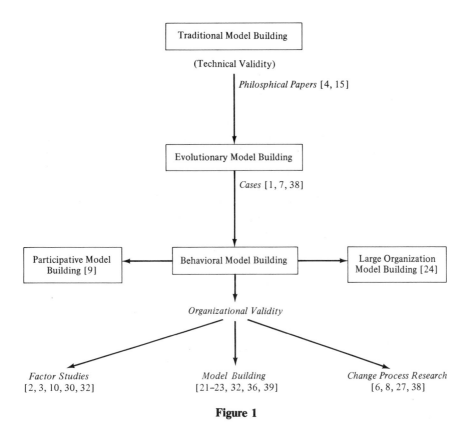

Figure 1

control over the learning process of the user (knowledge of the model and of management science) and also a sense of shared values (or at least goals). This model building paradigm has been proposed by Urban and Karash [39] and employed in a number of studies by Urban [38] and by Little [15, 16]. A significant advantage of this strategy is that marginal analysis of costs versus benefits can be made, although the benefits may only accrue in the longer run and costs, to be estimated accurately, should probably include costs of organizational change associated with the implementation process itself.

An attempt to deal with the behavioral and organizational impact of the model development/implementation process is behavioral model building. This strategy requires more than simple interaction between the researcher and the manager; a formal assessment of the desired fit between a decision model and an organization is made and the change necessary to achieve this fit (or "organizational validity") is measured using instruments developed for this purpose. Organizational validity can be measured at the individual, small group, and organizational levels, as studies by Robey and

Zeller [27], Larŕeché [11], and others have shown. Many of the determinants of implementation success can be evaluated within this framework, that is, by evaluating the gap between desired (postimplementation) and actual (preimplementation) attitudes, cognitive style, goals, communication patterns, organizational structure, and so forth.

Two independent extensions of the behavioral model building concept have been made by Hildebrandt [8] and by Manley [22]. The first, called participative model building and developed within the context of social planning applications, is a strategy designed to move the analyst from a role of providing others with solutions to their problems to one of enabling others to solve their own problems more effectively. In Hildebrandt's view, behavioral model building is too restrictive in that the researcher is still the "expert"—only now one with behavioral as well as technical talents—and thus too little attention is given to more complex relationships that exist between various interest groups within and outside of social organizations. Participative model building, then, would seem to bring a political dimension to implementation where goals are based on collective judgments of social welfare.

The second extension, by Manley, called large organization model building, also arises out of a special context, in this case the application of management science in large organizations such as the Department of Defense. In Manley's experience, behavioral model building and other approaches do not adequately fit a very large organization because of the vast scope of certain projects and correspondingly extensive communication problems. Large organization model building establishes the operations research activities in a planning or research office that provides a "front" for model development and masks "outsider" status to the organization in general. Then, through a series of formal lines of direct communication to many parts of the organization and through special, informal communication tools such as "straw men" (used as attitude objects to trigger valuable behavioral feedback), the same kind of behavioral data sought in behavioral model building is collected in a more practical and politically feasible way. In fact, Manley notes that attempts by top management to collect such information directly from the bottom levels of the organization, and vice versa, were found to be relatively less effective or not effective at all.

All of these strategies suggest that the model building process is changed due to implementation considerations. Models may be developed in an evolutionary fashion. Model characteristics may be based on salient attitudes and decision-style constraints. Model development may even involve participatory groups or organizational subunits that facilitate the process of communication and implementation. The point is that, as opposed to traditional model building, strategies designed to achieve implementation necessarily imply a more sensitive, controlled, and reactive model building procedure.

In addition, if what is required to obtain successful implementation is a good fit between the model and the organization, then this fit can be gained by changing the model or by changing the organization. Both cases involve costs: the cost of what might be called suboptimality and the cost of organizational change. Naert and Leeflang [24, p. 344] consider the case of models that simultaneously deal with multiple decisions such as advertising budgeting, copy preparation, and media planning. Not only would such models be complex, they argue, but they might also miss the sequence and level of such interrelated decisions. Thus, the nature of the model should depend on the nature of the organization. In the sequel, Naert and Leeflang propose hierarchical models and model sequences that may accomplish just such a fit.

Finally, implementation strategies should either implicitly or explicitly consider power relationships. It is in precisely this way that the work of Hildebrandt and Manley is prescient. Management science implementation is a special case of organizational innovation and so the fundamental issue is how to introduce change into organizations. For staff specialist groups such as OR/MS departments, or for anyone wishing to implement change in an organization who does not have a power base, the problem becomes one of managing behavior to meet certain objectives.

Philosophical Papers

As an approach to the implementation problem, a series of conceptual papers were written, two of which have had considerable impact on implementation research. The first paper, by Churchman and Schainblatt [4], describes the notion of mutual understanding between researcher and manager, a point first raised by Morse and Kimball [23] in their pioneering text on operations research. They identified four positions of the model builder–model user interface: separate function (neither understands the other), communication (user understands builder), persuasion (builder understands user), and mutual understanding (both understand each other). The separate function position is akin to what we have called traditional model building and is not recommended. The communication position has some merit in that a sophisticated manager could specify the nature of the model building effort. Presumably, evolutionary model building results in increasing sophistication on the part of managers to achieve just such control over the model. The persuasion position implies a marketing concept on the part of the model builder: in other words, a behavioral model building approach.

Mutual understanding, of course, is argued to be the best position and, in principle, it is. Neither evolutionary nor behavioral model building strategies would reject the spirit of this approach. But as a philosophical dictum, mutual understanding until recently lacked operational meaning.

Now, empirical research on implementation that has revealed such factors as goal congruence, attitudes, and personal stake to be determinants of implementation success has given new definition to this concept. In striving for a better match between model and manager [cf. 10] mutual understanding is a strategic goal if not a tactical objective.

A more personal view of implementation is reflected by Little's [14] concept of a decision calculus. Decision models, according to Little, should be simple, robust, easy to control, adaptive, complete on important issues, and easy to communicate with. These criteria arise out of the model building experience of Little and his associates [15–18, 38] rather than from empirical research on implementation. The characteristics of simple and complete, seemingly at odds, can be reconciled in an evolutionary model building context, especially if simple is taken to mean understandable to the user and complete is understood to mean relative completeness [24]. It is easy to see how models that are adaptive and robust appeal to managers, although like all model characteristics, they are not absolute ideals [cf. 13] nor are they always to be desired [24, p. 118].

The characteristic of easy to control, meaning that the model is constructed in such a manner that it can be made to behave the way the manager wants it to, is more of a problem since, together with the usual emphasis in decision-calculus models on subjective parameter estimates, it can lead to models that may make managers "feel good" rather than think (or decide) well. Although this problem has been discounted by Naert and Leeflang [24, p. 348], it has been seriously questioned by Parsons and Schultz [26, p. 33], who would add to Little's criteria an additional one, representativeness, as a test of the validity of the sales response component of a decision model. This test is a crucial one since, in the final analysis, models must be judged by the level of objective improvement in decision making due to their use.

Naert and Leeflang [24, p. 25] discuss this point in terms of what they call the direct benefits of decision models:

> Companies invest in model building presumably because it leads to better decisions. "Better" is understood here as contributing to the fulfillment of the company's goals. For example, if the firm's single objective is to maximize profit, benefits of a model could be defined as the discounted differential profit generated by having the model as opposed to not having it.[3]

The authors also note a number of side benefits of model building such as improved understanding, help in problem finding, and improved information handling, but since such benefits can also accrue from non-

---

[3] Copyright 1978, Martinus Nijhoff Publishers, the Hague, the Netherlands.

management science interventions (such as consulting, organizational development, and executive training programs), it is more appropriate in such discussions to confine cost–benefit analysis to the intrinsic management science contribution, in this case the model.

Little's final criterion, ease of communication, is also one that appeals to managers and has received some empirical support [24, pp. 349–352]. Still, with rapidly advancing technology, it would be an oversimplification to equate ease of communication with interactive computer terminals. Like all model characteristics, the most appropriate ones are those that facilitate implementation by providing a fit between the model and the organization; and as we have seen, this fit can be achieved by changing the manager as much as the model.

Cases

A rich source of anecdotal material about implementation comes from cases describing successful or unsuccessful operations research projects. We have already discussed evolutionary model building, an implementation strategy derived from attempts to implement successively more complex versions of a new product evaluation model [39]. More typically, the cases are written by observers or participant-observers who are not actually model builders but who attempt to record the history of a model implementation [6] or to study common problems associated with a number of implementation efforts [1].

Gibson [6] studied implementation in a bank as a participant-observer. He found that personality types, business history, and social structure influence both individual users' attitudes toward the OR/MS project and the model builder's knowledge of the company. These factors plus model characteristics then influence implementation. By learning more about the culture of organizations, Gibson argues, operations researchers can learn more about how to proceed with successful model building and implementation.

By studying case histories of 56 decision support systems, Alter [1] defined eight risk factors that suggest how any actual implementation situation can differ from an ideal (no-risk) situation: nonexistent or unwilling users; multiple users or implementors; disappearing users, implementors, or maintainers; inability to specify purpose or usage pattern; inability to predict and cushion impact; loss or lack of support; lack of experience with similar systems; and technical problems and cost effectiveness. Alter's idea here is not so much to measure risk as to increase awareness of contingencies bearing on a model implementation project. Like most case studies, the purpose is to provide a descriptive background for the model builder to increase understanding.

Factor Studies

Philosophical discussions and case studies have formed a foundation upon which implementation research can be built. They have shown that organizational validity as well as technical validity is needed for successful implementation. But specific behavioral factors influencing implementation must be identified before an operations researcher or management scientist can be given constructive guidelines toward creating more easily implementable models. Identifying such key behavioral factors has been the goal of a number of factor studies.

Since the Churchman and Schainblatt article [4], the importance of mutual understanding between the researcher and manager has been recognized. Huysmans [9] and Larféché [11] argue that organizational validity can be enhanced through mutual understanding, helping to create a model that better matches the manager's style and ability. Huysmans suggests that differences in cognitive style between a researcher and a manager serve as a constraint to model implementation. Managers are classified into two groups: analytic reasoners and heuristic reasoners. Researchers are assumed to build models requiring integral understanding by the manager, necessitating continual researcher assistance, or explicit understanding, requiring no continual researcher assistance. Huysmans concludes that if the researcher uses an explicit understanding approach, heuristic managers generally reject the model, while analytic managers respond more positively. If an integral understanding approach is used, however, both heuristic and analytic managers more readily accept the model. If the cognitive style of the manager can be determined, then the researcher can use this information to modify the model building approach to better match the manager.

Larféché argues that the integrative complexity theory of Schroder, Driver, and Streufert can be used to determine the optimal model complexity for a given manager. This theory states that the level of information processing attained by a manager is dependent on both the level of integrative complexity and the environmental complexity of the model. An optimal level of environmental complexity may exist for which a manager attains the highest level of information processing. If there are differences in individuals' integrative complexity, then models can be developed to create the level of environmental complexity that maximizes the information processing ability of each manager.

Schultz and Slevin [31] believe it is necessary to determine the attitudes and perceptions toward a project at the personal, small group, and organizational levels in order to design a model that is organizationally valid. They isolated seven attitudinal dimensions affecting implementation success. Urgency of the problem, personal stake in the model, and feelings toward change were identified on the personal level. At the small group level, the importance of interpersonal relationships and feelings toward the researcher were most important. The amount of top management support and the level of congruence between the goals of the organization and the model were most important at the organizational level.

A series of studies at Northwestern University [e.g., 2, 3, 28] examined several management science groups in an attempt to discover key organizational factors affecting implementation. Although agreeing that mutual understanding between a researcher and a manager will help implementation, Bean et al. [2] question the extent to which managerial attitudes can be changed and the importance of these changes. They argue that structural variables such as life cycle stage of the OR group, portfolio of projects, organizational location of MS, mediators (if any) used, top management support, and resources are more important. Bean and Radnor [3] believe that mutual understanding between a researcher and a manager may not always be possible. They argue that in certain cases functionally related intermediaries may be necessary to supply the needed communication between the researcher and the manager.

Model Building

Since implementation can be regarded as a special case of organizational innovation, researchers have attempted to build explanatory models of the implementation process. At this time, however, the most useful of these models are primarily descriptive, since they organize the findings from current studies and identify areas for further research. Some attempts have been made to formulate predictive models of implementation [21, 37], but a lack of knowledge of relevant factors and the means of measuring them make these attempts exploratory at best.

In one of the earlier descriptive models, Schultz and Slevin [32], propose that the probability of success of a management science model depends on both technical validity (how capable the model is in solving the problem) and organizational validity (how compatible the model is with the organization). Individual variables, small group variables, and organizational variables all must be considered in measuring the organizational validity of a model. Schultz and Slevin conclude that identifying these variables and developing techniques for their measurement are critical areas for further study.

Vertinsky, Barth, and Mitchell [40] used an expectancy–valence theory approach to develop a model to describe and explain the process of social change in organizations with established OR/MS activities. This model indicates that motivation to expend effort to implement OR/MS is due to three factors (type I expectancy, type II expectancy, and valence) and several factors that provide feedback affecting these variables. Type I expectancy refers to a manager's expectation that use or implementation of the OR/MS will lead to task accomplishment or performance. A manager's type II expectancy is the belief that this performance based on model use will produce certain outcomes or payoffs. The degree of preference for the different payoffs that can be directly contingent on a manager's performance as a result of the use of OR/MS defines valence. The sum of the product of all type II expectancies and their valence multiplied by the type I expectancy gives the probability that the OR/MS will be implemented.

A more comprehensive model of implementation has evolved in the work of Lucas [20], who has conducted nine empirical studies to test its validity. This model consists of two interdependent functional relationships. In an intermediate relationship, attitudes and perceptions are hypothesized to be a function of model quality and management support. Implementation is theorized as being a direct function of these attitudes and perceptions as well as of model quality, management support, decision style, and situational and personal factors. So model quality and management support exert both a direct and an indirect effect upon implementation, whereas attitudes and perceptions, decision style, and situational and personal factors provide only a direct effect. Lucas concludes that, in general, the relationships hypothesized in the model are supported by the empirical data; but further research is needed, especially to provide more evidence on the possible causal links in the model.

An example of such a causal study is the work of Lucas and Schultz (in progress). They develop a simultaneous equation or structural model of the implementation process. The case dealt with involves the class of implementation problems where management initiates model building to provide an aid to making recurring decisions by multiple users, such as investment advisory models for brokers or sales forecasting models for sales managers. Research such as this is promising in that previously isolated findings on determinants of implementation success are integrated in a general theory of implementation and tested as a whole in an empirical econometric model.

Change Process Research

Implementation of management science involves the adoption of new decision-making techniques within an organization. With the introduction of any innovation, certain changes must occur within individuals before a new idea will be accepted. Tradition must be rejected. New ideas must be learned and integrated. So the implementation of OR/MS requires a change process to occur within the organization. Therefore, in order to improve implementation, it is necessary to understand this change process and discover ways to manage it; change process research is an attempt to acquire this understanding.

Sorensen and Zand [36] adopted the Lewin–Schein theory of change to study the change process involved in the implementation of operations research. This theory posits that there are three stages in a change process: unfreezing, changing, and refreezing. Unfreezing entails overcoming resistance to change by introducing disequilibrium into a present stable environment. Encouragement of dissatisfaction with current behavior, or just the lack of confirmation of this behavior, can produce this state of disequilibrium. Once unfreezing has occurred, changing can begin. Changing involves exposing individuals to new information, attitudes, and theories in order to create new perceptions and develop new behavioral patterns. Implementation has not been accomplished, however, merely with the establishment of new perceptions and behavior. These new perceptions and behavior must be totally absorbed into the manager's day-to-day decision making. Refreezing utilizes reinforcement and confirmation to assure that the OR/MS output, a model say, becomes "frozen" into the accepted decision-making process of the organization. Unless this refreezing is accomplished, managers may regress to their old perceptions and behavior once the influence of the researcher is removed.

Narasimhan and Schroder [25] develop a three-phase theory of the change process involved in implementation that is very similar to Sorensen and Zand's. They stress that a management scientist who intervenes in an organization acts as the principal change agent within the organization and has much more influence over implementation than other organizational factors. Since such influence is so important, according to these authors, the scientist must take great care in managing the change process.

The Kolb–Frohman model of consulting activity is used by Ginzberg [7] to study the implementation of 29 computer-based management science projects. Although the Kolb–Frohman model separates the change process into seven stages (scouting, entry, diagnosis, planning, action, evaluation, and termination), it still includes the more general unfreezing, changing, and refreezing relationships. Ginzberg discovered major differences between the manager and researcher on both the perception of the process and its outcome. He stresses the need for a planned-change approach to implementation involving a joint effort by the manager and researcher so that the researcher can better understand the user's perspective of the process. The greatest difference in perception concerning the process occurred during the termination (refreezing) stage. Ginzberg concludes that this problem may be caused by the researcher's tendency to terminate the project before complete refreezing has occurred. If this is true, then the researcher must place more emphasis on the refreezing stage by continuing involvement with the firm for much longer than previously believed necessary.

When totally new technology is being introduced into an ongoing operation, Galbraith [5] proposes that a diffusion model is most appropriate for managing the change process. Initially, "management islands" should be employed to differentiate the new technology from daily opera-

R. L. Schultz and M. D. Henry

tions and protect it from short-run pressures. These management islands should be autonomous units receiving funding and expertise from corporate levels. As the new technology is allowed to mature in this protected environment, young managers are trained in its use and sent to all areas of the firm, thus facilitating the diffusion of these new ideas. As these managers become more established, their support can be used to help integrate the technology into the entire operation. Use of this type of diffusion process for OR/MS implementation can be very powerful since support for the technology is developed internally.

Managing Implementation

As emphasized throughout this chapter, management science inherently attempts to improve decision-making processes of organizations. Recent experience, however, has shown that most management science applications have failed in this regard. Consider that an organization can be thought of as a living organism, not unlike a human body, composed of many separate parts, each interdependent on all others for survival. If a foreign substance is introduced into a human body, defense mechanisms immediately confront the invader and, depending on its compatibility with the body, the substance is either accepted or destroyed. We might then regard management science as a foreign agent being introduced into an organization; and just like a human body, an organization possesses defense mechanisms that may reject management science. So if decision models, for example, are to be accepted or implemented in an organization, then they must fit the organization or they may be rejected by strong organizational resistance. The research approaches discussed above are attempts at finding ways to improve the management of implementation by making management science more compatible with organizations. Although further research is needed, important generalizations have resulted from these studies that provide insight for operations research practitioners.

To create the organizational climate necessary for successful implementation, a management scientist must understand the organization so that strategies can be designed to fit specific situations. Just as a physician realizes the importance of conducting a complete medical history and physical examination before treating a patient, a management scientist should realize the importance of obtaining a thorough knowledge of both the past and present workings of a living organization. Information needs to be collected at the organizational, small group, and individual levels to assure that all important factors are considered. This information leads, in turn, to a better fit between a decision model and an organization, that is, organizational validity, and hence to an increased probability of implementation success.

Organizational Validity

At the organizational level, factors of interest include life cycle stage of an OR/MS group (if present), amount of top management support for management science, and congruence between goals of an organization and researcher. These factors define the structural setting where a management scientist must work. If an internal OR/MS group is involved, then the group's life cycle stage will affect implementation. In early stages, when strong organizational support has not developed, implementation is much more difficult than in later stages, when successful performance has created support; so implementation strategy should adjust as a group's life cycle changes. Top management support is vital for acceptance of any idea; if information from an organization shows that such support is lacking, care must be taken to nurture it by educating managers as to the benefits available from management science. Should little congruence exist between goals of an organization and of a researcher, the value of any model developed will be minimal. By diagnosing such a situation, a researcher is able to adapt to better match an organization's goals and create a model that is more implementable.

While knowledge at the organizational level provides a view of the structural environment that faces a management scientist, information at the small group level focuses more on behavioral problems. When working within an organization, close interaction with various managers is a necessity, and personality conflicts, such as negative feelings between a manager and researcher, can serve as roadblocks, greatly inhibiting chances for implementation. A researcher must become aware of any conflicts that develop and take steps toward finding workable solutions, because if problems are not recognized or are ignored altogether, then implementation may prove impossible. In addition, for organizations where small group interactions are of high social importance, disruption of interpersonal relationships caused by use of a model may also create resistance to implementation. Researchers should recognize such situations and design models that preserve as much of an organization's interpersonal structure as possible.

Solving problems at the organizational and small group levels greatly enhances chances for successful implementation; however, certain unique problems exist at an individual level that must also be resolved. For instance, individuals have a natural reluctance toward change, especially if doubt exists as to its potential value. Managers must be convinced that a model's use will lead to improved performance and payoffs worth the frustrations involved. Also, the importance of a problem affects a manager's feelings toward change; for example, the more urgent a problem is, the more willing a manager is to accept new ideas for its solution.

A manager's decision-making (cognitive) style should also be considered, since evidence exists that certain model building approaches are most effective with certain styles. Whether it be cognitive style or integrative complexity, some classification of style needs to be used to help determine the best strategy for teaching a manager to interact competently with a model. A manager may feel so threatened by a model that is developed and presented in an inappropriate manner for a given decision style that no attempt will be made to understand or implement it.

Not only must a researcher acquire a thorough knowledge of an organization and develop an appropriate strategy, but also a state of mutual understanding should be reached where an organization understands the researcher. To create mutual understanding, managers should become involved in the entire research project, beginning with agreement as to the goals of the research, for common goals are essential for a unified problem-solving effort. After goals are established, a joint definition of the problem should be developed to assure that the correct problem is being solved. Research is useless when it solves the wrong problem (a type III error).

As mutual understanding develops, managers must learn to interact competently with a management science model. Different approaches (including decision calculus, evolutionary model building, and behavioral model building) have been recommended for helping a manager understand a model, and an appropriate choice should be made for each situation. If managers are not instructed how to interact with a model, then we can hardly expect them to use it or use it correctly. Because of great disparity in background, training, and personality between some researchers and managers, situations may arise where direct communication between them is impractical. In such cases, use of functionally related intermediaries may prove helpful in facilitating a flow of necessary information. Marketing research, for example, may serve as an effective interface between OR and marketing management.

A final point that must be remembered in any discussion of management of implementation is that implementation involves a process of change within organizations. Organizations must pass through a series of stages before implementation is achieved. Traditional decision-making processes must be rejected while new processes are learned and accepted. A management scientist or model builder must learn to manage this change process to assure that all necessary stages are reached. For example, complete implementation may not occur unless researcher support is extended beyond a period of initial use of a model to assure the "refreezing" of the model into an organization. So care must be taken not to terminate a project prematurely. Also, when totally new technology is being introduced, it may be wise first to differentiate the project from daily operations, and then slowly to diffuse it throughout an organization as it becomes more accepted.

The process of managing implementation will become more systematic in the future. For now, general guidelines such as these serve to minimize problems associated with model implementation and, what is perhaps more important, the results of implementation research suggest how the very process of building models can and should be altered.

Denouement

We have seen how research on implementing operations research/management science has led to certain findings about the process of organizational innovation. We have also seen how such research relates to managing implementation. The outcome of this work on the implementation problem, however, is still in doubt. What impact will increased awareness of these issues have on model builders? How will organizational arrangements for conducting operations research projects be changed? When will the development of decision models be integrated into the more general (and accepted) practice of marketing research? It would seem that the answers to these questions lie in progress along three important and parallel tracks: research, practice, and training.

Research

The trends in implementation research have been in apparently opposite directions. On the one hand, the very nature of the implementation problem has forced some management scientists and implementation researchers to develop simple, pragmatic strategies to cope with barriers associated with organizational change. Decision calculus, contingency approaches, risk analysis, implementation profiles, and other such strategies were developed out of OR/MS experience and research to provide analysts with a means to better control the results of their work. The implementation profile, for example, represents an attempt to reduce the large number of factors affecting implementation success to a more manageable number of variables that can be measured in checklist fashion for any implementation situation [cf. 34]. It is difficult to argue with the spirit of this research, since implementation findings ought to be implemented!

On the other hand, it is entirely appropriate to investigate further the behavioral phenomenon of implementation. We currently utilize knowledge about consumer behavior in day-to-day marketing management; at the same time we pursue more complete understanding of the process of consumer choice. In similar fashion, we should continue to study the complex side of implementation, expanding the number of variables considered simultaneously (as in Lucas and Schultz noted above), and we should do so precisely because this is an aspect of human choice that deserves to be studied.

These two trends in implementation research are, of course, complementary. New work should be encouraged in both directions with continual cross checking of scientific versus managerial constraints. Perhaps the best example that such progress is not only possible but desirable is the research of Lucas [19] on implementing computer-based models. As the implementation knowledge base expands, the practice of management science will benefit greatly.

Practice

Most business firms and an increasing number of nonprofit organizations utilize marketing research to support marketing decisions. The same thing cannot be said about marketing decision models. This discrepancy between the use of decision aids and the application of other sophisticated marketing research techniques can probably be explained by the normative versus descriptive or prescriptive nature of the models. In our experience, when working with business organizations it makes a considerable difference (to implementation success) whether a consultant is viewed as providing *information* as opposed to *answers*. Sales forecasts, attitudinal studies of consumers, market positioning, and other "standard" research fare are treated as information inputs by managers; control over decisions, although always subject to the quality of research, is still in the hands of managers.

But decision models, as the name implies, are more of a threat to management control. This threat arises not so much because managers cannot reject the models (they of course do this regularly), but because the models, if they are to be successfully implemented, must be relied on, that is, trusted. When a manager is told that an advertising budget can be reduced to maximize profit, based on some decision model, the manager must believe in the model. The manager must trust the model as another experienced colleague would be trusted. It should be no surprise that such elevation of models to equal or even dominating status with marketing managers causes all of the sorts of problems that arise in implementation research.

Moreover, no one who has ever developed a model designed to aid decisions has not had similar doubts, or at least they should have had them. Every decision model must be based on a description of sales response, and methodology designed to assure the representativeness of this crucial aspect of technical validity has been an important topic of recent marketing literature [cf. 24, 26]. Equally important questions can be raised about the solution of models, regardless of how sales response is measured, and new approaches to optimization are being reported [cf. 41]. The burden on the model builder, then, is not trivial. Progress in the application of marketing decision models will require not only better implementation, but better model building as well.

Training

Research on implementation and practical considerations of marketing management would have you believe that model builders should have a combination of technical skills and behavioral savvy, and perhaps this is just the case. Or it may be that the role of change agent should be formalized as a mediator between analytical model builders and heuristic managers. In either case, there are clear implications for the training of operations researchers.

First, as elementary as this sounds, students of operations research and management science (and maybe practitioners as well) should be exposed to a formal treatment of the implementation problem. We do not expect management scientists to use brute force in the way they develop models; thus, we should not expect analysts to approach implementation as amateurs. A survey of basic management science texts reveals that almost all neglect implementation; in most cases the topic is not even mentioned. Students are not well prepared to face the behavioral and political realities of applied operations research, and the experience of practitioners may also fall short of a clear understanding of the problem. Technical training is not enough.

Second, most management scientists could benefit from better behavioral training, that is, in education aimed at increased awareness of individual and social actions. At ORSA/TIMS joint national meetings, some of the more popular sessions are those dealing with straightforward insight into implementation based on practitioners' experiences, including such behavioral factors as how to dress and how to act! The message here seems to be that a well-prepared M.B.A. could do a better job of selling OR than an operations researcher. Moreover, the point is well taken; since implementation is the bottom line, management scientists should know more about management and behavior.

Third, operations researchers should be educated in the output of implementation research, implementation strategies, and procedures. A course focusing on implementation ought to be as important to the academic preparation of a management scientist as a course on programming. In practice, we know that each is essential to the other in achieving OR success. Short courses for practitioners could serve much the same role. Exposure to the implementation problem, awareness of behavioral science, and education in implementation technology should be essential ingredients of training in operations research.

In the final analysis, marketing management science will be judged by its impact on organizational decision making. Better models will be built and better methods developed for implementing them. One of the most exciting aspects of this enterprise is the synergy between marketing science and marketing practice, for marketing decision models, above all else, are rooted in fact and valued in use.

References

1. Alter, Steven. "Implementation Risk Analysis," in Robert Doktor, Randall L. Schultz, and Dennis P. Slevin (eds.), *The Implementation of Management Science.* Amsterdam: North-Holland, 1979, pp. 103–119.
2. Bean, Alden S., Neal, Rodney D., Radnor, Michael, and Tansik, David A. "Structural and Behavioral Correlates of Implementation in U.S. Business Organizations," in Randall L. Schultz and Dennis P. Slevin (eds.), *Implementing Operations Research/Management Science.* New York: American Elsevier, 1975, pp. 77–132.
3. Bean, Alden S., and Radnor, Michael. "The Role of Intermediaries in the Implementation of Management Science," in Robert Doktor, Randall L. Schultz and Dennis P. Slevin (eds.), *The Implementation of Management Science.* Amsterdam: North-Holland, 1979.
4. Churchman, C. West, and Schainblatt, A. H. "The Researcher and the Manager: A Dialectic of Implementation," *Management Science* 11 (February), B69–87 (1965).
5. Galbraith, Jay R. "A Change Process for the Introduction of Management Information Systems: A Successful Case," in Robert Doktor, Randall L. Schultz, and Dennis P. Slevin (eds.), *The Implementation of Management Science.* Amsterdam: North-Holland, 1979, pp. 219–233.
6. Gibson, Cyrus F. "A Methodology for Implementation Research," in Randall L. Schultz and Dennis P. Slevin (eds.), *Implementing Operations Research/Management Science. New York: American Elsevier, 1975, pp.* 53–73.
7. Ginzberg, Michael J. "A Study of the Implementation Process," in Robert Doktor, Randall L. Schultz, and Dennis P. Slevin (eds.), *The Implementation of Management Science.* Amsterdam: North-Holland, 1979, pp. 85–102.
8. Hildebrandt, Steen. "From Manipulation to Participation in the Operations Research Process," in K. B. Haley (ed.), *OR'78.* Amsterdam: North-Holland, 1978, N8f, pp. 1–18.
9. Huysmans, Jan H. B. M. "The Effectiveness of the Cognitive-Style Constraint in Implementing Operations Research Proposals," *Management Science* 17 (September), 92–104 (1970).
10. Larréché, Jean-Claude. "Managers and Models: A Search for a Better Match," unpublished Ph.D. dissertation, Stanford University, 1974.
11. Larréché, Jean-Claude. "Integrative Complexity and the Use of Marketing Models," in Robert Doktor, Randall L. Schultz, and Dennis P. Slevin (eds.), *The Implementation of Management Science.* Amsterdam: North-Holland, 1979, pp. 171–187.
12. Larréché, Jean-Claude, and Montgomery, David B. "A Framework for the Comparison of Marketing Models: A Delphi Study," *Journal of Marketing Research* 14 (November), 487–498 (1977).
13. Lilien, Gary L. "Model Relativism: A Situational Approach to Model Building," *Interfaces* 5 (May), 11–18 (1975).
14. Little, John D. "Models and Managers: The Concept of a Decision Calculus," *Management Science* 16 (April), B466–B485 (1970).
15. Little, John D. "BRANDAID: A Marketing Mix Model, Part 1: Structure," *Operations Research* 23 (July–August), 628–655 (1975).

16. Little, John D. "BRANDAID: A Marketing Mix Model, Part 2: Implementation, Calibration, and Case Study," *Operations Research* 23 (July–August), 656–673 (1975).

17. Little, John D., and Lodish, Leonard M. "A Media Planning Calculus," *Operations Research* 17 (January–February), 1–35 (1969).

18. Lodish, Leonard M. "CALLPLAN: An Interactive Salesman's Call Planning System," *Management Science* 18 (December), 25–40 (1971).

19. Lucas, Henry C., Jr. *The Implementation of Computer-Based Models*. New York: National Association of Accountants, 1976.

20. Lucas, Henry C., Jr. "Empirical Evidence for a Descriptive Model of Implementation," *Management Information Systems Quarterly*, 2 (June), 27–42 (1978).

21. Manley, John H. "Implementation Attitudes: A Model and a Measurement Methodology," in Randall L. Schultz and Dennis P. Slevin (eds.), *Implementing Operations Research/Management Science*. New York: American Elsevier, 1975, pp. 183–202.

22. Manley, John H. "Implementing Change in Very Large Organizations," in Robert Doktor, Randall L. Schultz, and Dennis P. Slevin (eds.), *The Implementation of Management Science*. Amsterdam: North-Holland, 1979, pp. 189–203.

23. Morse, Philip M. and Kimball, George E. *Methods of Operations Research*. New York: Wiley, 1951.

24. Naert, Philippe A., and Leeflang, Peter S. H. *Building Implementable Marketing Models*. Leiden: Martinus Nijhoff Social Sciences Division, 1978.

25. Narasimhan, Ram, and Schroeder, Roger G. "An Empirical Investigation of Implementation as a Change Process," in Robert Doktor, Randall L. Schultz, and Dennis P. Slevin (eds.), *The Implementation of Management Science*. Amsterdam: North-Holland, 1979, pp. 63–83.

26. Parsons, Leonard J., and Schultz, Randall L. *Marketing Models and Econometric Research*. New York: North-Holland, 1976.

27. Robey, Daniel, and Zeller, Richard L. "Factors Affecting the Success and Failure of an Information System for Product Quality," *Interfaces* 8 (February), 70–75 (1978).

28. Rubenstein, Albert H., Radnor, Michael, Baker, Norman R., Heiman, David R., and McColly, John B. "Some Organizational Factors Related to the Effectiveness of Management Science Groups in Industry," *Management Science* 13 (April), B508–518 (1967).

29. Schultz, Randall L. "The Legitimacy of Management Science," *Interfaces* 5 (August), 26–28 (1975).

30. Schultz, Randall L., and Slevin, Dennis P. "Implementation and Management Innovation," in Randall L. Schultz and Dennis P. Slevin (eds.), *Implementing Operations Research/Management Science*. New York: American Elsevier, 1975, pp. 3–20.

31. Schultz, Randall L., and Slevin, Dennis P. "Implementation and Organizational Validity: An Empirical Investigation," in Randall L. Schultz and Dennis P. Slevin (eds.), *Implementing Operations Research/Management Science*. New York: American Elsevier, 1975, pp. 153–182.

32. Schultz, Randall L., and Slevin, Dennis P. "A Program of Research on Implementation," in Randall L. Schultz and Dennis P. Slevin (eds.), *Implementing Operations Research/Management Science*. New York: American Elsevier, 1975, pp. 31–51.

33. Schultz, Randall L., and Slevin, Dennis P. "The Implementation Profile: Assessment Center Technology Applied to the Implementation Problem," presented at the Joint National Meeting, ORSA and TIMS, Los Angeles, November 13–15, 1978.

34. Schultz, Randall L., and Slevin, Dennis P. "Introduction: The Implementation Problem," in Robert Doktor, Randall L. Schultz, and Dennis P. Slevin (eds.), *The Implementation of Management Science*. Amsterdam: North-Holland, 1979, pp. 1–15.

35. Schultz, Randall L., Slevin, Dennis P., and Henry, Michael D. *A Bibliography on the Implementation of Operations Research/Management Science*. Krannert Graduate School of Management, Purdue University, 1978.

36. Sorensen, Richard E., and Zand, Dale E. "Improving the Implementation of OR/MS Models by Applying the Lewin-Schein Theory of Change," in Randall L. Schultz and Dennis P. Slevin (eds.), *Implementing Operations Research/Management Science*. New York: American Elsevier, 1975, pp. 217–235.

37. Souder, Wm., E., Maher, P. M., Baker, N. R., Shumway, C. R., and Rubenstein, A. H. "An Organizational Intervention Approach to the Design and Implementation of R & D Project Selection Models," in Randall L. Schultz and Dennis P. Slevin (eds.), *Implementing Operations Research/Management Science*. New York: American Elsevier, 1975, pp. 133–152.

38. Urban, Glen L. "Building Models for Decision Makers," *Interfaces* 4 (May), 1–11 (1974).

39. Urban, Glen L., and Karash, Richard. "Evolutionary Model Building," *Journal of Marketing Research* 8 (February), 62–66 (1971).

40. Vertinsky, Ilan, Barth, Richard T., and Mitchell, Vance F. "A Study of OR/MS Implementation as a Social Process," in Randall L. Schultz and Dennis P. Slevin (eds.), *Implementing Operations Research/Management Science*. New York: American Elsevier, 1975, 253–270.

41. Zoltners, Andris A., and Sinha, Prabhakant. "Integer Programming Models for Sales Resource Allocation," *Management Science* 26 (March), 242–260 (1980).

Index